After the Postcolonial Caribbean

"Meeks presents an erudite and unexcitable interpretation of the dark times which engulf us. In sprightly, dancing prose he locates the Caribbean in the global currents which organize who we now are and who we can become. Refusing the programmatic nostrums which see only the darkness, his is a democratic sensibility which affirms the creativity of the oppressed, expansively conceived. Working from an immovable materialism, he unearths the subterranean forces which mark emergent futures and in which life itself can flourish. 'Memory. Imagination. Hope.' Indeed. Meeks offers us a book of rare beauty."

— Bill Schwarz, Queen Mary University of London

"Brian Meek's *After the Postcolonial Caribbean* is a clarion call. He reminds us that only a state, understood as a fully democratized postsecular deity of our collective making, can save us. *After the Postcolonial Caribbean* is exemplary of C.L.R. James's grounded creative universality at its best."

— Francio Guadeloupe, University of Amsterdam and Royal Netherlands Institute for Southeast Asian & Caribbean studies

Black Critique

Series editors: Anthony Bogues and Bedour Alagraa

We live in a troubled world. The rise of authoritarianism marks the dominant current political order. The end of colonial empires did not inaugurate a more humane world; rather, the old order reasserted itself.

In opposition, throughout the twentieth century and until today, anti-racist, radical decolonization struggles attempted to create new forms of thought. Figures from Ida B. Wells to W.E.B. Du Bois and Steve Biko, from Claudia Jones to Walter Rodney and Amílcar Cabral produced work which drew from the historical experiences of Africa and the African diaspora. They drew inspiration from the Haitian revolution, radical Black abolitionist thought and practice, and other currents that marked the contours of a Black radical intellectual and political tradition.

The Black Critique series operates squarely within this tradition of ideas and political struggles. It includes books which foreground this rich and complex history. At a time when there is a deep desire for change, Black radicalism is one of the most underexplored traditions that can drive emancipatory change today. This series highlights these critical ideas from anywhere in the Black world, creating a new history of radical thought for our times.

Also available:

Moving Against the System: The 1968 Congress of Black Writers and the Making of Global Consciousness
Edited and with an Introduction by David Austin

Anarchism and the Black Revolution: The Definitive Edition
Lorenzo Kom'boa Ervin

A Certain Amount of Madness: The Life, Politics and Legacies of Thomas Sankara
Edited by Amber Murrey

Of Black Study
Joshua Myers

Cedric J. Robinson: On Racial Capitalism, Black Internationalism, and Cultures of Resistance
Edited by H.L.T. Quan

Black Minded: The Political Philosophy of Malcolm X
Michael Sawyer

Red International and Black Caribbean Communists in New York City, Mexico and the West Indies, 1919–1939
Margaret Stevens

The Point Is to Change the World: Selected Writings of Andaiye
Edited by Alissa Trotz

After the Postcolonial Caribbean

Caribbean

Memory, Imagination, Hope

Brian Meeks

PLUTO  PRESS

First published 2023 by Pluto Press
New Wing, Somerset House, Strand, London WC2R 1LA
and Pluto Press Inc.
1930 Village Center Circle, 3-834, Las Vegas, NV 89134

www.plutobooks.com

British Library Cataloguing in Publication Data
A catalogue record for this book is available from the British Library

ISBN 978 0 7453 4790 5   Paperback
ISBN 978 0 7453 4793 6   PDF
ISBN 978 0 7453 4792 9   EPUB

This book is printed on paper suitable for recycling and made from fully
managed and sustained forest sources. Logging, pulping and manufacturing
processes are expected to conform to the environmental standards of the
country of origin.

Typeset by Stanford DTP Services, Northampton, England

Simultaneously printed in the United Kingdom and United States of America

Contents

List of Photographs   vi
Acknowledgments   vii
About the Cover   x

Introduction: A Bend in History's River   1

PART I: REMEMBERING

1. Reminiscing in Black, Gold, and Green   35
2. Reading the Seventies in a Different "Stylie": Dub, Poetry,
    and the Urgency of Message   41
3. The Politics of Edna Manley: A Preliminary Appraisal   69
4. Lamming's Politics and the Radical Caribbean   95
5. Jamaican Roads Not Taken, or a Big "What If" in Stuart Hall's
    Life   110

PART II: IMAGINING

6. Beyond Neoliberalism's Dead End: Thinking Caribbean
    Futures through Stuart Hall and *The Kilburn Manifesto*   127
7. Hegemony and the Trumpian Moment   145
8. Roadblock on Hope Road: The End of Imagination and
    Capital's Late Afternoon   163
9. On the Question of Optimism in Troubled Times: Revolution,
    Tragedy, and Possibility in Caribbean History   182

Index   206

List of Photographs

1. Edna and Norman Manley in Jamaica c. 1933   79
2. *Boy with Reed* (1928)   83
3. *Adam and Eve* (1930)   84
4. *Negro Aroused* (1935)   84
5. *Diggers* (1936)   85
6. *Market Women* (1936)   87
7. *Youth* (1938)   88
8. *Strike* (1938)   89
9. *Brother Man* (1961)   90
10. *The Voice* (1980)   91
11. *Ghetto Mother* (1981)   92

Acknowledgments

It is an absolute privilege to have been able to devote most of my working life in trying to understand and discuss the social as well as political contours of the Caribbean and particularly to engage with the people and movements that have sought to bring about meaningful change in the region. Alongside this, I have had the good fortune of sharing this exploration, conversation, and debate with a community of fellow travelers, many of whom have become steadfast friends and whose sharp minds and keen insights have helped sharpen mine. Among them are my colleagues and collaborators who over the years have been part of a lively discourse on the Caribbean at many venues, symposia, and conferences. Those still here include (and my apologies if I have left anyone out) Rupert Lewis, Anthony Bogues, Patsy Lewis, Percy Hintzen, Pedro Noguera, Anton Allahar, Linden Lewis, Deborah Thomas, Carole Boyce Davies, Alissa Trotz, Paget Henry, Cecilia Green, Maureen Warner-Lewis, Lewis Gordon, Jane Anna Gordon, Neil Roberts, Kari Levitt, Erna Brodber, Alex Dupuy, David Scott, Faith Smith, Belinda Edmondson, Charles Carnegie, Trevor Munroe, Don Robotham, Gina Ulysse, Aaron Kamugisha, Rachel Manley, Rivke Jaffe, Jay Mandle, Mervyn Morris, David Lehmann, Anthony Payne, Hilbourne Watson, C. Y. Thomas, Obika Gray, Velma Pollard, Gordon Rohlehr, David Austin, Patrick Goodin, Bill Schwarz, Carolyn Cooper, Hubert Devonish, Kate Quinn, Shalini Puri, Tennyson Joseph, Sunity Maharaj, Pat Northover, Kim Robinson-Walcott, Wendy Grenade, Yarimar Bonilla, Rhoda Reddock, Clinton Hutton, Esther Figueroa, Anthony Harriott, Naghmeh Sohrabi, Folke Lindahl, Sonjah Stanley Niaah, Jermaine McCalpin, Don Marshall, Pat Mohammed, Fragano Ledgister, Shanti Singham, Maziki Thame, Donna Hope, Donette Francis, Ariella Azoulay, Vazira Zaminder, Honor Ford-Smith, and Francio Guadeloupe; as well as those who have passed on to meet the ancestors, among them Charles Mills, Norman Girvan, Kamau Brathwaite, Andaiye, Barry Chevannes, Rex Nettleford, Manning Marable, Leith Mullings, Stuart Hall, Kamau Brathwaite, Carl Stone, Edwin Jones, Richard Jacobs, Bill Riviere, Pat Emmanuel, Lloyd Best, Selwyn Ryan, and George Lamming.

More immediately related to *After the Postcolonial Caribbean*, I thank the hosts, organizers, and editors who facilitated the keynotes, seminars, and edited collections in which several of the chapters were initially presented or published. I start by thanking Dilip Menon, director of the University of Witwatersrand's Johannesburg Centre for Indian Studies in Africa, for inviting me to deliver an early reading of my chapter "On the Question of Optimism in Troubled Times" as part of his Centre's series of Distinguished Lectures from the Global South. At University College London, I thank Charlotte Al-Khalili, Narges Ansari, Myriam Lamrani, and Kaya Uzel for hosting and inviting me to the 2019 gathering of anthropologists for the conference "After the Event: Prospects and Retrospects of Revolution," at which I further elaborated on this chapter. Thanks to David Scott, Donnette Francis, and the Small Axe collective for their thoughtful 2017 "Symposium on the Jamaican 1970s," held both at CUNY Graduate School and Columbia University, which provided me space to think about my own poetry. Gratitude to Christine Chivallon and the team at the Université Paris Diderot for inviting me to speak on the significance of the Kilburn Manifesto for Caribbean futures at their 2016 conference "Une Journée avec Stuart Hall"; to Sonjah Stanley Niaah and the Institute of Caribbean Studies and Reggae Studies Unit at the University of the West Indies Mona, for inviting me to deliver the Annual Walter Rodney Lecture "Roadblock on Hope Road: The End of Imagination and Capital's Late Afternoon" in 2018; to the Edna Manley Foundation and the Edna Manley School for the Visual and Performing Arts in Kingston, Jamaica, for inviting me to give the annual Edna Manley Memorial Lecture in 2015 and to Kim Robinson-Walcott, editor of *Caribbean Quarterly*, who first published it; to Adi Ophir at Brown University for inviting me to be a panelist at the 2017 conference "The Trump Edition" in their remarkable Political Concepts series; to Bill Schwarz, who was editor of *The Locations of George Lamming*, the Macmillan volume in which my chapter on Lamming first appeared; to Rachel Mordecai, editor of *Small Axe*'s online journal *S/X*, for publishing my short reminiscence on Jamaican independence; and to Paul Bové and *boundary 2*'s online journal *B2O*, for publishing my 2017 reflection on Stuart Hall "Jamaican Roads Not Taken."

I offer here special thanks to my colleagues and students across many departments and in the administration of Brown University, who through their generosity and kind words have made the last seven years memorable, in which, after decades at the University of the West Indies, I came in 2015 to Brown as Chair of the Africana Studies/Rites and Reason Theatre Department. Among them, too many to mention all, I thank my Africana colleagues, Tony Bogues, Tricia Rose, Lundy Braun, Francoise Hamlin, Keisha-Khan Perry, Matthew Guterl, Elmo Terry Morgan, Lisa Biggs, Geri Augusto, Paget Henry, Dotun Ayobade, Karen Allen Baxter, Alonzo Walker, Kathy Moyer, and the late, indomitable Anani Dzidzienyo. And a shout-out to all the brilliant Africana graduate scholars who have seriously informed my thoughts these past seven years!

Special thanks to my long and dear friend and colleague Tony Bogues, who remains the examplar of steadfast intellectual leadership, for his tremendous work in building, as its inaugural director, the Center for the Study of Slavery and Justice (CSSJ) at Brown while constantly reinventing his own scholarly trajectory. Tony has blossomed far beyond his initial spheres of interest in political philosophy and intellectual history, into curation and art history and I am certain that soon he will enter newer, even more exciting fields. Thanks again to you, Tony, and Bedour Alagraa for your vision in initiating the Black Critique series with Pluto Press in which this volume is published. Thanks to the anonymous readers who gave very useful directions in strengthening the manuscript. Thanks to Pluto Press, especially David Shulman, Robert Webb, Emily Orford, Natalie Jones, Melanie Patrick (for her great cover), and all who enthusiastically agreed to publish this volume.

And during this extraordinarily difficult moment in the world, a time of rising authoritarianism and fascism, a time when, in early 2022, the COVID-19 pandemic is still very much a clear and present danger, I want to express thanks to my children for their love and fortitude. To Neto, who has taught us what it means to literally pick yourself up and dust yourself off. To you, Neto Maceo, and your children, Nialli and Zeni, forward ever! And to Anya and Seya, for your thoughtfulness, care, and affection. We watch you in awe and wonder at how you have grown as you pursue your own brilliant paths with creativity, grit, and (mostly) good humor.

Finally, to my dear wife and lifelong companion, Patsy Lewis, without whom this volume would not have seen the light of day. Thanks for your unquestioning support, encouragement, and unremitting presence during the darkest COVID days and nights. You have managed to hold me up even under the strain of your own prodigious efforts to direct a major center and complete your own quite daunting, multiple publication projects. One Love and eternal respect, Patsy.

About the Cover

The book's cover is the frontispiece of an etching on plexiglass by renowned Haitian artist Edouard Duval Carrié. It is titled *Le Royaume de ce Monde* (*The Kingdom of This World*). Like Alejo Carpentier's famous novel of the same name, it is a meditation not only on the meaning of the Haitian Revolution and Haitian independence, but on more expansive questions of the possibilities, vagaries, and prospects facing all postcolonies. I wrote to Edouard, asking him whose eyes were staring out and what its meaning was. His response was: "The eyes are those of the 'witness' in the novel, Ti Noel. He does represent the eyes of the Haitian people who have witnessed and endured so much and are also looking toward an even more uncertain future, which today looks even more troublesome than ever!" I agree entirely with Edouard but add my own coda, proposing that captured beyond the uncertainty, fear, and even paranoia of the independence moment is the enduring and unconquerable will to be free. For what else is the insertion of Laferrière, Christophe's monumental Citadelle just below Ti Noel's line of vision for but to concretely manifest this desire for liberty? Yet we can't avoid noting that the Citadelle was built in an authoritarian manner, with inordinate human sacrifice and blood, thus even further complicating the original postcolonial narrative.

Le Royaume de ce Monde (2017), Etching on plexiglass in painted wood frame, Edouard Duval Carrié, Collection of Patsy Lewis and Brian Meeks.

Introduction
A Bend in History's River

If there was ever a moment when the river of history inflected and percep-
tibly shifted her course, it was 2019. The housing and then financial crash
of 2008–2009 had passed, and a decade later, Western states were still
trying to recover from "the slowest and most uneven economic recovery
in living memory."[1] There was, it seems, evident in the limited indices
of "growth," and its increasingly sluggish pace, something rotten at the
core of this revival. The first signals came, interestingly, from the global
forces of the Right, with the victory and consolidation of regimes veering
toward extreme nationalism and neofascism in Russia, Hungary, Poland,
India, Brazil, Egypt, the Philippines, and Turkey, to mention only some of
the most egregious instances. And then in 2016, first in the summer with
the British vote to exit the European Union and in the fall with Donald
Trump's presidential victory (despite losing the popular vote), the trend
was confirmed. It is not that popular and anti-dictatorial progressive
forces were inactive at this time. The street demonstrations against Brexit
were some of the largest and most impressive in British history, and the
anti-racist, anti–police brutality movement under the slogan "Black Lives
Matter" emerged with real energy in the United States in 2015; but in
almost every instance, these nascent movements seemed to be outflanked
and outmaneuvered by the contingents of reaction, harking back with
nostalgia to romanticized pasts, calling for closed borders, exclusion,
repression, and one narrow, racist national order.

Then 2019 came and upended all of that. Robin Wright in the *New
Yorker* vividly describes the significance and impact of that year:

> the tsunami of protests that swept across six continents … engulfed
> both liberal democracies and ruthless autocracies. … Throughout
> the year, movements emerged overnight, out of nowhere, unleashing
> public fury on a global scale. From Paris and La Paz, to Prague and

---

1   Joe Guinan and Martin O'Neill, "The 'Third Way' May Have Worked for New
Labour, but It Is Impossible Now," *Guardian*, May 13, 2021.

2 · AFTER THE POSTCOLONIAL CARIBBEAN

Port-Au-Prince, Beirut to Bogota and Berlin, Catalonia to Cairo, and in Hong Kong, Harare, Santiago, Sydney, Seoul, Quito, Jakarta, Tehran, Algiers, Baghdad, Budapest, London, New Delhi, Manila and even Moscow.[2]

Each instance of upheaval was, of course, rooted in national narratives, but the common causes were also plain to see. In Chile, economic grievances dating back to the long history of entanglement with neoliberal experiments under the Pinochet dictatorship were at the forefront. In Lebanon, grievances over the cost of living, stagnant wages, and charges of corruption forced Prime Minister Hariri to step down. In Iraq, protests over the government's failure to address declining living standards commingled with deep historic divisions exacerbated, no doubt, by the fragmentation of society and the state in the wake of the US-led invasion. In France, the "Yellow Vests'" protests opposed President Macron's austerity measures, purportedly to end economic malaise. All, as Henry Carey suggests, were united in a common anger and exhaustion with the status quo: "Fed up with rising inequality, corruption and slow economic growth, angry citizens worldwide are demanding an end to corruption and the restoration of the democratic rule of law."[3]

Not only were there unprecedented numbers in the streets, but this global wave, like its predecessor—the worldwide uprising of 1968— brought into being new forms and tactics of popular mobilization. Thus, while the youthful protesters of 1968 were everywhere in the streets, they operated within a political culture, influenced by Fanon, Guevara, and the Black Panthers,[4] that valorized guerrilla warfare and revolutionary violence as favored methods of engagement. The street warriors of 2019, however, learning from available technologies of the cell phone and social

2   Robin Wright, "The Story of 2019: Protests in Every Corner of the Globe," *New Yorker*, December 30, 2019.
3   Henry Carey, in Tony Walker, "2019 Was a Year of Global Unrest, Spurred by Anger at Rising Inequality—and 2020 Is Likely to Be Worse," December 10, 2019, https://theconversation.com. On global inequality at the turn of the twenty first century, see Goran Therborn, "Two Epochal Turns of Inequality, Their Significance and Their Dynamics," *Journal of Chinese Sociology* 8, no. 9 (2021); and Facundo Alvaredo, Lucas Chancel, Thomas Piketty, Emmanuel Saez, and Gabriel Zucman (eds.) *World Inequality Report* 2018, Belknap Press Harvard, Cambridge, MA, 2018.
4   See Robyn Spencer, *The Revolution Has Come: Black Power, Gender, and the Black Panther Party in Oakland*, Duke University Press, Durham, NC, 2016.

media, operate within their own culture of dispersed and spontaneous mass mobilization.[5] If the politics of the 1960s was driven by charismatic (male) leaders, political parties, and trade unions, the new wave often has women in the vanguard, or might be defined as an almost leaderless movement, brought together by social media tweets and with equally rapid demobilization when necessary. This absence of a center that can be identified, arrested, and broken makes the new movement particularly difficult to defeat and therefore suited for an articulated, tactical resistance. As Paolo Gerbaudo suggests, "these protests are popular insurgencies. They reflect the failure of nation states in the global era. They're not a passing crisis that can be remedied through the regular lever of the state … these movements may be the early symptoms of a new global crisis."[6]

Then, at the tail end of 2019, the COVID-19 virus surfaced, first in Wuhan, China, and then rapidly spreading across the globe until the World Health Organization classified it as a pandemic on March 11, 2020. Earlier prognostications on the continued vibrancy of the popular protests were initially pessimistic, as the view held by many was that the accompanying quarantine measures would stem, along with COVID, the viral spread of popular upheaval. But on May 25 in Minneapolis, Minnesota, George Floyd, an African American man, was arrested by Derek Chauvin, a white policeman, who, while Floyd was on the ground and immobile, sunk his knee into Floyd's neck for more than nine minutes until he was dead. This tragic horror, one of a now-familiar pattern, often recorded on cellphone cameras of brutal police violence directed against Black people, sparked outrage across the United States. By June the demonstrations under the "Black Lives Matter" (BLM) slogan had brought millions into the streets, with hundreds of marches daily, and were being described in the New York Times as the largest in US history. The marches—persistent, multiracial, urban, and rural—surpassed by far the one-day Women's March against Trump's inauguration in January 2017 and the Tea Party right-wing rallies that followed Obama's coming to office in 2009.[7]

---

5   See Wright, "The Story of 2019."
6   Paolo Gerbaudo, quoted in Wright, "The Story of 2019." Gerbaudo develops his analysis of the new movements in Paolo Gerbaudo, *The Mask and the Flag: Populism, Citizenship and Global Protest*, Oxford University Press, Oxford, 2017.
7   See Larry Buchanan, Quoctrung Bui, and Jugal K. Patel, "Black Lives Matter May Be the Largest Movement in U.S. History," *New York Times*, July 3, 2020; Lara Putnam, Jeremy Pressman, and Erica Chenoweth, "Black Lives Matter beyond America's Big Cities," *Washington Post*, July 8, 2020; and Keeanga Yamahtta Taylor,

Black Lives Matter, however, refused to remain within the confines of US borders. By the middle of June, the internet news service *VOX* noted in a headline that "BLM has become a global rallying cry against racism and police brutality"[8] and continued to note people taking to the streets in London, Seoul, Sydney, Monrovia, Rio de Janeiro, and Idlib, Syria. And as one Belgian activist noted, "outrage at an event in the upper Midwest of the USA, was transformed into people thinking how it was relevant where we were."[9]

Floyd's murder arose out of the specific history of US racism and police abuse of Black people, but it is fitting and deeply significant that it found resonance globally, in a world in which the history of modernity is deeply intertwined with the consolidation of capitalism, European suzerainty, and the consequent imbrication of race and racism.[10] In this sense, then, the Floyd mobilization is not only a sustaining and continuation of the turn in the river and the popular upwelling of 2019; it also suggests a deepening with the central problematics of race and racism more firmly affixed to the banner of protest alongside authoritarianism, corruption, and the state itself.

PUERTO RICO AND HAITI

The Caribbean, too, at least in some constituencies, has been active in this new turn to popular protest. Puerto Rico's long and fraught history of quasi-colonial status with the United States was further aggravated by the 2006 final phasing out of the federal tax credits that US businesses had traditionally received when investing on the island. This came close to coinciding with the 2008 financial crisis, and the subsequent rapid decline in Puerto Rico's economic fortunes led to the establishment in 2016 of a Financial Oversight and Management Board, called by Puerto Ricans, with significant chagrin, "La Junta," which was appointed by Congress to manage the island's finances. The following year, Hurricane

---

From *#BlackLivesMatter to Black Liberation*, Haymarket Books, Chicago, 2016.
8   Jen Kirby, "BLM Has Become a Global Rallying Cry against Racism and Police Brutality," *VOX*, June 12, 2020.
9   Kirby, "BLM."
10   See, for instance, Cedric Robinson's thesis exploring the historical inter-relationships of capitalism and race: Cedric Robinson, *Black Marxism: The Making of the Black Radical Tradition*, University of North Carolina Press, Chapel Hill, 1983; and Minkah Makalani, "Cedric Robinson and the Origins of Race," *Boston Review*, accessed February 11, 2021, www.bostonreview.net.

Maria devastated the island, with an official death toll of 2,975 persons. This closely connected sequence of economic and natural catastrophe, exposing for all to see the territory's liminal status,[11] was further aggravated by the abysmal response of the Trump regime, which refused to release sufficient disaster funds, appearing to punish the island for not seeming to be sufficiently in the Republican political camp.

The immediate call to the streets, however, was none of these, but the release of a series of social media tweets[12] with Governor Ricardo Rosello speaking with his aides and political associates and suggesting his arrogance and contempt for ordinary Puerto Ricans, who were still deeply traumatized by their dire social and economic plight. The tweets hit the news on July 1, 2019. Within fifteen days, a series of island-wide demonstrations and strikes, with increasing numbers and fervor, had forced him to resign. An unprecedented alliance of feminists, LGBTQ activists, and entertainers, as well as overwhelming support from swaths of the population who had never before been involved in politics, brought the government to its knees and changed the temper of Puerto Rican politics.[13]

The problem of Puerto Rico's political future and the increasing desire for statehood remain unresolved. Meanwhile, Puerto Ricans who are all US citizens vote with their feet and relocate to the mainland. Since 2008, the population, according to a Pew poll, has declined by 15 percent.[14] Puerto Ricans increasingly seem to have, on the one hand, abandoned sovereignty as understood by the twentieth-century anti-colonial yearning for independence of *La Patria*,[15] but this has not assuaged the desire for

11 See Yarimar Bonilla and Marisol LeBron, *Aftershocks of Disaster: Puerto Rico before and after the Storm*, Haymarket Books, Chicago, 2019.
12 See "What Is behind the Protests in Puerto Rico?" *New York Times*, August 3, 2019.
13 See Simon Romero, Francis Robles, Patricia Mazzei, and Jose A. Del Real, "15 Days of Fury: How Puerto Rico's Government Collapsed," *New York Times*, July 27, 2019.
14 Francis Robles and Patricia Mazzei, "After Protests, Will Real Change Come to Puerto Rico?" *New York Times*, August 3, 2019.
15 In the 2020 election plebiscite on the question of statehood, on a straight Yes or No vote, 52 percent voted in favor of statehood and 47 percent against. In five previous votes, there had always been three options, with, alongside independence and statehood, the existing option of "Commonwealth" or the existing and now generally despised form of "Free Associated State." See Cristina Corujo, "Puerto Rico Votes in Favor of Statehood. But What Does It Mean for the Island?" www.abcnews.go.com, November 8, 2020. However, even if statehood were to be voted

a unified Puerto Rican people. As Ed Morales suggests, the movement of 2019 presented the possibility of a new, intersectional unity of Puerto Ricans beyond the old patriarchal formations, including women and LGBTQ people. "What unifies everyone," Morales asserts "is the pride and love for Puerto Rico. Puerto Ricans have this outsized nationalism because it's been a colony for its entire existence. It's this tremendous need to have national unity because the sovereign nation doesn't exist."[16]

This was also a year of distress and protest in Puerto Rico's neighbor, the state of Haiti, which shares Hispaniola with the Dominican Republic and occupies the western third of the island. Haiti's traumas are uniquely Haitian, yet she shares resonances with Puerto Rico and the world. The second independent country in the hemisphere after the United States, Haiti has suffered through quarantine and economic strangulation, debt, invasion, and dictatorship. More recently, following the military overthrow of Jean-Bertrand Aristide's Fanmi Lavalas government in 1991, and his return three years later as a "tamed," more moderate leader,[17] a series of regimes have careened toward corruption and increased the poverty of the already pauperized majority. Destitution and tragedy, however, hit unimaginable turning points after the 2010 earthquake that destroyed much of the capital Port-au-Prince and killed an estimated 250,000 people.[18] International rescue and recuperation efforts have been a failure, and subsequent regimes, particularly those led by Martelly and Moïse, have been accused of extensive corruption. Most shockingly, development funds provided by the Venezuelan government, through the Petrocaribe agreement, have gone missing, even as President Moïse, under direction from the International Monetary Fund (IMF),

on by referendum, as is possible arising out of two distinct bills put before the House Committee on Natural Resources in April 2021, there remains significant opposition on both sides of the aisle, including from no less a notable person as Democratic leader in the Senate, Chuck Schumer. See Pedro Caban, "The End of the Commonwealth of Puerto Rico," *Portside*, June 7, 2021, https://portside.org,2021-05-20.
16   Ed Morales, quoted in Isabella Herrera, "'It's Not Full Citizenship': What It Means to Be Puerto Rican Post-Maria," *New York Times*, September 19, 2019. See also Ed Morales, *Fantasy Island: Colonialism, Exploitation and the Betrayal of Puerto Rico*, Bold Type Books, New York, 2019.
17   See Alex Dupuy, *The Prophet and Power: Jean-Bertrand Aristide, the International Community and Haiti*, Rowman and Littlefield, Lanham, MD, 2007.
18   See Alex Dupuy, "Class, Power, Sovereignty: Haiti before and after the Earthquake," in Linden Lewis (ed.) *Caribbean Sovereignty, Development and Democracy in an Age of Globalization*, Routledge, New York, 2013, 17–34.

indicated his intent to remove the few remaining subsidies on food and fuel.[19] Further ire was directed at Moïse when he sought to interpret the constitutional and electoral arrangements to extend his term in office.[20] Through 2019, demonstrations continued and amounted to as many as eighty-four per day[21] as the end of the year approached.

And then, on July 7, 2021, Jovenel Moïse was assassinated.[22] Despite the arrest of a group of Colombian mercenaries charged with carrying out the tragic act, months later it was still not clear who was responsible. In September 2021, chief prosecutor for Port-au-Prince Bed-Ford Claude asked a judge to charge Prime Minister Ariel Henry in connection with the killing, but before this could be carried out, Henry fired Claude.[23] This tragedy and the accompanying uncertainty has thrown an already shattered country into further turmoil; and then in August another unimaginably damaging magnitude 7.2 earthquake rocked southern Haiti, killing hundreds and displacing thousands.[24]

Haiti and Puerto Rico: neighbors in the Caribbean Sea, but with dramatically different histories. Puerto Rico was the mid-twentieth-century showcase for American success and what it meant to be within the sphere of the Western superpower in the Cold War, though now cast aside, her example superfluous in a world of neoliberal globalization. And Haiti, the victorious exception in the age of slavery that brought Europe and white colonialism to their knees two centuries before and therefore had to be simultaneously punished, denied, and erased from history. Yet both seem now united in the second decade of the twenty-first century, in a common struggle against corruption and liminality and desperately searching for modalities of control and autonomy from a distant, uncaring sovereign.

---

19   See Kirk Semple, "'There Is No Hope': Crisis Pushes Haiti to the Brink of Collapse," *New York Times*, October 20, 2019.

20   See Azam Ahmed, "Haiti Gripped by Violent Protests amid Calls for President's Ouster," *New York Times*, September 28, 2019.

21   Arvind Dilawar, interview with Kim Ives, "Haiti's Massive Protests Are a Repudiation of Authoritarianism and US Intervention," *Jacobin*, March 5, 2021.

22   British Broadcasting Corporation, "Haiti's President's Assassination: What We Know So Far," July 7, 2021.

23   Anthony Faiola, "A Haitian Prosecutor Sought Charges against the Prime Minister in the President's Assassination. He Was Fired," *Washington Post*, September 14, 2021.

24   Henry Fountain, "Strong Earthquake Rocks Haiti Killing Hundreds," *New York Times*, August 14, 2021, updated August 23, 2021.

CUBA

Then, on July 11, 2021, Cuba, too, erupted in widespread anti-government demonstrations that on the surface bore remarkable similarities to the global uprisings of 2019. There was the initial demonstration in San Antonio do los Banos that, in the era of smartphone communication, quickly spread to other cities and to the capital, Havana, itself.[25] The underlying demands were also similar—against rising inflation, the seemingly interminable economic crisis, debilitating power outages, and, from some, the six-decade-long regime of the Partido Communista de Cuba (PCC). The anti-government protests were matched with parallel demonstrations and celebrations in the Cuban exile community in Miami, where, as in the past, following the collapse of the Soviet Union in the early 1990s and the ensuing "Special Period" and following Fidel Castro's death in 2016, there was anticipation that the end of communism was imminent.[26] That the Cuban context might possess its own peculiarities, however, became apparent when in response to the protests, the government and its supporters held their own massive rally in Havana on July 17,[27] suggesting that even with evident erosion, the Revolution still maintains significant popular support.

If this is indeed the case, then it is cause for scrutiny. Surely there is a story to be told of the tenacity of those who, against all odds, continue to support the Revolution, unless we cynically conclude that all the people in the street were herded out for the sake of the cameras. Cubans are suffering from economic depredation not seen on such a scale and intensity since the Special Period and the existential threat that followed the withdrawal of Soviet assistance. The reasons are compound and include the drastic reduction in energy subsidies from Venezuela; the deepening of US sanctions, particularly the banning of remittances imposed by Trump and continued without relent by Biden; and a concatenation of pandemic-related factors, including the crash of the vital

25   See Marc Frank and Sarah Marsh, "Cuba Sees Biggest Protest for Decades as Pandemic Adds to Woes," accessed July 17, 2021, https://www.reuters.com/world/americas/street-protests-break-out-cuba-2021-07-11/. For a more textured reading of the protests, see Comunistas Editorial Board, "From Cuba: A Description of the Protests," July 17, 2021, in *Socialist Worker*, issue no. 2764.
26   See Patricia Mazzei, "Miami Embraces Cuba Protests: 'I Never Thought This Day Would Come,'" *New York Times*, July 17, 2021.
27   See Adam Taylor, "After Unrest and Arrests, Cuban Government Holds Flag-Waving Rally as Show of Strength," *New York Times*, July 17, 2021.

tourism industry and the rapid spread of the virus itself.[28] One of the supreme ironies of the present moment is that the globally outstanding Cuban health system, which has the capability to research and design its own vaccine, is hamstrung by the sheer wreckage of the Cuban economy, which has severely inhibited its production and effective distribution.

Yet even with these extreme economic conditions, and the continuing support of large numbers of Cubans for the regime, the July protests seemed to signal something qualitatively new. There were more people in the streets than ever before, they were younger, and based on social media images and the presence of hip-hop messaging, especially the anthem of the protesters "Patria y Vida" (Homeland and Life),[29] the crowds were more visibly Black in composition.

The cynical character of US foreign policy in helping to foster this crisis is quite obvious. For six decades, apart from the brief interregnum late in Obama's second term, the policy of squeezing Cuba until her people squeal for hunger and hopefully revolt has been paramount. In response, Cuba has built a fortress society and economy in which central, authoritarian control is the only clear alternative to US intervention. Centralized state hegemony has effectively undermined either "overthrow" strategies of CIA and military intervention or "underthrow" strategies of IMF policy manipulation. In relatively good times, with assistance from the Eastern Bloc or even Venezuela, the state has been able to provide excellent health services, a free and effective educational system, and a modicum of basic goods and services. This is the reason why Cuba survives while Left-leaning regimes in Guatemala, Chile, Jamaica, Nicaragua, and across the Americas have vanished at great human cost. Central authoritarian control is simultaneously, however, deeply corrosive and can only continue as a viable policy of a popular government in times of war or crisis and not as a permanent way of life.

But even at the best of times, the centrally planned economy engendered supply chain inefficiencies, shortages, and concurrent dissatisfactions, which have been overlooked in the past by a significant majority in the interest and defense of the *patria* and the Revolution. The Cuban dilemma has always been how to maintain the integrity of a sovereign, independent, socialist state that will be able to provide a prosperous and

---

28   See Oscar Lopez and Ernesto Londono, "'Everyone Has a Tipping Point': Hunger Fuels Cuba's Protests," *New York Times*, July 12, 2021.
29   See Megan Janetsky, "'Patria y Vida'—Homeland and Life—Watchwords in Cuba's Protests," *New York Times*, July 13, 2021.

egalitarian future for her people without returning to the suzerainty of the United States and, more immediately, without succumbing to the revanchist forces in Miami. For anyone who believes that Cuba will make a smooth transition from socialism to Miami-style capitalism should think again of what occurred in Chile under Pinochet, Argentina under the generals, and the rivers of blood it would require to seek to return the country to her sordid, dependent, capitalist past.

The policy answers, however, that would turn around the present moment of erosion while preserving the ideals of a social and egalitarian state are by no means immediately apparent. They must head at minimum in the direction of a "revolution in the revolution" that would recognize the alienation, hostility, and concerns of urban youths, particularly Black urban young women and men,[30] and bring them, LGBTQ Cubans, and disenchanted intellectuals into a new expanded and more inclusive coalition with the rural and urban working class. This, however, would also require a new international situation in which, pressured by popular opinion, the United States, Europe, and Latin America were to become more open to doing business with Cuba and, internally, for the emergence of new permutations of market and state that would preserve the integrity of a socialist society alongside a buoyant private sector.

THE ANGLOPHONE CARIBBEAN

The states of the Anglophone Caribbean, united in the loose alliance of the Caribbean Community (CARICOM), surprisingly and somewhat ironically, in light of their location at the heart of the radical upheavals of the 1960s,[31] remain for the most part dormant. There is certainly, beyond the collapse of the radical projects of the 1970s, an active and vibrant feminist movement. Various feminist organizations, including Red Thread and Tamùkke Feminist Rising in Guyana; the Sistren Theatre Collective and more recently the Tambourine Army in Jamaica; Code Red in Barbados; the Caribbean Feminist Action Network (CAFRA)

---

30   For a plaintive statement on the continued alienation of Black people in Cuba and a call for reform, particularly of the police and carceral state, see Cuba Liberacion Negra, "Statement of Colectivo Cuba Liberacion Negra" (The Cuba Black Liberation Collective), accessed September 2, 2021, https://medium.com/@ cuba.liberacion.negra.

31   See, for instance, Kate Quinn (ed.) *Black Power in the Caribbean*, University of Florida Press, Gainesville, 2014; and Rita Keresztesi, *Literary Black Power in the Caribbean: Fiction, Music and Film*, Routledge, New York, 2021.

and Womantra in Trinidad and Tobago; Productive Organisation for Women in Action and Toledo Maya Women's Council in Belize; and Life in Leggings, a Caribbean Alliance against Gender-Based Violence, have fought against domestic violence, lobbied to change laws, and fought to change attitudes that perpetuate sexual harassment, violence, and rape in and out of the workplace.[32] And increasingly in the first two decades of the twenty-first century, a vigorous LGBTQ movement, working in a region in which homophobia is rife, has battled on all fronts to change laws, societal norms, and mores that discriminate against and make life exceedingly dangerous for gay and queer communities.[33] There has also been an uplifting renaissance of popular protest music as in the instance of Jamaica, where the "reggae revival" of the past decade has brought brilliant young artists like Chronixx, Lila Ike, Protégé, Jah9, and Koffee to the fore.[34] Singing with lyrics that hark back to the radical themes of cultural resistance and Black liberation of the 1960s and 1970s, the new music is nonetheless fresh and current in its incorporation of driving dancehall tracks and increasingly with the incorporation of feminist messages.

Beyond these important exceptions, however, the absence of popular movements and certainly of mass upheavals, along lines evident across the globe, is cause for consideration. One possible answer, at first somewhat compelling, is the proposal first mooted three decades ago by Jorge Dominguez and colleagues, that there is quiescence in the Anglophone Caribbean precisely because here, relatively speaking, things have gone well and post-independence parliamentary democracy has flourished. The logical conclusion, therefore, is that there is no toxic

32   See, for instance, Patricia Mohammed (ed.) *Gendered Realities: Essays in Caribbean Feminist Thought*, The University of the West Indies Press, Kingston, 2002; Rhoda Reddock, *Women Labour and Politics in Trinidad and Tobago*, Zed Books, London, 1994; Michelle V. Rowley, "Whose Time Is It? Gender and Humanism in Contemporary Caribbean Feminist Advocacy," *Small Axe* 14, no. 31 (2010): 1–5; and Alissa Trotz (ed.) *The Point Is To Change the World: Selected Writings of Andaiye*, Pluto Press, London, 2020.

33   See Cornel Gray and Nikolai Attai, "LGBT Rights, Sexual Citizenship and Blacklighting in the Anglophone Caribbean: What Do Queers Want/What Does Colonialism Need?" in Michael Bosia et al., *The Oxford Handbook of Global LGBT and Sexual Diversity Politics*, www.oxfordhandbooks.com, Oxford, 2020.

34   See Reshma B., "The Reggae Revival," www.read.tidal.com, December 27, 2019; Aileen Torres-Bennet, "Reggae Making a Revival in Jamaica, Recalling Golden Era of 70s," Reuters, August 24, 2017; and Kezia Page, "Bongo Futures: The Reggae Revival and Its Genealogies," *Small Axe* 21, no. 52 (2017): 1–16.

brew of authoritarian leadership imposing draconian, foreign-derived economic policy, such as was at the heart of many of the upheavals of 2019.[35] The Anglophone Caribbean has notably, with the exception of the 1979 Grenada Revolution, managed to maintain electoral systems that, despite severe strains (Jamaica in 1980, a few regimes that have dominated parliament for prolonged periods in St. Vincent and Grenada, as well as the persistent problem of race and its impact on elections in Guyana, for instance), still appear to facilitate succession.[36] This, however, is at best only partially true, and at worst a mirage. The moment of relative calm is not the clear blue lagoon of a successful polity, but a dead pool of malaise, deep cynicism, and withdrawal from politics as well as from the postcolonial vision of the political kingdom as the avenue through which social and human improvement and "betterment" must pass.

I suggest elsewhere in this volume, and indeed through much of my work,[37] that though confronted with the sheer might of empire, it is the political folding and collapse of the progressive movements and regimes that led and inhabited the "Long Seventies" that has yielded an articulated twilight of disillusionment. While all the Caribbean territories have their own social and political trajectories,[38] it is worthwhile to think of

35 Though written in and referring to an earlier period, the best expression of the position that Anglo-Caribbean democracy might make the region an exception among "developing nations" is to be found in Jorge Dominguez, Robert Pastor, and R. Delisle Worrell, *Democracy in the Caribbean: Political, Economic and Social Perspectives*, Johns Hopkins University Press, Baltimore, 1993.

36 For a discussion of Caribbean electoral systems, suggesting their relative resilience, see Cynthia Barrow-Giles, "Democracy at Work: A Comparative Study of the Caribbean State," *Round Table* 100, no. 414 (June 2011): 285–302.

37 See Brian Meeks, "The Political Moment in Jamaica: The Dimensions of Hegemonic Dissolution," in Manning Marable (ed.) *Dispatches from the Ebony Tower: Intellectuals Confront the African American Experience*, Columbia University Press, New York, 2000, 52–74; and Brian Meeks, *Envisioning Caribbean Futures: Jamaican Perspectives*, The University of the West Indies Press, Kingston, 2007.

38 I think of Barbados, in particular, where despite a decade or more of recession, the election of a new and vibrant leader in Mia Mottley in 2018 has given hope for the possibility of a more engaged conversation with the Barbadian people and greater commitment to a broader Caribbean unity. But this hope is running against the current. See, for instance, Mottley's compelling 2021 address to the 76th UN General Assembly: "Barbados: Prime Minister Addresses General Debate," September 24, 2021, https://media.un.org/asset/k1r/k1rfi800fw. Most of all, the 2021 decision to break with the British monarchy and make Barbados a republic confirms a boldness of leadership only too rare in the contemporary Anglophone Caribbean. See, for instance, Danica Coto, Associated Press,

Jamaica's declining voter turnout rates as less of an outlier than a portent of things likely to come for the rest of the region. In the 2016 general elections, the turnout rate of 48.37 percent of registered voters was the lowest since the PNP boycotted the 1983 elections, but the 2020 elections eclipsed this with an even lower 37 percent turnout.[39] The stark analysis of a column with the heading "Turn Out for What?" in the *Jamaica Observer* bluntly encapsulates the sense of a looming disenchantment at the end of things:

> years of political skullduggery and broken promises have turned off a great many voters. And to make matters worse, deliberate acts of political benightedness and deprivation, tribalization, trivialization of our democratic process, lack of civic pride and interest, big money influence and involvement—without regard for ethical altruism or institutional morality—the absence of inspirational leadership, and just sheer intellectual dishonesty are but a few of the reasons for the steady decline in voter participation.[40]

The range of statistics from across the region pointing to a crunch moment is overwhelming. In his insightful book *Beyond Coloniality*, Aaron Kamugisha gives a snapshot of some highlights, including: Guyana being among the countries with the highest suicide rates in the world; unemployment in Grenada between 2013 and 2015 averaging over 30 percent; the rates of sexual assault in three Caribbean countries ranking among the top-ten countries with the highest rates of sexual assault; the seven countries with the highest rates of educated workers emigrating to OECD countries all coming from the Caribbean; and every Anglophone Caribbean country except Trinidad and Tobago being in a formal structural adjustment agreement with the IMF.[41] To these must be added that among 180 countries measured on the 2019 Corruption Perception Index, three countries—Jamaica, Guyana, and Trinidad—were ranked

"Barbados Becomes a Republic after Bidding Farewell to British Monarchy," accessed June 21, 2022, https://www.pbs.org/newshour/world/barbados-becomes-a-republic-after-bidding-farewell-to-british-monarchy.

39   Electoral Commission of Jamaica, "General Election 2020 Preliminary Results," https://ecj.com.jm, September 4, 2020.

40   Christopher Burns, "Turn Out for What?" *Jamaica Observer*, September 20, 2020.

41   See Aaron Kamugisha, *Beyond Coloniality: Citizenship and Freedom in the Caribbean Intellectual Tradition*, Indiana University Press, Bloomington, 2019, 54.

among the most corrupt[42] and, tragically, that in terms of global murder rates per 100,000 persons, four Anglophone Caribbean countries ranked in the top ten, with Jamaica at four, while seven altogether ranked in the top twenty-one.[43] For the Anglophone Caribbean this is not a moment of happy cohabitation with the neoliberal model, nor is it one of peaceful complaisance with a functioning and successful parliamentary democracy. Rather, as Norman Girvan[44] has warned, this is a time of growing existential crisis in which the failure of the postcolonial model to deliver a better life for the majority, their perception of rising prosperity for only a small minority, and the growing possibility of environmental disaster on the horizon, has led not to popular revolt but rather an emerging consensus of all-around hopelessness, with a surge to the exits, and for those who can't make it, a turn to the bending and breaking of rules to survive, and to try to achieve the good life, by any means necessary.

One of the clearest indicators of a new situation has been the gradual erosion and then more rapid erasure over the past four decades of the notion of sovereignty as a worthwhile and achievable objective. In a survey of the late colonial and immediate postcolonial struggle for liberation in Africa and the Caribbean, Adom Getachew focuses on the efforts of N. W. Manley, Eric Williams, Michael Manley, Kwame Nkrumah, and Julius Nyerere, among others, to not only transform the relationship of the newly independent states to the Western world, but to reconfigure the entire world itself, in the direction of one grounded in the principle of "nondomination." This project, arising from a profound and assertive sense of confidence in self and of the historical role that Black people were called upon to play, she coined as their ambitious attempt at "world-making":

the combination of nationalism and internationalism that Nkrumah and others articulated was increasingly tethered to the territorial form of the nation-state. Thus, the world-making of decolonization should be understood as an internationalism of the nation-state. But

---

42   See "Corruption Perception Index 2019," accessed June 2019, www.transparency.org/cpi.

43   "Murder Rate by Country 2021," *World Population Review, 2021,* accessed May 1, 2021, https://worldpopulationreview.com/en/country-rankings/murder-rate-by-country.

44   See Norman Girvan, "Assessing Westminster in the Caribbean: Then and Now," *Commonwealth and Comparative Politics* 53, no. 1 (2015): 95–107.

even in this phase where anticolonial nationalism was bound to the institutional form of the nation-state, its vision of the world order went far beyond demanding an inclusion in and expansion of an existing international society. Instead the pursuit of international nondomination entailed a thoroughgoing reinvention of the legal, political and economic structures of the international order.[45]

If this prepossession of leadership, no doubt also present in popular perceptions of the immediate postcolonial period, has been in steep decline, surely one signal of its nadir must have been the 2011 poll conducted in Jamaica's venerable *Gleaner*, which found that 60 percent of the Jamaican people supported the view that the country would have been better off had it remained a British colony, with 17 percent disagreeing.[46] And the final nail in the coffin must certainly have been the March 22, 2019, meeting in southern Florida at Donald Trump's residence at Mar-a-Lago, of a handful of Caribbean leaders at the president's insistence. In the ongoing US efforts to isolate and possibly overthrow the Maduro government in Venezuela, the Anglophone Caribbean (CARICOM) countries have been a sticking point. Most, like Haiti, were beneficiaries of Venezuelan solidarity through the Petrocaribe agreement that provided them with generous credit lines and development funds connected to the purchase of Venezuelan oil. The United States pressured Jamaica, St. Lucia, Haiti, and the Bahamas to break CARICOM solidarity and secure sufficient votes in the Organization of American States to help reelect their preferred anti-Maduro candidate Luis Almagro as secretary general. The sorry photograph of five Caribbean leaders (including the Dominican Republic, which is not a member of CARICOM) waiting in the anteroom of Trump's office for his summons and directive spoke

---

45 Adom Getachew, *Worldmaking after Empire: The Rise and Fall of Self-Determination*, Princeton University Press, Princeton, NJ, 2019, 25; and Adom Getachew, "When Jamaica Led the Fight against Exploitation," *Boston Review*, February 5, 2019, http://bostonreview.net/race.

46 "Jamaicans Would Have Been Better Off British," *BBC News*, June 28, 2011. Ironically, as many citizens of "independent" Caribbean states contemplate the imagined pleasures of colonialism, "non-sovereign" Caribbean territories, beginning with the 2009 demonstrations in the French DOMs, are chafing and revolting against the continued presence and domination of the metropolitan power. See Adlai Murdoch (ed.) *The Struggle of Non-Sovereign Caribbean Territories: Neoliberalism since the French Antillean Uprisings of 2009*, Rutgers University Press, New Brunswick, NJ, 2021.

volumes. The bold decision of Barbados Prime Minister Mia Mottley to break with the Monarchy and make Barbados a republic in 2021 led to renewed soundings from Jamaica's Prime Minister Andrew Holness that his country would soon become a republic, too,[47] and despite scattered anti-royal protests and calls for reparations when Prince William and his wife, Kate Middleton, the Duchess of Cambridge, visited Jamaica in March 2022,[48] there is no vibrant sense of urgency arising from a burning desire to claim full, unambiguous sovereignty coming from the state. Rather, there is a suspicious scent of one-upmanship, in which the government of Jamaica, perceiving tiny Barbados as having stolen a march on her leadership status in the Anglophone Caribbean, sought to reassert her prestige.

This is the dead-end space that the Caribbean occupies in the third decade of the century. The Caribbean states have become a "scuffling of islands"[49] with limited principle and purpose to guide them. Provided they follow the rules of the Fund and obey the twists and turns of US foreign policy, they might be left alone in benign neglect by the empire to try to make ends meet; but as St. Vincent Minister of Finance Camillo Gonsalves asks ironically:

Will CARICOM as an organization disappear? Of course not. We are a bunch of islands and states clustered closely together. Geography and reality will undoubtedly force us to cooperate in our own self-interest on various functional tasks. The logic of integration economics remains compelling. But the idea of CARICOM, the principle of solidarity the

47   See Christopher Thomas, "Holness Says Becoming a Republic Should Not Be Empty Symbolism," *The Gleaner*, December 10, 2021, https://jamaica-gleaner.com/article/news/20211210/holness-says-becoming-republic-should-not-be-empty-symbolism.
48   See Kate Chappell and Brian Ellsworth, "British Royals' Jamaica Visit Stirs Demands for Slave Reparations," Reuters, March 23, 2022, https://www.reuters.com/world/americas/jamaicans-protest-slavery-reparations-ahead-visit-by-british-royals-2022-03-22/.
49   For this notion, see Gordon Rohlehr, "A Scuffling of Islands: The Dream and Reality of Caribbean Unity in Poetry and Song," in Brian Meeks and Folke Lindahl (eds.) *New Caribbean Thought: A Reader*, The University of the West Indies Press, Kingston, 2001, 265–305; and Patsy Lewis, "A Scuffling of Islands, or a Nation?" in Aaron Kamugisha (ed.) *Caribbean Political Thought: Theories of the Postcolonial State*, Ian Randle Publishers, Kingston, 2013, 363–73.

ethos of one for all, has died. And with it, the dream of a more perfect union. RIP CARICOM: 1973–2020.[50]

NEW THINKING

The real-world evaporation of any vestigial space for sovereignty has been accompanied by a growing and lively theoretical debate[51] in Caribbean studies as to its continued utility, or how it might be reconfigured to more appropriately work with novel emancipatory projects for the Caribbean people.

Linden Lewis, for instance, suggests that sovereignty as a form of relative autonomy was always more myth than substance. What little of the myth that persisted was disabused even before formal independence, with the 1953 ouster of the PPP government in British Guyana, reconfirmed with the 1983 invasion of revolutionary Grenada and sealed with the overthrow of Aristide in Haiti in 1991 and the 1997 "Shiprider" agreements that gave US warships the right to freely patrol "sovereign" Caribbean waters. For Lewis, the only answer must be to abandon the empty notion of political sovereignty and return to the older concept of the "sovereignty of labor," placing labor and the power of the people at the center of a society based on freedom, equality, and social justice.[52]

Yarimar Bonilla, in her granular, ethnographic study of the 2008–2009 strikes and demonstrations in Guadeloupe and Martinique, protesting the persistent racial and colonial character of the departements d'outre mer (DOMs) constitutional arrangements with France, imagines the possibility of "non-sovereign futures" that do not necessarily follow the "the decisive breaks with the past associated with modernist models of

---

50 Gonsalves's immediate reference was a vote in the OAS on December 6, 2020, when Jamaica broke with Trinidad and Tobago and voted with unelected Venezuelan representative Juan Guaido, condemning Trinidad and Tobago for an incident in the waters between Venezuela and Trinidad that had led to the deaths of a number of Venezuelan migrants. Camillo Gonsalves, "Every Island for Itself…," *iwitness news*, accessed April 21, 2021, www.iwnsvg.com/2021/03/09/every-island-for-itself.
51 For a useful exploration of recent trends, see Tennyson Joseph, "The Intellectual Under Neo-Liberal Hegemony in the English-Speaking Caribbean," *Social and Economic Studies* 66, no. 3/4 (2017): 97–122.
52 See Linden Lewis, "The Dissolution of the Myth of Sovereignty in the Caribbean," in Lewis (ed.) *Caribbean Sovereignty, Development and Democracy*, 68–87.

sweeping revolutionary success."[53] More to the point, she identifies specifically two notions arising from the popular demonstrations: the first, its opposition to *pwofitasyon*, a Creole word that encompasses exploitation and profiteering; and the second, *Liyannaj*, another Creole term that implies the coming together for common goals. Both terms, she suggests, agreeing with Edouard Glissant, are part of a new "poetic formation"[54] that lays the foundation for novel ways to imagine community outside the traditional categories of citizen and nation.[55]

And in a similarly close, ethnographic reading of another major Caribbean catastrophe of recent times—the 2010 invasion of Tivoli Gardens in Kingston to capture the community's "Don" Christopher "Dudus" Coke[56]—Deborah Thomas also seeks to repurpose the use of sovereignty. She explores, chronicles, and meditates on the tragic killing of an unknown number of citizens—somewhere between seventy-five and two hundred—by the police and military in the Tivoli raid, and argues that any return to the question of sovereignty and the political must be closely bound to questions of the ethical, of affect,[57] of repair, and of love.[58] Thomas asks:

53 See Yarimar Bonilla, *Non-Sovereign Futures: French Caribbean Politics in the Wake of Disenchantment*, University of Chicago Press, Chicago, 2015, 177.
54 Bonilla, *Non-Sovereign Futures*, 151.
55 See *Non-Sovereign Futures*, 177. See also Bonilla's essay "Ordinary Sovereignty," in which she argues that the notion of political sovereignty in the Caribbean is a fiction and calls for greater attention to the congruences between the independent and non-independent Caribbean territories. See Yarimar Bonilla, "Ordinary Sovereignty," *Small Axe* 17, no. 3 (2013): 153.
56 See also my chapter "Jamaica on the Cusp of Fifty: Whither Nationalism and Sovereignty," where an attempt is made, exploring the Dudus events, to complicate political sovereignty as multifaceted, with some aspects of it still very much present. In Brian Meeks, *Critical Interventions in Caribbean Politics and Theory*, University Press of Mississippi, Jackson, 2014, 183–95.
57 For a useful discussion of affect in Caribbean postcolonial theory, see Jonathan Pugh, "Postcolonial Development, (Non)Sovereignty and Affect: Living on in the Wake of Caribbean Political Independence," *Antipode* 49, no. 4 (2016): 867–82.
58 In an equally compelling reflection on the peculiar history of Haiti, with the juxtaposition of a severely compromised political sovereignty beside a prevalent and vibrant popular culture, Thomas argues against the grain that sovereignty, if seen from the perspective of Haiti and her long history of peasant resistance, feels like "endurance, as something that can be lived in the everyday, something people carry with them even as the material moments that promised alternatives fail." Deborah Thomas, "Haiti, Politics and Sovereign (Mis)recognitions," in Alessandra Benedicty-Kokken, Kaiama A. Glover, Mark Schuller, and John Picard Byron,

Is the political the sphere through which ethical relations can mean-
ingfully emerge? Of course, Rastafari have long answered this question
in the negative, grounding ethical life instead in marronage, a state of
being in which "agents struggle psychologically, socially, metaphys-
ically, and politically to exit slavery, maintain freedom, and assert a
lived social space while existing in a liminal position." I want to argue
that it is in conditions of marronage that repair is possible.[59]

Thomas's gesture toward an internally generated sovereignty and in the
direction of an ethic of love finds surprising resonance in Aaron Kamugisha's *Beyond Coloniality*, where he juxtaposes C.L.R. James's Caribbean
Marxism alongside Sylvia Wynter's critical, epistemic reading of Western
modernity and assertion of a new project beyond Western man, toward
the human.[60] In his synthetic conversation with these and other critical
thinkers in the Black radical tradition, Kamugisha doesn't sideline the
political: there is room for both a Caribbean nation[61] and a reassertion
that the political project must be one of "revolutionary socialism."[62] But
his novel turn occurs when, reading with both George Lamming and
Audre Lorde, he proposes that in building itself anew, the Caribbean
must be guided by that "most elusive of human emotions. Love."[63]

These four important, critical Caribbean scholars, from various
disciplines and with differing objectives, nonetheless reflect a common
intellectual imperative of the early twenty-first century. There is the need
evident in all to think beyond the grand strategy of the anti-colonial
generation, which is that of taking state power, of capturing the "political
kingdom" as the surest route to building a new society.

The Haiti Exception: Anthropology and the Predicaments of Narrative, Liverpool
University Press, Liverpool, 2016, 137–56.
59 Deborah Thomas, *Political Life in the Wake of the Plantation: Sovereignty,
Witnessing, Repair*, Duke University Press, Durham, NC, 2019, 214. The quote
within her excerpt is from Neil Roberts, *Freedom as Marronage*, University of
Chicago Press, Chicago, 2015, 10.
60 It is nearly impossible to single out any of Wynter's many, complex and
subtle writings, without listing them all as Kamugisha does. Nonetheless, on the
foregrounding of the quest for a reconstituted notion of the human, I have found
this article particularly useful: Sylvia Wynter, "Unsettling the Coloniality of Being/
Power/Truth/Freedom: Towards the Human, after Man, Its Overrepresentation—
an Argument," *CR: The New Centennial Review* 3, no. 3 (Fall 2003): 257–337.
61 See Kamugisha, *Beyond Coloniality*, 207.
62 *Beyond Coloniality*, 213.
63 *Beyond Coloniality*, 214.

However, beyond asserting a set of new and critically important ethical principles, there is in all a relative silence or hesitance as to what comes next. Thomas most clearly confronts the old state sovereignty objective head-on, in her reassertion of Neil Roberts's notion of marronage as an option. But where is the virgin territory, the "Cockpit Country" for the maroons to survive, flourish, and hopefully launch occasional guerrilla forays? Are they not inevitably always under surveillance, subject to arbitrary taxation, in danger themselves of always being attacked, imprisoned, and subject to erasure? In Bonilla's foregrounding of *Liyannaj*, we see a compelling alternative ethos of human living and nascent principle of community organizing, while seemingly sidelining traditional political approaches and "the decisive break with the past" of earlier revolutionary strategies. But where is the room for the new community organizations arising out of this principle to maneuver in the context where there is still the overarching power of the centralized French state? What has changed in the dynamic that Aimé Césaire faced half a century ago, when he and other French anti-colonial fighters chose to maintain a status with France as opposed to the Anglo-Caribbean path of separation from the empire? And isn't it that very dynamic which allowed colonial racial and class hierarchies to survive and consolidate that in turn led to the strikes and demonstrations of 2009? Kamugisha gives nominal recognition to a more meaningful Caribbean integration and reintroduces revolutionary socialism but spends no time at all explaining what these might entail and how these new initiatives might be different in ways that would make them compelling, particularly in light of the historic tragedy that occurred the last time an experiment with "revolutionary socialism" in its title was tried. Lewis in his important foregrounding of the ethos of labor and the working class, in a manner reminiscent of George Lamming (as discussed elsewhere in this volume), nonetheless leaves hanging a glaring set of questions: In the first rise of the Caribbean labor movement after the uprisings of the 1930s, wasn't there the clear recognition that without influence and control over the state, its laws and statutes, the labor movement couldn't consolidate its successes and make further advances? Doesn't this return us to the question of control over the state? Even when that state is largely gutted by structural adjustment agreements, does it not still possess overwhelming power and force within its boundaries?

I ask these questions not to disagree at all with their fundamental conclusions. There has been a gaping lacuna in discourse on the philosophical, the ontological, and the ethical that these and other scholars like Anthony Bogues, Eudine Barriteau, Paget Henry, David Scott, Charles Mills, Lewis Gordon,[64] and so many others have labored to introduce, rethink, and elaborate in the dark years beyond the collapse of the Caribbean radical movement of the 1970s. The assertion of an ethic of love, as straightforward as it sounds, the assertion of the central relevance of popular cultures of survival, ways of being, modes, to use the Rastafarian word of "livity," are profound and must be moved to the center of any theoretical notion of liberation and, needless to say, of the programs of future movements aimed at social and political transformation. The question, however, must inevitably be asked: And what of the political? How do the new formations work in, around, and beyond the political system, which despite decrepitude and ineffectiveness is still very much there? What appears to be missing is a necessary and equally robust parallel conversation on how to imagine, construct, and fight for a new politics, alongside the essentially philosophical and theoretical effort, present in abundance here, to think about its guiding ethos.

Few studies have sought to move beyond the confines of limited Westminster constitutional reform to think through what a new politics might look like in a world of new informational networks and emerging transnational linkages. In his short piece "Towards a New Democracy in the Caribbean," Percy Hintzen breaks new ground by suggesting that there are possibilities to outflank the limiting and exhausted national politics of the Caribbean islands via new counter-hegemonic transnational networks that include transnational social movements, transnational labor, transnational women's movements, and the global indigenous movement:

> opportunities for effective development and genuine democracy can be opened up by global processes and practices occurring outside the space of governance, or by possibilities provided by global actors who are relatively free from the state effects of global capitalist power and

64 See for example, Anthony Bogues, *Black Heretics, Black Prophets: Radical Political Intellectuals*, Routledge, New York, 2003; Eudine Barriteau, "The Construct of a Postmodernist Feminist Theory for Caribbean Social Science Research," *Social and Economic Studies* 41, no. 2 (1992): 1–43; Paget Henry, *Caliban's Reason: Introducing Afro-Caribbean Philosophy*, Routledge, London, 2000; David Scott, *Refashioning Futures: Criticism after Postcoloniality*, Princeton University Press, Princeton, NJ, 1999; Charles Mills, *Radical Theory, Caribbean Reality*, The University of the West Indies Press, Kingston, 2010; and Lewis Gordon, *An Introduction to Africana Philosophy*, Cambridge University Press, Cambridge, 2008.

from their capacity to impose their will on national apparatuses of government. Such processes are organized around counter-hegemonic transnational actors.[65]

Though the question must be asked of Hintzen, where do these new alliances lead? Are we looking at radical transnational alliances that subvert the power of the existing state? If so, who determines law, taxes, traffic rules, and the like, within the territorial space? I ask these questions not to be difficult, but because we urgently need them to be answered in this uncertain moment. In her recent, sweeping attempt to grasp Haiti's contemporary crisis and her approach as to how to move beyond it, Mimi Sheller charts, as the title *Island Futures*[66] implies, an urgent and vivid roadmap from the minutes of a meeting of twenty-six Haitian organizations and social movements and seventeen from the Dominican Republic. From their conclusions I mention just the leading points, each of which requires far more elaboration, including: 1) breaking with policies of exclusion of women, minorities, youths, and other marginal groups; 2) breaking with economic dependence with an emphasis on and return to domestic agricultural production along with a reduction in dependence on fossil fuels; 3) breaking with the excessive centralization of power and utilities; and 4) breaking with destructive land ownership patterns, including comprehensive rural and urban land reform. These "breaks" are to be accompanied by a new approach to popular mobilization, a new system of public education, a reorganization of the health system, and a new justice system with equal rights and to fight against corruption. The organizations end with a call, important for both its historic and contemporary significance, to cancel all of Haiti's debts.[67]

I find the declaration from these Haitian and Dominican organizations and Sheller's use of them illuminating, as an indication of the tenor and temper of the people on the island of Hispaniola as well as a leading signal for a new politics for the future of the Caribbean. In 2007, I published my own vision for the region, *Envisioning Caribbean Futures: Jamaican Perspectives*, but as I develop elsewhere in this volume, events since then

---

65   Percy Hintzen, "Towards a New Democracy in the Caribbean: Local Empowerment and the New Global Order," in Brian Meeks and Kate Quinn (ed.) *Beyond Westminster in the Caribbean*, Ian Randle Publishers, Kingston, 2018, 189.
66   Mimi Sheller, *Island Futures: Caribbean Survival in the Anthropocene*, Duke University Press, Durham, NC, 2020.
67   Sheller, *Island Futures*, 154–56.

have taken us far beyond the settings of that book's relatively modest conclusions. In *Envisioning*, I proposed a "development state" approach, but with greater democracy and accountability in its central organs. The economic direction, too, was relatively limited. Aside from a thorough-going land reform as a central effort to end inequalities, it proposed a central placement of cultural industries as the cutting edge of future Jamaican development. The third plank, or the Constituent Assembly of the Jamaican People at Home and Abroad, is still highly relevant. The Assembly would constitute both residents in the island and the diaspora and would convene at regular intervals to address questions of generational change and what these might mean for new constitutional, economic, and social relations.

URGENT QUESTIONS

World events since the 2008 Great Recession, however, now more urgently framed in the face of incontrovertible climate change[68] and looming environmental collapse in addition to a burgeoning popular, global upwelling for rights and justice, demand that we move beyond these timid steps in incremental reform to boldly imagine a more expansive future for the Caribbean in the world, and where we are unable to provide clear answers, to place the burning questions that open the doors to those futures decisively on the table. Among them, I propose the following questions.

What does it mean to consider reconstructing an economy not based on "extractivism"?[69] The technology now exists and continues to improve that allows us to consider leaving the oil and coal that is left in the ground. The environmental disaster of the last two hundred years demands that we consider this. It also demands that we look at broader

---

68   For the disturbing summary of the latest findings on climate change, see Masson-Delmotte et al., Intergovernmental Panel on Climate Change (IPCC), *Summary for Policymakers, in Climate Change 2021: The Physical Science Basis. Contribution of Working Group 1 to the Sixth Assessment Report of the IPCC*, Cambridge University Press, Cambridge, 2021.

69   See the conversation on extractivism as a colonial enterprise, whether practiced by right- or left-wing regimes, in Walter D. Mignolo and Catherine E. Walsh, *On Decoloniality: Concepts, Analytics, Praxis*, Duke University Press, Durham, NC, 2018, 6. I am thankful to Esther Figueroa for her film *Fly Me to the Moon*, which explores the complex nature of human interconnectedness with the environment, as it exposes the damage wrought on Jamaica by the extractive bauxite industry. See Esther Figueroa, *Fly Me to the Moon*, Kingston, 2019.

notions of extractivism, such as the destruction of mangrove swamps for the building of hotels, the degradation and pollution of beaches, and the extermination of coral reefs. When does the carnage end, and what are the sustainable means of living and thriving that can replace this reckless and unsustainable mode in which we live?[70]

How do we sustain a functioning, manageable, humane, and sustainable health system for all, beyond the narrow profit motives of the market? Most Caribbean territories operate with a bifurcated and unequal health model in which the few benefit from good health care, while the majority suffer through crowded, inadequately staffed, and poorly supplied hospitals and health systems. The remarkable success of the Cuban health system, in providing free primary health care for the entire population, first-rate specialist services, and front-ranking research, as well as in Cuba's early development of their own COVID-19 vaccine, is beyond outstanding. It illustrates what is possible from a system focused on people and not profits, even in a country that has been under siege for more than six decades. The experience of the COVID-19 pandemic confirms that there can only be one decent health system,[71] or ultimately the entire populace will pay the price.

What kind of educational system would both provide for free, quality education up to the tertiary level, while reducing the gaping inequalities between elite schools and the rest and the archaic bifurcation between technical and "grammar" modes of education?[72] And closely connected to the form, what of the content of education? How do we end, through schooling and other measures, the sordid persistence of racism, colorism, and other manifestations of self-hatred inherited from slavery and colonialism?

What are the constitutional, legal, social, educational, and cultural changes that need to be made to end the prevalence of misogyny, gendered

---

70 For a discussion of the climate crisis and its consequences as well as a radical blueprint for a possible way out, see Noam Chomsky and Robert Pollin, *Climate Crisis and the Global Green New Deal*, Verso, London, 2020.

71 See, for instance, Daniel A. Rodriguez, *The Right to Live in Health, Medical Politics in Postindependence Havana*, University of North Carolina Press, Chapel Hill, 2020; and Julie Feinsilver, "Cuban Medical Diplomacy," in Aviva Chomsky, Barry Carr, and Pamela Maria Smorkaloff (eds.) *The Cuba Reader; History, Culture, Politics*, Duke University Press, Durham, NC, 2013, 590–94.

72 See, for instance, Anne Hickling-Hudson, "Towards Caribbean 'Knowledge Societies': Dismantling Neo-colonial Barriers in the Age of Globalization," *Compare* 34, no. 3 (September 2004): 293–300.

violence, and all forms of gender discrimination? What are the legal, social, and educational steps that need to be taken to end homophobia and all modes of sexual discrimination and accompanying violence[73] directed against LGBTQ people? It is an irony of history that in a region marked by the history of slavery and indentured labor—where racism, degradation, and violence were embedded into the very fabric of these societies—while the fight against racial oppression, incomplete as it is, is acknowledged as legitimate, other forms of othering, marginalization, and exclusion remain pervasive and are considered acceptable. These, too, need to be thoroughly exorcised.

For the Caribbean and the entire African diaspora, how would an effective program of reparations serve to rebalance global inequalities without insidiously serving to exacerbate local inequalities?[74] And what is our relation to Pan-Africanism? The call to closer relations between the peoples of continental Africa and the peoples of the overseas African diaspora have been a persistent and vital component of all the major anti-colonial and postcolonial movements. What would a meaningful, economically beneficial, and culturally uplifting Pan-African network look like? And does Pan-Africanism have a future in a world in which we are moving away from distant, powerful centers and toward local, popular empowerment? Or is there room alongside the local for a powerful trans-national coming together of peoples with deep historical, cultural, and social memories and connections that empowers the local while allowing unanticipated spaces for popular interaction across distant geographical locations?[75]

73 See M. Jacqui Alexander, "Not Just (Any) Body Can Be a Citizen: The Politics of Law, Sexuality and Postcoloniality in Trinidad and Tobago and the Bahamas," *Feminist Review* 48 (Autumn 1994): 5–23.
74 See Hilary Beckles, *Britain's Black Debt: Reparations for Caribbean Slavery and Native Genocide*, The University of the West Indies Press, Kingston, 2013; William A. Darity Jr. and A. Kirsten Mullen, *From Here to Reality: Reparations for Black Americans in the Twenty-First Century*, University of North Carolina Press, Chapel Hill, 2020; and the important *Caricom Ten Point Plan for Reparatory Justice*, accessed February 21, 2019, https://www.caricom.org/caricom-ten-point-plan-for-reparatory-justice/.
75 To this point, I find Claire Vergerio's argument exploring the history and future prospects of the Westphalian order persuasive. She suggests that it might be useful to think in the near future not necessarily about the absolute disappearance of nation-states but of the growth of a variety of international forms of collaboration and cooperation—in other words, of an international order that "could make space for a greater diversity of polities and restore some

And what of the Indo-Caribbean? Indian Caribbean people constitute a rich, vital, and central component of Caribbean culture and life but have been historically relegated to its margins. What are the active measures that need to be taken to recognize, as Walter Rodney[76] so effectively began to elaborate, the colonial roots of the divide between African and Indian communities, particularly in Guyana, Suriname, and Trinidad and Tobago,[77] and what steps need to be taken to overcome embedded histories of racial othering, discrimination, division, and violence, in the interests of a more united, democratic, and multicultural Caribbean?

How do we think about Caribbean diasporas as part of broader Pan-African, Pan-American, and Pan-Asian networks of solidarity and collaboration? Stuart Hall was right in recognizing that the diaspora was not simply "us over there."[78] The Caribbean diaspora is deeply caught up in the North American and European communities in which they reside; yet the salience and relevance of the diaspora as a source of remittances and potentially a stream of human resources as well as social and political reinvigoration for the island home is huge.[79] None of these potentials come without contradictions, but the future of the Caribbean without its diaspora playing an outsized role is unimaginable.

How do we rethink the role of the indigenous and of indigeneity in the Caribbean region? Beyond the outstanding need to recognize and respect the existing indigenous populations in the mainland territories, particularly of the Guianas[80] and Belize, there is the urgent imperative to provide

balance between the rights of states and the rights of other collectivities," such as indigenous groups and transnational movements. Claire Vergerio, "Beyond the Nation-State," *Boston Review*, May 27, 2021, www.bostonreview.net.

76   See Walter Rodney, *A History of the Guyanese Working People, 1881–1905*, Heinemann, Kingston, 1981.

77   For a rich, comparative discussion of Indian self-perception and the historical roots of racial divisions in Guyana and Trinidad and Tobago, see Dave Ramsaran and Linden Lewis, *Caribbean Masala, Indian Identity in Guyana and Trinidad*, University Press of Mississippi, Jackson, 2018.

78   See Stuart Hall, "Through the Prism of an Intellectual Life," in Brian Meeks (ed.) *Culture, Politics, Race and Diaspora: The Thought of Stuart Hall*, Ian Randle Publishers, Kingston, 2007, 269–91.

79   See, for instance, D. Alissa Trotz and Beverly Mullings, "Far from Home but Close at Heart: Preliminary Considerations on Regional Integration, Deterritorialisation and the Caribbean Diaspora," in Patsy Lewis, Terri-Ann Gilbert-Roberts, and Jessica Byron (eds.) *Pan-Caribbean Integration: Beyond Caricom*, Routledge, London, 2017, 187–205; and Carole Boyce Davies, *Black Women, Writing and Identity: Migrations of the Subject*, Routledge, London, 1994.

80   See Desrey Fox, "Continuity and Change Among the Amerindians of

social and economic support to the remaining Carib[81] populations in the Windward Islands and also to deepen the effort of researching and memorializing the history of the Taino in the Greater Antilles. The model for a reinvigorated approach should remember the example of the Black victors of the revolution in St. Domingue, who, with remarkable perspicacity, respect, and generosity, chose to return their newly freed country to the name the Tainos had originally given her: Haiti.

How do we rethink self-government, democracy, and empowerment beyond the Westminster-oriented nation-state? How do we move beyond the severe limitations of representative democracy that limit and restrict popular participation, generate tribalism, and enforce top-down relationships with representatives without succumbing to the dangers of single-party overlordship? Do we want to consider here a borderless Caribbean region with common laws, with power devolved as much as feasible to the communities?[82] On the other hand, how do we avoid a devolution of power from the center that leads to the accumulation of arbitrary power in the hands of semi-feudal principalities? How do we imagine and consider anew a Caribbean of the people and not of the politicians, the bankers, and the private sector?

How do we think about the Caribbean as a borderless region, and do we imagine it conceivably as a template for a borderless world[83] in the not-too-distant future?

Finally, how do we think beyond capitalism?[84] Surely the world of capital as a free agent roaming the globe, exploiting, conquering, and destroying entire peoples, animals, and the environment at will, to the point of looming climate disruption and disaster on a heretofore unimag-

Guyana," in Rhoda Reddock (ed.) *Ethnic Minorities in Caribbean Society*, ISER, St. Augustine, Trinidad and Tobago, 1996, 9–104.
81 See Crispin Gregoire, Patrick Henderson, and Natalia Kanem, "Karifuna: The Caribs of Dominica," in Reddock (ed.) *Ethnic Minorities in Caribbean Society*, 107–71.
82 For recent reading on Caribbean integration and its limitations, see Patsy Lewis, Terri-Ann Gilbert-Roberts, and Jessica Byron (eds.) *Pan-Caribbean Integration: Beyond Caricom*, Routledge, London, 2017.
83 See Achille Mbembe, "The capacity to decide who can move, who can settle, where and under what conditions is increasingly becoming the core of political struggles," in "The Idea of a Borderless World," November 11, 2018, https://africasacountry.com.
84 See, for instance, Adam Fishwick and Nicholas Kiersey, *Postcapitalist Futures: Political Economy Beyond Crisis and Hope*, Pluto Press, London, 2021.

inable scale[85] while dividing and dehumanizing peoples of color, is drawing to a close. What will replace it? Can we imagine a world beyond *pwofitasyon*? Can human beings be inspired to invent and develop new agricultures, modes of transport, energy sources, means of entertainment, and all the myriad needs of contemporary society without the lure of wealth as the only meaningful basis of human social and economic interaction? Can we imagine a world of high technology with its resources and benefits shared and without domination by a handful of masters of the universe whose ability to corrupt and destroy any project of social and political upliftment is already out of control? Can we, then, imagine a new modus of social living for the Caribbean people that would incorporate, adapt, and perhaps also exclude some of the ideas mooted here, always conscious of the central reality of motion and that new situations will inevitably demand new policies, new positionings, and new perspectives?

MEMORY, IMAGINATION, HOPE

The influences behind these urgent questions and more generally on my thinking in this period are many. Overarching all, as this entire introduction has argued, is the gathering mood of the times, in which the wind of resistance and uprising is once more gaining speed. Another, certainly, has been living in the United States and teaching at Brown University since 2015. This, in retrospect, must be considered a period of popular upheaval, rivaling 1968 as conjunctural moment of anti-systemic awakening around questions of race, class, gender, sexuality, and the very definition of the American nation, even as the forces aligned against it have also gained traction. I am thankful, in particular, to my many graduate and undergraduate students in Africana Studies and all across Brown, who have reminded me what it means to be enthusiastic, inquisitive about the past, and selflessly committed to trying to change the world we live in for the better. Another major stream arose from the 2012 celebration of fifty

---

85   I point to the details of the Sixth (2021) IPCC report, which outlines a series of possible outcomes from relatively serious to extreme if the world continues along its present path of emissions production or effectively decreases pollution. Most frightening is the recognition that there is the possibility of the loss of entire island countries in the Pacific without drastic curtailment. The saving of the world requires new radical policies that carry us far beyond the limits of private-sector-led reductions and urgently raises the need for new public, social, and global action. See IPCC Report 2021 and Kate Lyons, "IPCC Report Shows 'Possible Loss of Entire Countries within Century,'" *Guardian*, August 9, 2021.

years of independence from the United Kingdom in both Jamaica and Trinidad and Tobago. I was at the time director of the Sir Arthur Lewis Institute of Social and Economic Studies (SALISES) at the University of the West Indies and led the organization and hosting of a mammoth series of intellectual encounters to reflect on the meaning and signifi-cance of the independence experience in the Commonwealth Caribbean. The many papers from the final conference were never published, but on rereading them, there was an air of solemnity and even despair surround-ing recent history and uncertainty for the future that pervaded them. The great expectations of independence had been exhausted, and the radical movements, from Black Power across the region to Democratic Socialism in Jamaica and the Grenada Revolution, had long been defeated and laid to rest. What was left appeared to be a moment of stasis and ennui, in which the (always tentative) possibilities for sovereign decision-making were at a dead end and the likelihood of radical change seemed close to impossible. What were the twists and turns in the postcolonial journey that brought the Anglophone Caribbean to this moment, and what, if any, are the prospects to rethink and possibly advance toward more just, democratic, and empowering futures? This book explores these questions and searches for new theoretical approaches as well as practical proposals that might help in identifying credible new directions.

The essays in this volume, which together attempt to grapple with these questions, were all written for distinct events, keynotes, and lectures spread over this past decade. They nonetheless serendipitously trace my thoughts along this arc of Anglophone Caribbean independence from 1962 until the present. I have preferred to leave them in their temporal context, rather than try to rewrite and update them, as I think that it is worthwhile to understand them as inhabitants of the distinct moments in which they were written. In Part One (chapters 1–5), I use the work of artists and scholars and my own early attempts at poetry-writing to help tell a story of the Caribbean postcolonial that myriad historians have done through more traditional means. Here, however, I retrace this ground in a more discursive way and with more biographical, personal, and close-up lenses to try to better understand how it has come to this denouement. In Part Two (chapters 6–9), I use some of the foundational thoughts, criticisms, and ideas mustered in Part One to begin imagining possible pathways and options for more liberating Caribbean futures after the postcolonial.

Chapter 1 uses the colors of the Jamaican independence flag to reflect, if fleetingly, on the moment of independence, August 6, 1962, and the actual ceremony of celebration in the nation's brand-new National Stadium. What were the sharp social and political divisions that had festered in the centuries of colonialism and, more immediately, the final decades of the colonial era? What were the effervescent hopes and expectations that were placed on independence and a future of freedom from the British? This introductory, discursive musing on these questions draws on shards of memory from my own presence as a child that night in the stadium to suggest the inherent tenuousness and fragility in the Jamaican moment of national ascendancy.

Chapter 2 utilizes my own poetry, largely written in the 1970s and published in the volume *The Coup Clock Clicks*,[86] as an archival source to explore the politics and zeitgeist of the Caribbean 1970s. Written over a period of intense engagement as a student and later activist in Trinidad, Jamaica, and Grenada, the poems suggest in new and revealing ways some of the hidden passions and motivations that inhabited the work and thinking of an entire generation in this era of radical upheaval in the Caribbean.

Chapter 3 explores the life and artistic production of Edna Manley, often considered in Jamaica as the matriarch of the anti-colonial and immediate postcolonial artists' movement. Manley's work as an artist and sculptor has been well documented, but little attention has been paid to her political role in the national movement. This lacuna is particularly serious when we note that she was the wife of Norman Manley, generally considered the leader of the movement for independence; cousin to their political nemesis Alexander Bustamante, who actually led Jamaica into independence; and mother of Michael Manley, the most consistently radical of the post-independence Jamaican prime ministers. This chapter begins to address these failings with a "preliminary assessment" that seeks to capture Edna's complex (and sometimes contradictory) fusion of Blakeian anarcho-spiritualism with Fabian socialism that helped define her own brand of radical/reformist opposition to Jamaica's stultifying racial and social order.

Chapter 4 focuses on the work of George Lamming, perhaps the most consistently political and radical member of the famous school of late colonial and early postcolonial Caribbean writers. The essay seeks to both

---

86   Brian Meeks, *The Coup Clock Clicks*, Peepal Tree Press, Leeds, 2018.

identify the qualities that made Lamming an insightful and prescient observer of Caribbean politics as it tries to understand the novel and creative ways that he sought to incorporate and shape Marxism and Black Power into his own unique approach to understanding the Caribbean.

Chapter 5 turns to the work of the Jamaican-born theorist of cultural studies Stuart Hall. His death in 2014 was a moment for reflection on his tremendous reach and significance, though his role in his home region was limited. The chapter returns to the politics of the Caribbean 1970s and asks the heuristic counterfactual "what if?" to muse on what it would have meant if Hall had decided, instead of laying his bed in Britain, to return to the Caribbean in the 1960s. Would his critical but flexible and humanistic approach to Marxist theory have made a difference to the radical movements that emerged in this period? And what would that have meant for their future courses? These questions can never be answered, but asking them is an avenue for both exploring Hall's oeuvre as well as critiquing the failed politics and theory of radical movements in the Caribbean of the radical 1970s.

Chapter 6 returns again to Hall's work, this time via the 2015 *Kilburn Manifesto*, in which Hall and a number of close collaborators published (for him posthumously) a manifesto for a new, radical politics for the United Kingdom. Not only was this a stunning response to those who considered Hall's work in cultural studies to be somewhat abstract and disconnected from the real world, but it raised common questions and proposals that extend beyond *Kilburn*'s immediate application to British politics. The chapter uses the manifesto to reflect on the parlous state of twenty-first-century social and political life in the Caribbean and to think about how *Kilburn* might help in stimulating the creation of similar manifestos for imagining new Caribbean futures.

Chapter 7 shifts focus to the United States in the year immediately after Donald Trump's presidential victory. I had moved to Rhode Island to assume the chair of the Africana Studies Department at Brown University in 2015 and so was a close witness to Trump's stunning victory in the November 2016 election. The entire atmosphere preceding and following his ascension to power reminded me of the course of Jamaican politics after Michael Manley's 1980 electoral defeat. Elsewhere I have referred to this state of anomie and uncertainty, in which no dominant social bloc is in charge of the direction of society, as one of "hegemonic dissolution." Trump lost the 2020 election to Joseph Biden, but "Trumpism," the toxic right-wing jingoism that he fostered, continued to dominate Republican

politics in 2021. The chapter explores how my usage of hegemonic dissolution in the Jamaican context might prove helpful in understanding and
perhaps transcending this fraught and dangerous Trumpian moment in
the United States and its fellow manifestations in world politics.

Chapter 8 argues, developing themes mooted in chapter 6, that
Caribbean politics is consumed with a dangerous infatuation with neoliberalism, even as that paradigm is in terminal decay. This is especially
ominous, I suggest, as capitalism itself is in existential crisis and there
is thus an imperative to imagine and bring to life new models of social
and political organization as well as new words, visions, and approaches
to social and political living that are capable of addressing questions of
survival in this post-postcolonial time.

Chapter 9 is partly a rejoinder to a very short interaction that took
place at a "Conference on the Jamaican Seventies" hosted by David Scott
and the *Small Axe* Collective at Columbia University in 2017. Despite
the defeats of the popular movements for revolutionary and radical
change in the Anglophone Caribbean, I retained a general optimism as
to the possibilities of learning from them and charting new paths for the
future. David, on the contrary and consistent with perspectives on "the
tragic" developed in his recent work, was far more cautious. What, then,
is the foundation for radical optimism or its converse, a tendency toward
foregrounding pessimism and tragedy? Inspired by the resurgence of
anti-systemic movements such as the 2020 global Black Lives Matter
demonstrations, I use Scott's work, particularly *Conscripts of Modernity:
The Tragedy of Colonial Enlightenment*, and read it alongside C.L.R. James's
The Black Jacobins in order to reimagine the foundations for a politics of
radical optimism in an era of epistemic and existential uncertainty.

PART I

Remembering

1

Reminiscing in Black, Gold, and Green

I don't know whether I can call myself an independence baby. I wasn't born in 1962—the year the flag went up—nor did I come of age in that time, with the implicit suggestion that I might possess some fuller understanding of what the whole occasion meant. Indeed, I probably don't qualify at all, being born in Montreal, Canada, despite my always reminding anyone curious enough to ask that I arrived on "the Rock" only a few months later. Even this minimal claim, though, I wryly discovered in the wake of Pluto Shervington's 1970s hit song, would inevitably fail the "I Man Born Ya"[1] examination of national authenticity.

Yet, in a fallback attempt to secure a pass, I submit that I was present in the National Stadium the night the black, gold, and green[2] unfurled, and

---

1 Shervington's song was an ode to Jamaicanness and a statement of resistance against the notion that patriotic Jamaicans would want to desert their island to go and live in the United States or Canada. "I man born ya, I naa leave ya fi go America." I recall hearing a crowd in the National Stadium stirringly sing this in unison at the Carifesta (Caribbean Festival of the Arts) celebrations in the summer of 1976 at the height of Democratic Socialism. Manley would win the December 1976 elections decisively, but a year later, with empty coffers and an IMF structural adjustment agreement in place, his government was on its way to crisis and defeat in 1980. Pluto Shervington was among the emigrants who eventually left for Miami. Pluto Shervington, *I Man Born Ya*, Federal Records 45 rpm release Kingston, 1976.

2 The symbolic meaning of the flag, with its distinctive gold saltire and black and green triangular inserts, is of more than passing interest. In 1962 a bipartisan committee of the House of Representatives agreed on its meaning: "Hardships there are, but the land is green and the sun shineth." www.brittanica.com/topic/flag-of-jamaica. Few at the time seemed to consider it tragically ironic that the black part of the flag, designating hardship, was also the color of the vast majority of Jamaicans, therefore equating blackness with hardship. This changed in the 1990s when, under PJ Patterson's PNP government, a committee chaired by Rex Nettleford agreed on the amended slogan: "The sun shineth, the land is green, and the people are strong and creative." www.jis.gov.jm/information/symbols. Another interesting note is that it is the only flag in the world that does not have in it red, white, or blue. www.worldatlas.com/flags/jamaica. For an important thesis

this must count for something. And though I was only a tender nine years old, I remember it sharply. There were these rapid strobe-like flashes, or at least I think it was a strobe, which I had never seen or heard of before. Or it might just have been the multiple flashes of hundreds of cameras as the red, white, and blue Union Jack slithered down and the new symbol of hope clambered up, illuminated intermittently and tentatively, like the new nation herself. Then it was up and fluttering as the strains of "Jamaica Land We Love" filled the already overflowing stadium for the first time.

I was perhaps, a little too young to understand all that was going on. There were the debates over the Federation[3] that had run very hot in the preceding months. Then there was the Referendum, in which Premier Norman Manley's People's National Party (PNP), with its argument for achieving sovereignty via a united group of West Indian states, was ultimately defeated by his cousin Alexander Bustamante and his Jamaica Labour Party (JLP) with its belated, though powerful, appeal for Jamaican independence as a solitary state. The Referendum was a huge disaster for Manley, the respected Queen's Council. The intellectual leader of the nationalist movement, he and his comrades had sat in opposition for the entire decade after Universal Adult Suffrage elections were first held in 1944. When the PNP eventually won in 1955, he worked tirelessly to advance the goal of national autonomy through what he thought was the only feasible avenue for economic and political viability—a West Indian Federation of Jamaica and the British territories in the eastern Caribbean.[4]

But the federal project was blighted from the start. The failure to engage Jamaicans in a genuine conversation from the beginning about the pros and cons of Federation meant that when the inevitable differences arose, there was no foundation of mutual understanding to fall back on. Conflicting and contradictory island-specific interests led to clashes around the citing of the capital, taxation policies, the design of a customs union, and myriad other details. There were also the inevitable personality-based conflicts as the newly emergent political elites jockeyed for power, seeking to balance the priority of securing national power bases with the necessity of protecting island interests at the federal level.

arguing how Jamaicans came to identify themselves as a Black nation, see Colin Palmer, *Inward Yearnings: Jamaica's Journey to Nationhood*, The University of the West Indies Press, Kingston, 2016.
3   See, in particular, John Mordecai, *The West Indies: The Federal Negotiations*, George Allen and Unwin, London, 1968.
4   See Trevor Munroe, *The Politics of Constitutional Decolonization: Jamaica: 1944–62*, Institute of Social and Economic Research, Kingston, 1972.

The game was virtually over when in the lead up to the first federal elections in 1958, the key players—Manley in Jamaica and brilliant historian Dr. Eric Williams in Trinidad—chose not to contest, effectively ceding the regional premiership to Barbados's Grantley Adams, an individual whose personality would prove wholly unsuited to forging unity out of regional indifference and adversity. Adams's petulant style of leadership, in which, from the distant (from Jamaica's perspective) federal capital in Chaguaramas, Trinidad, he issued edicts that seemed to dictate policy to Jamaica, only served to inflame suspicions about the "small islanders" that were simmering beneath the surface.[5]

The federal idea was always somewhat alien and artificial in Jamaica, with her historical ignorance of and distance from the Eastern Caribbean. Her traditional patterns of migration looked either north, to the United Kingdom, Cuba, and the United States, or west, to Panama and Costa Rica. The British Colonies of the Eastern Caribbean, aside from minor contact through the West Indies cricket team and the still-tender University College of the West Indies (UCWI) founded at Mona, Jamaica, in 1948, were far beyond the horizon of most Jamaicans and existed in the imaginary, if at all, as backward, dependent, "small islands." When, during the brief federal moment, these distant, vaguely perceived second cousins appeared in the popular mind to wish to dictate local policy, the door was left ajar for the intervention of determined opposition.

Into this opening rode Bustamante. The leonine, charismatic hero of the 1938 labor riots had lost much of his glamour in the previous decade when the JLP served in office. The limited power offered by the early constitutions, with the governor having the decisive vote, was in part the cause, giving Bustamante responsibility without genuine authority. But his own brand of unpredictable authoritarianism also contributed to his gradual eclipse, as the PNP countered this with a mass base built on more democratic, grassroots-based organizational principles. Many assumed that when the PNP triumphed convincingly in 1955 it signaled the banishment of Busta and the JLP to the political wilderness for a long time. But this was to underestimate Busta's wiliness and canny grasp of Jamaican folkways and politics.[6]

Initially lukewarm to the federal idea, Busta eventually embraced it to the point where the federal party to which the JLP was allied was

---

5   For a rich discussion of the various causes and arguments for the break-up of the Federation, see W. Arthur Lewis, "Epilogue," in Mordecai, *West Indies*, 455–62.

6   See George Eaton, *Alexander Bustamante and Modern Jamaica*, LMH Publishing, Kingston, 1995.

victorious in the 1958 elections, and in Jamaica herself the JLP gained more votes than the PNP. When, however, he sensed growing dissension in the federal ranks and a groundswell—particularly among the elites—for a Jamaican solution, he pirouetted from his pro-federal stance to become, seemingly overnight, the supreme advocate of Jamaican secession.[7] In the end, Bustamante's simple slogan of independence for Jamaica proved far more comprehensible than the more convoluted concept of independence via the avenue of Federation. In retrospect, it was probably only Manley's remarkable personality and the trust that many invested in him that prevented an even more convincing JLP victory in the 1961 plebiscite, instead of the relatively modest, though decisive, margin of 54 percent against and 46 for continuing in the regional government.

I came from a federal family. My mom[8] was Trinidadian and she met my Jamaican dad while they were both students at McGill in Montreal; she was a liberal arts major and he was studying dentistry. They returned to Jamaica in 1956, just as the PNP had come to power and Federation was gaining momentum. As bright young professionals, they soon gravitated to the small but influential crowd of young thinkers and artists gathered around the UCWI. Douglas Manley—Norman's elder son—and his charming, talented wife, Carmen, were among their best friends, as were the St. Lucian student/poet Derek Walcott, the novelist John Hearne, and the iconoclastic painter Karl Parboosingh. This was a PNP crowd, but also essentially a federal crowd. People like my parents had studied in Canada, while others like Douglas had studied in the UK. There, for the first time, they met other West Indians. They came home with a burning sense of belonging to a wider West Indian space, bolstered, as in my father's case, by marriage to a partner from another island. My best friend was Carmen and Douglas's son Norman, named, I

7   See Richard Hart, *The End of Empire: Transition to Independence, in Jamaica and Other Caribbean Region Colonies*, Arawak Publications, Kingston, 2006, 246–79.
8   Corina Aurelia Achong (1930–2013) was born in Port of Spain, Trinidad, and became the first female island-wide Government Scholarship winner in 1948. This took her to McGill University in Montreal, where she met Charles William Meeks, a dental student from Kingston, Jamaica, with whom she fell in love and married in 1952. Their decision to settle in Jamaica and not return to Trinidad (or stay in Montreal) was, I learned, a cause for some consternation in her family. Corina Meeks would later, in the 1970s, play an important role in the Democratic Socialist era as assistant/advisor to Michael Manley and then director of the government Agency for Public Information (API).

think unfortunately, after his famous grandfather. So, if our parents were PNP (and in Norman's case, his grandparents too), we by default were also PNP and, though somewhat distanced from the incessant debates surrounding the stubbornness of Williams, the arbitrariness of Adams, and Busta's opportunism verging on calumny, we were, by osmosis, also pro-Federation.

Thus, we were more than mere bystanders as the disaster of the Referendum defeat unfolded all too rapidly into Manley's decision—against the advice of many of his supporters—to hold an early election to decide who would lead the country into independence. I recall that on the night of the election, I was visiting with Norman and his parents at a guest house near Port Antonio. Douglas, who was a sociologist at the University, also had an English professor who was a polling expert staying with them. I remember when the results started coming in on the radio, the friend almost immediately said that it looked bad and that the PNP was likely to lose. We sat with trepidation, dejected, without franchise and voiceless, reflecting, no doubt, the feeling of thousands of PNP supporters nationally on the cruel irony through which Busta and the labourites, who had never been strong advocates of national sovereignty, had now, as pretenders to the throne, swept into power with the popular mandate to lead Jamaica into independence.

Yet on that fecund and fateful August night in the new National Stadium—the stadium conceived and built by Manley despite the many detractors who argued that it was a waste of time and money—the entire country, or at least a thirty-thousand-odd representation of the whole, seemed to be gathered for a common cause. How quickly and painlessly everyone had put Federation behind them and come over as one to the new notion of independence![9]

But now some of these very detractors were sitting alongside Her Royal Highness Princess Margaret in the Royal Box. And suddenly there was grumbling and unrest in the crowd as dense rumors circulated in the grandstand and beyond that Opposition Leader Norman Manley and his artist wife, Edna, had been denied seating and turned away from the Box; this action was thwarted only when Prime Minister Bustamante

9   Perhaps explained by Ewart Walters in his argument that the movement for independence, based on popular culture and the emergence of a Black middle class and intelligentsia, preceded and ran far deeper than the narrowly conceived Federation. See Ewart Walters, *We Come from Jamaica: The National Movement 1937–1962*, Boyd McRubie, Ottawa, 2013.

himself intervened and silenced the young Turks in his Cabinet with the command to "let my cousin in."[10] And that is why when the Kingston crowd, the majority traditionally loyal to the PNP, heard that Norman was in the stadium and being treated impolitely, they rose in adulation but also anger, drowning out, to their consternation, the polite applause accorded Bustamante and his ministers.

And that is in retrospect why my mother—"decent, brown, middle-class" lady that she was—and others in the crowd gathered after the ceremony outside the stadium waiting expectantly on Norman's Jaguar to emerge from the VIP parking, and why she, along with many others, began shouting and running behind the Jaguar to the embarrassment and consternation of my nine-year-old sensibility. And though my memory fades, they offered him words of comfort that must have said, "Never mind, Mr. Manley. Don't let the labourites worry you. We, your comrades, will stand with you through thick and thin."

Yet, when the British sun set on this uncertain evening and at midnight the black, gold, and green fluttered in the gentle breeze, we all, comrades and labourites, paused in awe and wondered together at the possibility and hope that this new nation offered—so small and frail in a world of immeasurable industry, commerce, and nuclear might. For Jamaica was herself, immeasurably beautiful, and filled with a dynamic and prepossessed, if also volatile and unpredictable, people who might still pen a new chapter in the history of the world.

For though it was never an urgent part of the nascent nation's celebrations, this was, after all, what had once been the wealthiest sugar plantation slave colony of Great Britain and was still only a hundred twenty years removed from enslavement. These children, overwhelmingly out of Africa but also of Asia, of the few Europeans who had stayed and the significant number of hybrids who had emerged along the way, were for the first time starting to write their own lyrics and sing their own song. And many hoped, perhaps tentatively, that when that song was written, the rest of the world might stop in its headlong rush, take note, and listen to an urgent rhythm accompanied by a new, enchanting melody.

Thus was born Jamaica; not in blood and thunder, yet riven with doubts and divisions, even as hope swelled in the hearts of many as they considered in the early morning hours the glorious possibilities that a new beginning might herald.

---

10   See Ewart Walters, "The Value of the National Stadium," *The Gleaner*, August 9, 2018.

2

Reading the Seventies in a Different "Stylie": Dub, Poetry, and the Urgency of Message

When Donette Francis asked me to write a paper for Small Axe's 2017 seminar on the Jamaican 1970s,[1] I had recently uncovered, dusted off, and compiled a collection of my own poems written between 1971 and 1988. These were published by Peepal Tree Press in 2018 under the title *The Coup Clock Clicks*, taken from a poem I wrote about the burgeoning violence in Jamaica in the mid-1970s.[2] The process of compiling and preparing those thirty-six short poems was in itself a somewhat longer story worth telling. From at least the age of fifteen, I felt I had to write. I had studied the usual range of Western, largely British poets for GCE English Literature and loved every moment of it. From Lord Byron's "The Prisoner of Chillon" and Alfred, Lord Tennyson's "The Lotos-Eaters" to Oliver Goldsmith's "The Deserted Village" and Samuel Taylor Coleridge's "Christabel," I found in poetry a vehicle and form that suited my own sense of pace and general impatience with seemingly long-winded narratives.[3] But if the English Romantics turned me on to poetry, two locally significant events suggested that my own poetry, if it ever appeared, could be written in an entirely different form.

The first was when our fourth-form literature teacher, a young Jamaican graduate of the University of the West Indies named Neville Bramwell, decided to play in class, on his scratchy, battery-powered Philips player, Hopeton Lewis's rock steady hit (later to become a classic) "Take It Easy," as quoted here:

---

1   The notion of "stylie," as used in 1970s Jamaican street talk, derives clearly from "style" but is its stylized version, as created by Jamaican deejays to refer to a new "wicked" version, dub, or iteration of a song or rhythm track.

2   Brian Meeks, *The Coup Clock Clicks*, Peepal Tree Press, Leeds, 2018.

3   All these poems are compiled in the short GCE text *An Anthology of Longer Poems*, edited by Thomas W. Moles and Arthur R. Moon, Longman's, London, 1965.

[Tek yu] time, …
No need to worry
[Tek] it easy, …
No need to worry

No slippin', no slidin', no bumpin', no borin'
I ride into town
If you fall from the race, it's no disgrace
Just pick yourself from off the ground.[4]

I don't remember Bramwell spending time parsing or even trying to extricate social and political meaning from the lyrics, yet just his act of playing rock steady, with its militantly laid-back rhythm (even though the necessary heavy bass was missing from his little turntable), was revolutionary. It forcefully brought home to me that this, too, was poetry and indeed a more urgent and immediate form that demanded to be listened to, read, analyzed, and understood. Poetry had instantly been freed in my mind from its English moorings and antecedents to become a different medium to do with what we wanted and wished. The earliest Jamaican toasters (deejays)—Count Machuki, Prince Buster, and King Stitt, among others—were of course already deeply involved in investing their dancehall selections with improvised lyrics and were not waiting on any signals of legitimacy from literature professors in order to do their toasting, but for me and, I suggest, many others in that class, this was the pivotal moment in which the possibility of writing for ourselves and making poetry our own became a reality.[5]

The second was listening to Eddy (not yet Kamau) Brathwaite read for the first time at the Creative Arts Centre (CAC) at the University of

4   Hopeton Lewis, "Take It Easy," accessed January 2018, www.genius.com/
Hopeton-lewis-take-it-easy-lyrics. Genius is typical of the many online sites that
transcribe Lewis's song, in that the words are translated into standard English.
I have inserted the Jamaican-inflected *tek* instead of "take" to convey a more
accurate sense of the rhythm and feel of it.
5   Among the many important critical histories and assessments of the
evolution of Jamaican dancehall music and culture, see Sonjah Stanley Niaah,
Dancehall: From Slave Ship to Ghetto, University of Ottawa Press, Ottawa, 2010;
Carolyn Cooper, *Sound Clash: Jamaican Dancehall Culture at Large*, Palgrave
Macmillan, New York, 2004; Norman C. Stolzoff, *Wake the Town and Tell the
People: Dancehall Culture in Jamaica*, Duke University Press, Durham, NC, 2000;
and Donna Hope, *Inna de Dancehall: Popular Culture and the Politics of Identity in
Jamaica*, The University of the West Indies Press, Kingston, 2006.

the West Indies, Mona (now the Philip Sherlock Centre for the Creative Arts), in 1969. This was the year after Walter Rodney's expulsion from the university, and Black Power and Rastafari sentiments were running hot among the Mona student population.[6] The students felt that the newly opened CAC was too European in its orientation, and therefore they decided to occupy it, lock it down, and demand that its curriculum and program change to feature more Black and Afrocentric scholars and artists. A group of us senior students at nearby Jamaica College left our campus and joined the occupation in solidarity. That evening, Brathwaite read from *Rites of Passage* to a small but enraptured audience.

> Drum skin whip
> lash, master sun's
> cutting edge of
> heat, taut
> surfaces of things
> I sing
> I shout
> I groan
> I dream
> about.[7]

I had yet to read any of his poems, but something about his hypnotic tone, calm demeanor, and trenchant delivery in that softened, stentorian Bajan accent presaged and predicted the style of his short, skinny, staccato wordplay as printed on the page. This was for me the Hopeton Lewis revelation made concrete. What Brathwaite did in *Rites of Passage* and eventually in the entire *Arrivants* trilogy was to use the vehicle of poetry as a finely honed tool and weapon to unmask and explain the long, sordid, but also glorious history of survival of Africans in the West.[8] Here was an endeavor truly worthwhile and a form that not only was accessible but also allowed room for both intellectual depth and rich, compassionate artistry.

6   See Rupert Lewis, *Walter Rodney's Intellectual and Political Thought*, The University of the West Indies Press, Kingston, 1998.
7   Edward [Kamau] Brathwaite, "Prelude," in *Rites of Passage*, Oxford University Press, London, 1967, 3.
8   See Edward [Kamau] Brathwaite, *The Arrivants: A New World Trilogy*, Oxford University Press, Oxford, 1973.

So, it was Bramwell playing Hopeton Lewis and Brathwaite reading himself who more than any others opened the door to my writing poetry, which became my dominant expressive art form for more than a decade, continuing sporadically in the 1980s and then ending altogether (of which more anon) before the end of that decade. In this (on reflection, relatively truncated) period, I was fortunate to cross paths with other young Jamaican poets, including, notably, Lorna Goodison, Jerry Small, Mikey Smith, Oku Onuora (then Orlando Wong), Mutabaruka (then Allan Hope), and, among the established writers, particularly Mervyn Morris.[9] And of course Brathwaite himself, who saw fit to publish an early poem of mine in the iconic *Savacou* 3/4 on new Caribbean poetry and included my poems with many of these and other emerging voices in *Savacou* 14/15, "New Poets from Jamaica," which appeared in 1979.[10] Some of these were republished in the iconic and pathbreaking 1986 *Penguin Book of Caribbean Verse in English*, which, although somewhat mechanical in its separation of the oral from the literary tradition, nonetheless opened the door to the full bandwidth of Caribbean poetic expression, including, from the "oral" end, Bob Marley, the Mighty Sparrow, Louise Bennett, and the newer reggae- and dub-influenced voices, alongside, from the "literary," Derek Walcott, Dennis Scott, and Jean Rhys, among others.[11]

---

9   Morris, it should be remembered, although separated by half a generation, was finely attuned to the new "wordsounds" coming out of Kingston and suggests that the formulation of dub poetry was first used in an interview conducted by him with Oku Onuora, though "prefigured" by the work and comments of Linton Kwesi Johnson. See Mervyn Morris, "A Note on Dub Poetry," *Wasafiri* 13, no. 26 (1997): 66–69; and "Dub Poetry?," *Caribbean Quarterly* 43, no. 4 (1997): 1–10. For an important comparative study of early performance poetry across the Anglophone Caribbean, see also Julie Pearn, "Poetry as a Performing Art in the English-Speaking Caribbean" (PhD diss., University of Sheffield, 1985).

10   *Savacou* was the journal of the Caribbean Artists Movement, publishing ten themed issues between 1970 and 1980, and one additional issue (no. 16) in 1989. It is useful to remember the stir that *Savacou* 3/4—"New Writing, 1970" (December 1970/March 1971)—and subsequent volumes caused in the tiny but vocal community of Caribbean literati. The use and style of Jamaican nation language, by Jerry Small especially, led to critical and condemnatory responses from, among others, Tobagonian poet Eric Roach and, in defense of the new forms, Guyanese critic Gordon Rohlehr. See Laurence A. Beiner, *Black Yeats: Eric Roach and the Politics of Caribbean Poetry*, Peepal Tree Press, Leeds, 2008; and Gordon Rohlehr, "West Indian Poetry: Some Problems of Assessment," in *My Strangled City, and Other Essays*, Longman, Port of Spain, 1992.

11   See Paula Burnett (ed.) *The Penguin Book of Caribbean Verse in English*, Penguin, Harmondsworth, 1986.

The project of exploring one's own creative work is fraught and dangerous. It can easily become and be perceived as a supreme instance of self-indulgent vanity or a somewhat restrained and dry attempt at merely annotating one's narrowly perceived meaning, reason for writing, and historical orientation. Despite these evident pitfalls, I persist for one simple reason, in that I think that these poems capture quite effectively not only a murky and half-forgotten decade and a half of my life but also the crucial period of post-independence radical Caribbean politics, what the calypsonian Brother Valentino refers to as "the Roaring Seventies."[12] When some fifteen years ago my wife, Patsy, urged that I "must publish" my poetry, echoing a sentiment initially given to me by my late mother, Corina, I demurred and found every excuse not to. The poems had been written too long ago; I was a different person then; they were too specific to events that were for the most part largely forgotten; they were all typed out on colored paper with accompanying sketches, and it would be too much trouble to retype them in contemporary digital format. Patsy solved the last problem by retyping them herself and presenting the results to me as a birthday gift. Still, I hesitated until arriving at Brown University in 2015 to chair the Department of Africana Studies, with its historic Rites and Reason Theatre. My presence in a superbly interdisciplinary center with a long literary and performing arts tradition, coupled with the distance from the Jamaican context, where I had headed a more traditional social sciences center heavily committed to policy-oriented studies, opened a window of possibility, and I unsealed my poetry file at last.

It was a revelation. Somehow in fewer than forty typed poems, I felt I had managed to capture the sequence and many of the critical moments that punctuated and helped define the zeitgeist of an era.[13] There were formative poems from the early 1970s, reflecting the Rastafari-inflected mysticism that was an integral part of the reemergence of radical traditions among young people in the short span between Emperor Haile Selassie's visit to Jamaica in 1966, the exclusion and banning of Walter Rodney in 1968, and the election of the Michael Manley government on a wave

---

12 Brother Valentino, "The Roaring '70s," accessed January 2018, www.youtube.com/watch?v=n75Pki_loZ4.

13 Elsewhere I have tried to recapture my peculiar personal history, moving between Trinidad, Jamaica, and Grenada in the period between 1970 and 1983, but the poems accomplish this, I suggest, far better than the formal prose. See my "Conclusion: Black Power Forty Years On; An Introspection," in Kate Quinn (ed.) *Black Power in the Caribbean*, University Press of Florida, Gainesville, 2014, 261–74.

of popular hope in 1972. There was the clear assertion of an emergent and still at the time insufficiently recognized urban popular culture of resistance, evident in both the utilization of Rasta-inflected Jamaican language and vistas drawn from Kingston's stark and graphic social and spatial landscapes. There was a distinct reflection in both content and form of my three years as an undergraduate in my mother's country, Trinidad and Tobago, between 1970 and 1973. These were the years immediately following the 1970 Black Power Revolution—when urban "Trinbagonian" young people, overwhelmingly Black, had demonstrated for three months for Black Power, a movement that ended with the Eric Williams government declaring a state of emergency and the arrest of the leaders of the movement, leading to an attempted coup by elements in the military, which was ultimately aborted.[14] The popular mood, however, did not subside with the state of emergency, and for my time in the twin-island state, radical ideas and tendencies continued to flourish—among them the guerrilla-oriented National United Freedom Fighters (NUFF), the death of whose leader, Guy Harewood, is the subject of one of these poems. There is, as the central part of the volume, an exploration of the 1970s during the Manley regime in Jamaica, when the country's hesitant steps toward a national democratic transformation were met with a determined, powerful, and ultimately successful reaction.[15] These poems, I think, capture the breadth of the social chasm that divided Jamaica in the 1970s and persists today, the urgency and poignancy of the popular expectations for change, and the sheer dangerousness and determination of power—both national and international—as it sought to outmaneuver, ambush, and ultimately strangle the popular movement. There is a brief reflection on the short-lived revolution in Grenada, where I spent two extraordinary years from 1981 until the weeks before the killing of Maurice Bishop, followed by the US-led invasion in October 1983. And in the end, if it can be said that the "Long Seventies" began with Rodney's exclusion and the Jamaican riots that followed in 1968 and ended in 1983 with Grenada, there are a series of reflections on the world

---

14   See Selwyn Ryan and Taimoon Stewart (eds.) *The Black Power Revolution 1970: A Retrospective*, Institute of Social and Economic Research, St. Augustine, Trinidad, 1995; and Quinn, *Black Power in the Caribbean*.

15   Still the best, graphic description of the reaction to Democratic Socialism is to be found in Manley's own retrospective of his two terms in power in the 1970s. See Michael Manley, *Jamaica: Struggle in the Periphery*, Writers and Readers, London, 1982.

that followed this period of popular upsurge—the years of returning home and confronting the long, difficult, articulated period of neoliberal domination and disillusionment that has continued into the present.[16]

In Lecture 7 of his 1988 series of talks at the University of Illinois Urbana Champaign, Stuart Hall spoke at length on the linked concepts of domination and hegemony. Riffing and expanding on an approach pioneered by Antonio Gramsci, in which both hegemonic and counter-hegemonic ideas are often seen as rooted in and emerging from commonly held perceptions or "common sense," Hall stresses the profound importance of exploring, seeking to understand, and logically attempting to change perceptions of what is common sense. Hegemony, Hall suggests, "can only be achieved as a historical process, not a thing achieved."[17] Likewise, counter-hegemony is best understood as a work in progress, requiring careful understanding of a historical conjuncture and the specific cultural, ideological, and linguistic apparatuses that ring with truth, give momentum to popular perceptions of "the truth," and provide justification for engagement, commitment, and untold personal sacrifices in support of the cause. This small personal archive, dusted off and uncovered almost as an intact time capsule, can hopefully initiate a conversation about what counter-hegemony in the Caribbean in the Long Seventies looked like and perhaps even suggest some of the reasons why the popular movements of the era achieved some initial success but failed to maintain momentum and were ultimately defeated, though, I underline, in the face of immense national, regional, and international opposition. I have grouped the referenced poems around the four themes mentioned previously—Rastafari/mysticism, resistance culture, injustice, and revolution—that describe and give context to the burgeoning counter-hegemonic discourse of the era. The fifth category—lamentation—explores poems written after the defeat of the movement as the decade of the 1980s moved on.

---

16 In a course on global Black radicalism that I teach with Geri Augusto at Brown University, we refer to the period between the radicalization of the civil rights movement in Lowndes County, Alabama, in the mid-1960s and the collapse of the Grenadian Revolution in 1983 as the "Long Seventies." It encompasses an unprecedented series of events in regions of the African diaspora that arc through the Caribbean movements discussed herein and the period of the Southern African Liberation victories against Portuguese colonialism.

17 Stuart Hall, "Domination and Hegemony," in Jennifer Darryl Slack and Lawrence Grossberg (eds.) Stuart Hall: Cultural Studies, 1983, Duke University Press, Durham, NC, 2016, 173.

RASTAFARI/MYSTICISM

To understand the soil out of which radical trends in Jamaican politics reemerged after the relative hiatus of the 1950s and 1960s is difficult, nigh impossible, without an appreciation of and reflection on the role of Rastafari. Emperor Selassie's visit to Jamaica in 1966 and the tumultuous welcome he received from tens of thousands of Rastas and non-Rastafari enthusiasts revealed the strength and tenacity of Black Nationalist currents within the popular culture, most immediately evident in the music.[18] Bob Andy's 1967 song, and his first big hit, "I've Got to Go Back Home" is emblematic of this moment, both in its capturing of urban alienation ("This couldn't be my home") and in its adherence to key tenets of Rastafarian redemptionist philosophy, asserting that there is a real home for all Black people in Africa.[19] It is the almost complete rebellion of Rastafari philosophy and praxis from established Euro-Creole Jamaican norms, its radical purity, that is of interest. Rastas shattered codes of appearance (particularly the wearing of beards and, most conspicuously, dreadlocks), language (via the transmutation, inversion, and subversion of already subversive Jamaican language), ritual (through the substituting of the rituals of "grounation," reasoning, and ganja, for those of the established church), and philosophy (God as Black; Africa as Zion; the West, particularly Jamaica, as Babylon) that provide the image and template for young Jamaican radicals.[20] That it was not without its own internal flaws is evident, in the traditional adherence to male supremacy in the patriarchal Old Testament aspects of the doctrine that were adopted and incorporated into various houses, including the Bobo Dreads, who eschewed contact with women during their menstrual periods, and the Twelve Tribes of Israel, who gave women one token position alongside their leadership of twelve men.[21] I use excerpts from my poems "Greetings two" and "one love Bra Daley" as examples of the

18   See Lewis, *Walter Rodney's Intellectual and Political Thought*.
19   See Bob Andy, "I've Got to Go Back Home," accessed January 2018, www.youtube.com/watch?v=lkqeCA4x6kk.
20   See Horace Campbell, *Rasta and Resistance: From Marcus Garvey to Walter Rodney*, Africa World, Trenton, NJ, 1987; Barry Chevannes, *Rastafari: Roots and Ideology*, Syracuse University Press, Syracuse, NY, 1994; and Nathaniel Samuel Murrell, William David Spencer, and Adrian Anthony McFarlane (eds.) *Chanting Down Babylon: The Rastafari Reader*, Temple University Press, Philadelphia, 1998.
21   See Maureen Rowe, "Gender and Family Relations in Rastafari: A Personal Perspective," in Murrell, Spencer, and McFarlane (eds.) *Chanting Down Babylon*,

power and seductiveness of the Rasta/mystic tradition in the late 1960s and early 1970s. "Greentings two" locates itself in an urban yard during a "reasoning" and partaking of herbs. None of the participants make any profound statements of philosophy or principle, but it is the reflections on shared experiences, the silences between the infrequent utterances, that are important. They are like the intermittent strums in a rock steady beat: checheh, checheh. Together, silences and companionship quietly forge unity and common purpose.

> IanI
> eyes I-
> servin'
> no sight
> of mud
> or water
> even sun
> baked cracks abs
> ent
> widdout leaves
> crabwalkin
> checheh::checheh
> checheh::checheh
> monotonously
> sunlight stirs
> smoky breeze
> denim eases
> shifts settles
> seedling grows
> green leaves
> sprout dust
> chlorofilled,
> covered broad
> "ili off?" seen[22]

72–88; and Imani Tafari-Ama, "Rastawoman as Rebel: Case Studies in Jamaica," in *Chanting Down Babylon*, 89–106.

22   Brian Meeks, "Greentings two," in *Coup Clock Clicks*, 14. I use short excerpts from the poems as illustration and to more effectively invoke the zeitgeist of the times. The complete versions are, of course, accessible in *Coup Clock Clicks*.

The second brings to the fore the late Brother Leonard Daley, "bra Daley," who was a genuine person, a painter, often mentioned among the panoply of outstanding Jamaican "intuitive" artists, a loyal husband and father, and an organic philosopher.[23] Daley was not Rastafari, at least not at the time that I reasoned with him, but if nothing else he was an iconoclast and an exemplar of a certain "mystic" tradition shared with Rastafari. His paintings, often dark and complicated, reminded me of the nightmarish quality of Hieronymus Bosch's. Yet Daley's philosophy was humanitarian; he believed in the redemption of even morally compromised people and was optimistic about the future of Jamaica and Jamaicans. In "One Love Bra Daley," Daley suggests how before the intensification of political divisions in the late 1970s and the consolidation of more popular intellectual approaches (Marxism, Black Power, and Rastafarianism), there was room in the Jamaican discursive space of the early 1970s for the flowering of a variety of quixotic perspectives as exemplified here:

yes beardman
a long time
now been tryin
to site
de hites an
couldn fin it
someplace up
a mountain
side a feel
a heart which
site a souns
an lik it up
real iri/
so from dis
time on a might
change a slight but
never be the same
again inside
site?
one love[24]

---

23   See National Gallery of Jamaica Blog, "Spiritual Yards—Gallery 3, Leonard Daley, William 'Woody' Joseph," accessed January 2018, www.youtube.com/watch?v=lkqeCA4x6kk.
24   Meeks, *Coup Clock Clicks*, 35.

RESISTANCE CULTURE

The movement of the 1970s was driven by the popular culture of the time. In Jamaica, reggae was the soundtrack, and Bob Marley, Peter Tosh, and Dennis Brown were among the leading prophets. But alongside the typical drums and bass of the reggae rhythms were other currents that competed for airtime. I wrote "Count Mystic" after a visit to Trinidad in 1973 of the East Kingston Rastafari/jazz band Count Ossie and the Mystic Revelation of Rastafari (MRR). Count Ossie and his group of Rastafari drummers had lived and played from their base near Wareika Hill in East Kingston for many years and were popular on a number of early ska recordings, most notably "Oh Carolina," which remains a turning point in the incorporation of akette drumming into the popular idiom.[25] Don Drummond and the Skatalites, Carlos Malcolm and his Afro-Jamaican Rhythms (who were profoundly influenced by Cuban Rumba and other rhythms), and others had also grounded with Rastafari, and with Ossie in particular, through the vibrant club scene in East Kingston and through further links with Rastafari groups in West Kingston's "Back-o-Wall" and the foreshore area of Southern St. Andrew. It was the chemistry, however, between saxophonist Cedric Brooks, bassist and flautist Joe Ruglass, and a group of young musicians influenced by the Coltrane, avant-garde tradition that led to the creation of the MRR and the iconic 1973 triple album *Grounation*.[26]

I was a student at the St. Augustine campus of the University of the West Indies when I met Count, Cedric, Joe, and the other members in somewhat difficult circumstances, after they had given a stirring concert at Queen's Hall in Port of Spain. They had been invited to Trinidad on an arrangement with a well-known Trinidadian calypsonian, who had lodged them in what was supposed to be a hotel but instead turned out to be a house of ill repute on Charlotte Street in downtown Port of Spain. What was worse, the calypsonian had subsequently abandoned them without any payment for their series of performances. Fortunately, along with colleagues in the Guild of Undergraduates (student government) at the University of the West Indies, we were able to plan at short notice a benefit concert on campus, headlined by the MRR themselves. This allowed them to pay their bills and return home to Jamaica with some

---

25   The Folkes Brothers, *Oh Carolina*, 45 rpm, Buster Wild Bells, Kingston, 1960.
26   Count Ossie and the Mystic Revelation of Rastafari, *Grounation*, Ashanti Records, Kingston, 1973.

cash in hand. On the night of the performance, tired from a hectic day of organizing the event, I arrived late. As I describe in "Jus felt Count Mystic," I heard from a distance in the night the steady heartbeat sound of the akette drums building above the combined moan of bowed acoustic bass, baritone sax, and slide trombone. For me it was as if a thunderstorm of Pan-African musical resistance had burst open.

TUNDAHSTAAM
a boltalightnin
tree fallin
down twelve
story glass
an stressed
concrete crackin
underneath the strain
a wealth a
academic talent
runs in fear
of rusty saxes
double bass
an goatskin
drums?
or the parting
of the waves[27]

The second instance of the power of insurgent culture is from May 1974, when Black American crooner Marvin Gaye was at the height of his popularity. He had managed to transcend the easy love-affair rhythm and blues of the early 1960s with the remarkably political 1971 album *What's Going On*[28] and then, in the following years, reinvented himself once again as a postrevolutionary lover man with *Let's Get It On*.[29] The Wailers—still with the full trio of Bob Marley, Peter Tosh, and Bunny Livingstone on board—were on an upward trajectory, with their albums *Catch a Fire* and the newly released *Burnin'*[30] climbing up local and

---

27 Meeks, *Coup Clock Clicks*, 17.
28 Marvin Gaye, *What's Going On*, Tamla, Detroit, 1971.
29 Marvin Gaye, *Let's Get It On*, Tamla, Detroit, 1973.
30 The Wailers, *Catch a Fire*, Island and Tuff Gong, April 1973; and The Wailers, *Burnin'*, Island and Tuff Gong, October 1973.

international charts. None of the promoters nor any of Gaye's agents, however, would have put the Wailers to open for him if there had been any fear of their eclipsing his star, which is exactly what happened. Gaye had arrived in Kingston, unfortunately for him, at the very moment when the effervescent, Jamaican urban Black culture, epitomized in the style, lyrics, and stance of the united Wailers, had risen to the surface. For Gaye it was perhaps a major booking error, but for the Wailers it was a triumphant arrival. "The Trench Town Assault Case," excerpted only in part here, sought to trace the fault lines in Jamaican society through a mapping of its microcosm in the placement and seating of people in the National Stadium on the night of the concert. Then the Wailers take the stage and, in the final stanza, excerpted here, shatter the already cracked facade of Jamaican (Kingstonian) normality.

> natty dread
> your guitar
> is a self
> loadin rifle
> your harmony
> is a thin
> black line
> of resistance
> natty dread
> blaze out
> your soun
> natty dread
> dont let i
> down
> natty dread
> wail out your
> soun
> natty dread
> dont let i
> down[31]

The poem "Langwidge&Culcha" is a meditation on nation language and the trials of growing up in postcolonial Jamaica. Much has been written about the failures of polarized Jamaican society, which stigma-

---

31   Meeks, *Coup Clock Clicks*, 44.

tizes the language of the majority and fails to accept the status of "nation language" as legitimate in its own right, fails miserably to find effective avenues through which to teach English as a distinct language, and then stigmatizes its own majority for failing to speak English "properly."[32] This poem tries to capture some of this tortured and still continuing conversation/argument/struggle.

aca
dem
ic
name
tame
ing
hi jack
ing
daily
i spirit/
skankin
nightly
lightly
roun
neat an
cozy
argu
circle
ments of
zoo lion
steel wire
a grip
i tongue
a shape
i mout(h)
a ben'
i lip [33]

32 See, for instance, Edward Kamau Brathwaite, *History of the Voice: The Development of Nation Language in Anglo-Caribbean Poetry*, New Beacon, London, 1984; Velma Pollard, *Dread Talk: The Language of Rastafari*, Canoe, Kingston, 1994; Hubert Devonish, *Language and Liberation*, Karia, London, 1986; and Carolyn Cooper, *Noises in the Blood: Orality, Gender, and the Vulgar Body of Jamaican Popular Culture*, Macmillan, London, 1993.
33 Meeks, *Coup Clock Clicks*, 27.

INJUSTICE

The prime motivation that inspired a generation into political activism was not, I suggest, religion, ideology, or philosophy but rather a burning sense of injustice. Who burned down Jones Town in Southern St. Andrew creating an exodus of refugees who ended up as a displaced community in the appropriately named Sufferers' Heights community of St. Catherine and why? Who set the vicious Orange Lane fire and why? Who burned down the Eventide senior living home and why? Who shot Bob Marley in an attempted assassination and why?[34] Who killed the golf caddy, as asked in the poem "March 9, 1976" (below), and why? Who, a hemisphere away, provided the weapons, resources, and logistics for the coup against Salvador Allende, the elected president of Chile, and then bombed him, leading to his decision to commit suicide in the Presidential Palace, La Moneda? Who supported with arms, diplomacy, and finances the regime of racist South Africa, enabling the invasion of independent Angola with the full intent to force, at the point of a gun, a free Black people back into servitude and oblivion? All these were considered by "the youth" as supreme acts of injustice, and all demanded resistance and commitment, as captured in these two poems. The first was written following a tragic yet typical report in the *Gleaner* of March 9, 1976, of the murder the night before of a number of people at a dance. One of the people killed—a golf caddy—stood out to me at the time, since the *Gleaner* had departed from its usual habit of devaluing the deaths of poor Black people, typically erasing their humanity and character by referring to them generically as "laborers." In this instance, the reporter deigned to actually mention the victim's modest, if distinct, profession.

could the golf
caddy know
who fired his life
inspired this crime

---

34 I am truly grateful to Marlon James, whose brilliant, Man Booker Prize-winning work of fabulous, speculative fiction brought this entire era and, in particular, the attempted assassination of Bob Marley to international attention in unprecedented ways. I had also sought to invoke the era in my earlier novel *Paint the Town Red*, Peepal Tree Press, Leeds, 2003. Far more work, both imaginative and forensic, needs to be done to unearth the deep layers of silence that surround this pivotal moment of Jamaican and Caribbean history. See Marlon James, *A Brief History of Seven Killings*, Riverhead Books, New York, 2014.

'gainst the youth
of the town?

crying i sight
brown grass
of a city
trying to out
dry flames
with i tears.[35]

The second example, "The Coup Clock Clicks," which is also used as the title of the collection, speaks to the notorious shooting up and burning of the entire community of lower Jones Town in South St. Andrew, leading to a mass migration of residents to establish a squatting settlement in Sufferers' Heights. Yet, as intimated, this was but one of many similar instances with victims from both sides of the political divide that give support to the claim that Kingston, and Jamaica more generally, was in a pre–civil war situation by the mid to late 1970s.

today
the west
burns down.
Jones town
cries out
for water.
the rat a tat
staccato/
automatic death
carves out its place
in history.
children fall
at barricades,
crumpled faces
age
before their
time[36]

---

35 Meeks, *Coup Clock Clicks*, 47.
36 *Coup Clock Clicks*, 57.

REVOLUTION

The belief in imminent revolution was an integral aspect of the movement, which gave it purpose and direction throughout the Long Seventies. In 1974, the Vietnamese had, after a bitter and bloody war with the French and then the Americans, won freedom through persistent and effective warfare against colonial and imperial interlopers. The conflict in Portuguese Africa was coming to a head, and it was the militant (and Marxist) revolutionaries of the Popular Movement for the Liberation of Angola (MPLA), Front for the Liberation of Mozambique (FRELIMO), and the African Party for the Liberation of Guinea-Bissau and Cape Verde (PAIGC) who were on the verge of taking power. A decade earlier Fidel Castro had taken power in Cuba and, after the successful defense at Playa Giron and the survival of the missile crisis, was holding it effectively in the face of incessant hostility from America. Even where the revolution had succumbed to the forces of imperialism, since, most notably in Allende's Chile, it was because, the narrative suggested, the approaches taken were insufficiently militant and revolutionary. Thus, the argument asserted that Allende was well meaning but naïve and this accounted in large measure for the success of Augusto Pinochet's coup and the bloody suppression of Unidad Popular. This presumption of revolution as not only achievable but also inevitable—not necessarily, though, perhaps, preferably via armed insurrection—was dominant and persuasive. The poem "To a Guy I knew but didn't meet" was written after I learned that Guy Harewood, a leader of the Trinidadian guerrilla group the NUFF, had been shot and killed by the police outside of Port of Spain.[37] The poem is unhesitating in its assurance of inevitable success, even in the face of tragic setbacks like the killing of Harewood.

and the rope lengthens
the crimes/
criminals
multiply
and oilfed SMGs
belch out

---

37   See Brian Meeks, "NUFF at the Cusp of an Idea: Grassroots Guerrillas and the Politics of the Seventies in Trinidad and Tobago," chapter 2 in Brian Meeks, *Narratives of Resistance: Jamaica, Trinidad, the Caribbean*, The University of the West Indies Press, Kingston, 2000, 48–74.

black blood
and countless
unnamed who fell
before you
brother G/
sisterB/
and Bogle,
Garvey,
Lumum
 ba,
Che,
Amilcar
Cabral,
will testify
for the tense
black hands
must dig
the hole
and the
hanging noose
must tighten
and the
living zombies
of this day/
nightmare
must fall-
out
in the night
light of our
tomorrow's
dawning[38]

With a similar sense of revolutionary optimism, though with a different country and struggle, "Angola Poem" heralds, in the wake of the Cuban role in successfully helping Angola to defend herself against South African invasion, the unstoppable nature of the international workers movement, bolstered by its newest contingents from southern Africa.

---

38 Meeks, *Coup Clock Clicks*, 33.

Cabinda
Benguela
Lobito
Caxito
Texeira
de Sousa
Luanda

Angola
is the
baby of
new Africa.

... back weh
Sout' Africa!
back weh
America!
Angola is
the baby of
new Africa.

next stop
JOHANNESBURG[39]

The Grenada Revolution burst on the Caribbean on March 13, 1979, with the New Jewel movement taking power by overthrowing, in an armed action, the arbitrary and authoritarian Eric Gairy regime. It was a year of revolutions, with events in Iran preceding and Nicaragua following hard on the heels of the Grenadian events. For the Anglophone Caribbean, with its traditions of Westminster-style parliamentary politics, Grenada came like a bolt out of the blue. For more than four years, the Revolution shone a light on alternative possibilities for small states to exercise sovereignty, new approaches to democracy, and novel initiatives in education and culture, among many others. However, there was another side to the process that suggested a leadership enthralled with questions of ideological purity, policies that weighed heavily against dissenters and increasingly hermetic, unrealistic notions of security,

---

39   *Coup Clock Clicks*, 47.

and the inevitability of the process that underestimated the real dangers facing revolutionary regimes in the Western Hemisphere. These perspectives contributed tragically to the sequence of events that led to the house arrest of Prime Minister Maurice Bishop by his own party in September 1983, his release by a crowd of supporters who then occupied the main military fort, the fort's recapture by soldiers loyal to the party, and then Bishop's death at the hands of his own People's Revolutionary Army.[40] The invasion of traumatized Grenada by the United States and regional allies a week later on October 19 not only sealed the fate of the short-lived revolution but also ended an era of radical Caribbean politics that had begun with the Rodney events of 1968 in Kingston.

The following poem, simply titled "Grenada," written shortly after Bishop's death and the wave of antirevolution sentiment that crested following the US-led invasion, tries to recapture that ephemeral moment of optimism and hope that surfaced for many in the period between 1979 and 1983. For my own mental survival, I needed to rescue a memory of the "revo" and its flawed but very real interlude of creative awakening and human flourishing that had been buried in the detritus of the October tragedy.

> though bombs drop amnesia
> and schooldays are over,
> i remember.
> a wood slatted bridge
> and the jungle green
> and the signs on every corner.

---

40   See, among more recent commentaries and analyses, David Scott, *Omens of Adversity: Tragedy, Time, Memory, Justice*, Duke University Press, Durham, NC, 2014; Shalini Puri, *The Grenada Revolution in the Caribbean Present: Operation Urgent Memory*, Palgrave Macmillan, New York, 2014; and Brian Meeks, "Grenada, Once Again: Revisiting the 1983 Crisis and Collapse of the Grenada Revolution," in Brian Meeks, *Critical Interventions in Caribbean Politics and Theory*, University Press of Mississippi, Jackson, 2014. And thankfully, a new generation of scholars is rethinking the history of the Revolution with fresh, critical gendered lenses. See, for instance, Laurie Lambert, *Comrade Sister: Caribbean Feminist Revisions of the Grenada Revolution*, University of Virginia Press, Charlottesville, 2020; Nicole Phillip-Dowe, "Women in the Grenada Revolution; 1979–1983," *Social and Economic Studies* 62, nos. 3 and 4 (2013): 45–82; and, though herself from a prior generation, the literary and theoretical work of Merle Collins, discussed in some detail in David Scott, "The Fragility of Memory: An Interview with Merle Collins," *Small Axe* 31, no. 14 (March 2010): 79–163.

i remember ...
smiling hopes on every corner
too thick to harness in a
May first shower,
mother and father
son and daughter
brother and sister
come together
these i will never
forget.[41]

LAMENTATION

The 1980 electoral defeat of Michael Manley, preceded that year by Walter
Rodney's assassination in Guyana and followed three years later by the
tragic collapse of the Grenada Revolution, signaled the end of the Caribbean's Long Seventies. Indeed, if one is to use the wider lens, it was also the
end of two decades of Black radicalism, evident in the collapse of the Black
Power movement in the United States and the funneling of Iran/Contra
funds both to wear down the Revolution and simultaneously to engineer
a drug crisis in American inner cities and the gradual reincorporation of
radical regimes in formerly Portuguese Africa into the mainstream of the
neoliberal world economy. Philosophically, Karl Marx and John Maynard
Keynes—strange bedfellows at best—had lost and Friedrich Hayek had
won. Allende's vision of a democratic road to socialism was replaced by
Pinochet's iron fist in politics and an open-market economy managed
intellectually and practically by the "Chicago boys." It was a time of lamentation but also a time to take stock and consider on what ground a new
and different kind of movement might arise again in the future.[42] These
poems, however, are not so much about future considerations but about

---

41   Meeks, *Coup Clock Clicks*, 67.
42   At the Small Axe conference on the Jamaican 1970s, I had a brief but
interesting exchange with David Scott on the meaning of tragedy, as exemplified
in the Caribbean radical movements of the 1970s, and whether, beyond them,
there were spaces for a politics of optimism. Suffice it to say that my approach
leaned to the side of optimism and David's did not. One outcome of that exchange
is described in the final chapter of this volume. See also David Scott, *Omens of
Adversity*; Brian Meeks, "After Tragedy, Searching for Liberation," *Cultural
Critique*, no. 93 (Spring 2016): 212–20; and Greg A. Graham, *Democratic Political
Tragedy in the Postcolony: The Tragedy of Postcoloniality in Michael Manley's
Jamaica and Nelson Mandela's South Africa*, Routledge, New York, 2018.

the lament of the moment. "October 80 night" imagines five inner-city
youths on the eve of the election, listening to the results and preparing for
the new world that will face them on the following day.

> roun' eight o clock,
> pressure ease up
> the radio start to crackle the news;
> Kingston gone;
> Clarendon gone;
> Spanish Town well hot.
> whol' heap a man get drop.
> cap start fe bawl,
> bobo him start crawl off the roof.
> me an' richie still flat.
> charlie? im still a sleep on im back.
> hours beat, charlie stop sleep
> rub im chin with expectant grin:
> "who win?" im ask me an richie.
> richie hol' on to im.
> "we lose. dem choose de green.
> is a different scene when mornin come."
> charlie start weep,
> I start fe cry,
> no one can sleep:
> bell start ring an shot still a pop.
> we light a spliff an get back flat
> an tek a stack, an hol' a watch
>   till morning come.[43]

The final poem shared in this chapter, "shattered glass," is a dirge in
honor of three young men, cadres of the Workers Party of Jamaica, killed
by the police "in a shootout" under typically murky and hotly contested
circumstances in 1984.

> o the morning dawned calm
> and the dewdrops stood
> on the sidewalk grass.

---

43 Meeks, *Coup Clock Clicks*, 60.

the nightingales sang in Red Hills Square.
schoolchildren sat in expectation
shading in the shadow of the mountain.
mist gave way to light.

then the watchers and the waiters
the hubbub and the clatter
the engines and the horns
the fumes and newspapers:
within sight, three young men alight
hands held high
in nervous posture ...

o the three young men with hands held high
backs against the concrete fence,
jaws toward the sky:
The cricket and the frog,
the silence and the wonder
the thunder then the silence
and the slow motion tumble.[44]

CLOSING CONVERSATION

The final conversation around these poems focuses on a number of dominant themes that run through the entire collection and that mark them out as intellectual products of a particular conjunctural moment of counter-hegemonic insurgency.

The first is the palpable sense of certainty as a dominant feature of the times. There is, through most of these, save perhaps those gathered under the section "Lamentation," the certainty of revolution and victory. There is the certainty of a positive victory in Angola that will inevitably extend to Johannesburg in apartheid South Africa. There is the sense that the currents of the world, of history, were inexorably in our favor, in favor of the youth, of Black people, of African emancipation, and of socialism. This goes far beyond the territory of cautious optimism. It is captured in "Angola poem," "The Trench Town Assault Case," and elsewhere. Its foundation derived, I suggest, not solely or even primarily from a

---

44 *Coup Clock Clicks*, 80.

Marxist reading of history, though Marxist dialectical progressivism certainly played an important role. However, I think it is the confluence of Marxist and Black radical notions of redemptive revolution cohabiting with biblical notions of revelation. Bob Marley and the Wailers' hit "Revolution," from the album *Natty Dread*, epitomizes this syncretism. It begins with the chanting of revelation "coming true," and only after this initial statement is made clear does it segue into the proclamation that "it takes a revolution, to make a solution." Yet this proves to be only an interlude; the climax returns to "lightning, thunder, brimstone, and fire" as the crescendo of a truly biblical chorus of cleansing flames.[45] This confidence was a feature of the times, and it gave young people an unsurpassed energy and optimism. However, it simultaneously, in its hubris, failed to prepare them for the looming confrontation with not only the power of locally entrenched oligarchies but also the overarching imperial power of the United States.

This naïveté is partly to be accounted for in the youthfulness of the movement, but also because of the crushing of radical traditions in the Anglophone Caribbean in the preceding decades, and therefore the absence of a solid contiguous memory and tradition of resistance to be drawn on from the recent past. Another undoubted feature was the Anglophone Caribbean's relative distance from the history of direct US intervention, which had largely taken place in the Latin Caribbean and Haiti and was therefore understood, at best, from a distance. However, the ideological, especially Marxist-Leninist, role in bolstering this sense of the inevitable cannot be underestimated. The Brezhnevian doctrine of overstating the power and consolidation of "really existing socialism," the parallel notion of the "non-capitalist path" as a feasible and viable alternative for all nations willing to follow the lead of the Soviet Union, and the relative success of the Cuban model in the 1970s all helped to give wings to the idea that revolution was just around the corner. In the end, given the resiliency of US hegemony and power, the failure to appreciate this was dangerous, not so much when in the verse of powerless poets but when translated into the policies and postures of popular movements, as evident in Manley's Jamaica and, most glaringly, in Grenada leading up to the crisis of 1983.

---

45 Bob Marley and the Wailers, "Revolution," *Natty Dread*, Island/Tuff Gong, Kingston, 1973.

The second theme is the emphasis placed on violence as an easily deployed, if not always first-avenue, means for advancing the progressive cause. There is of course a solid historical explanation as to why violence was so prominent, particularly in the Jamaican political imagination, where by the early 1970s there was already a long and sordid history of violence used to advance party political positions, both during and between elections.[46] However, there is also a wider international moment described by the Cuban Revolution, by the Vietnam War, and, as an example of the failure to use armed force, by the aforementioned overthrow of the elected Allende regime in Chile in 1973. Chile's history suggested that the careful preparation for armed struggle was necessary if the Revolution was to be successful, but there was also Vietnam in the years after the Tet Offensive and up until the US withdrawal; the growing and increasingly effective insurgencies in Angola, Mozambique, and Guinea-Bissau; and, toward the end of the decade, the successes of the Nicaraguan and Iranian Revolutions and, closer to home, Grenada—all confirming that revolutionary violence was necessary and integral to revolutionary success. Poems, of course, are not political strategy and refract, at best, a partial picture of complex theoretical calculations; and we also must not underplay the engrained history of violence in Jamaica and its use as part of the toolkit, if not the prerogative, of powerful Jamaican conservative forces. Yet it is still striking how often violence was invoked and placed at the center of the conversation.

A third feature, and among the more striking ones, in revisiting these poems is their evidently masculinist bias. It is not only the repeated reference to male heroes (Bob Marley, Count Mystic, Bra Daley, Guy Harewood) but also the masculinist references embedded in violence as a solution and male dominance asserted through sexual references, as in "The Trench Town Assault case" and elsewhere. Indeed, the greatest hesitancy in republishing these poems, going back to a point made earlier, is related to these glaring commissions and omissions. If I were to write these poems again, surely room could be found for mention of other heroines. Thus, Bra Daley's wife, Sis D, is mentioned as a concrete wall, a bulwark supporting the family, but inevitably as an infrastructural support and not an agent in her own right. In similar vein, "To a Guy I knew" mentions sister B (Beverly Jones, one of the NUFF militants

---

46 See Obika Gray, *Radicalism and Social Change in Jamaica, 1960–1972*, University of Tennessee Press, Kingston, 1991.

who was killed in a military ambush) but goes on to celebrate Paul Bogle, Marcus Garvey, Patrice Lumumba, Che Guevara, and Amílcar Cabral—all popular and noteworthy icons of the era. But where are the mentions in this collection of Angela Davis, Claudia Jones, Amy Jacques Garvey, Haydée Santamaría, or Guinea-Bissau's Ernestina Titina Silá. None gain sufficient favor to be highlighted. These lacunae were certainly integral to the times, and it would be invidious to rewrite the world of 1974 to pretend that it was 2018; yet I recall that in my room on the St. Augustine campus were two large posters, one of Ho Chi Minh and the other of Angela Davis. So even at that moment there was recognition of the central role of women in the movement. So why not their more prominent location at the heart of the poems?

A fourth dimension requiring consideration is the notion of audacity. The fearlessness evident in the numerous demonstrations by teenagers and young people, standing up in the face of the police and local power; even more so, the willingness to oppose in words and deeds the over-arching power of the hegemon; the readiness of unnamed communities and their residents to resist violent incursions and imagine and develop creative forms of self-defense, a few instances of which are captured in these poems—these are legion. Think, for example, of the simple yet profound act of embattled citizens removing the grates in the streets and lanes to prevent drive-by massacres. Think of inventions like the "twin barrel bucky"—a shotgun built out of a bicycle frame—as a self-fashioned but effective means of self-defense (the "bucky" is the subject of a poem in the volume not used here). Think of, in a different vein, the audacity of Bob Marley in many of his interviews, speaking to the international press confidently and without compromise in his Jamaican nation language; of the audacity of the Rasta singers/artists at the height of reggae in its first global blush of success, flashing locks on- and offstage in a world that remained, throughout and beyond these times, hostile to the very appearance of natural hair, much less the "unkempt," unruly dreadlocks. This consolidation of a culture of audaciousness, captured intermittently in these poems, deserves further thought and consideration as a critical and indeed central feature of the 1970s, which bore aloft the movement at home and gave Jamaican rebel culture credibility and purchase far beyond the small island's shores.

By far, however, to return to and underline an earlier thematic, the greatest motivation for these poems was a deep sense of injustice and the need to correct it. At the heart of my poetry is a perception of the vast inequalities in Jamaica and, more broadly, the Caribbean. There is an appeal against economic injustice as captured in the glaring inequalities portrayed throughout: political injustice is at the forefront of *The Coup Clock Clicks*; police injustice is prominent in "shattered glass"; imperial injustice takes center stage in "March 9, 1976" and "Grenada." It is rage against injustice, superseding the more abstract notions of social revolution or even biblically derived revelation, that drives these poems, that drove many in the popular movement and largely inspired me in the tumultuous Long Seventies in which I was privileged to live out my youth.

THE END(S) OF POETRY?

The Coup Clock Clicks closes in 1988, but my momentum as a poet had slowed long before that, and since then I have written a few lines but not at the pace nor, I think, with the inspiration of the earlier compositions. Why this sudden decline and then complete halt in poetic expression? This, as intimated at the beginning of this chapter, is a matter worth considering in itself and critical in helping to understand the character of the 1970s. I propose three reasons for the decline and ending of my poetic writing. The first has to do with politics. The movement, as it gathered pace, placed a premium on the activist, perceived as the person who could plan, agitate, distribute, and win over converts to the movement. The poet or prose writer was never as highly valued. It is true that rallies, meetings, and other political events were interspersed with cultural items, and the far more widely received reggae music was in its heyday of message and content and formed the soundtrack of that decade. No one actively discouraged poetry, but it seemed to occupy, at least in my reckoning, second or third place to more "political" activities, such as organizing and agitating in the traditional sense.

The second reason has to do with the defeat of the movement, beginning with the People's National Party electoral loss in 1980 and ending decisively with the Grenada debacle in 1983. That the popular movement was defeated is an assumption that runs through this narrative; the results were complex and obviously affected different people in different ways, depending, critically, on their social location and the vagaries of personality and luck. I felt that the best response I could give to explain the 1970s, to describe as well as possible what happened and suggest what mistakes needed to be avoided in the future, was to decenter my poetic voice, learn to the best of my ability the arcane skills of the scholar, and seek to carefully record, articulate, and interpret the critical moments of this remarkable era. This seemed to me the best option of remaining true to some of my core beliefs yet still being positioned to capture the granular details of those remarkable times for future generations. However, in reflection, and with respect to these very poems, was this the best path to have taken? Now I am not so sure.

The third proposed reason, linked also to the question of defeat, was the hard economic imperative to survive, to pay rent and school fees, and to buy food. The occupation of the academic, though somewhat poorly paid, particularly in the Jamaica of the 1980s, was nonetheless relatively steady and safe. However, it also came with the advantage of keeping one closer to spaces where critical ideas and conversations were generated, and thus it seemed like less of an existential compromise than other possible occupations. Poetry as a profession then, now, and for the foreseeable future will likely place the true practitioner closer to the margins of bare survival than academic labor or most other modes of possible employment. And so, regretfully, in the 1980s I closed the poetry file.

3

The Politics of Edna Manley:
A Preliminary Appraisal

When Joseph Manley first asked me to give the lecture that became this chapter, without further thought, but with great humility, I said yes, as for many reasons, none stated here, it would have been quite impossible for me to say otherwise. But then I immediately began to reflect on the mountain that I would have to climb, and the task became increasingly daunting and indeed frightening; because others have ascended this hill before and with extraordinary success. Thus, Wayne Brown's biographic reflections on Edna's private, early years in England and in Jamaica before the 1938 uprising,[1] David Boxer's wonderfully produced *Edna Manley: Sculptor*,[2] and Rachel Manley's memoirs *Horses in Her Hair*[3] as well as her carefully edited collection of Edna's *Diaries*,[4] are all, in their own way, sensitive, thorough, and in many respects complete assessments of the life of this remarkable Jamaican woman. Yet when I began rereading them all, as the inevitable prelude to my own reflections, it struck me that there was a clear and evident lacuna. Though it is impossible to consider Edna Manley without taking into account her evident role and insertion into the mainstream of modern Jamaican politics, and though politics runs through the interstices of all these important assessments, there is to date no attempt to understand the *politics* of Edna Manley in its own right. This absence is particularly noteworthy if we recall that she was cousin and wife to one Jamaican national hero, often considered the father of the national movement; cousin to a second who actually led the country into independence; and mother to two sons, both of whom became members of parliament, with one, Michael, becoming the fourth and arguably

1   See Wayne Brown, *Edna Manley: The Private Years, 1900–1938*, Andre Deutsch, London, 1975.
2   See David Boxer, *Edna Manley: Sculptor*, National Gallery of Jamaica and Edna Manley Foundation, Kingston, 1990.
3   See Rachel Manley, *Horses in Her Hair: A Granddaughter's Story*, Key Porter, Toronto, 2008.
4   See Rachel Manley (ed.) *Edna Manley: The Diaries*, Heinemann Caribbean, Kingston, 1989.

most outstanding, if not always most lauded, prime minister of postcolonial Jamaica.

And of course, by politics here, I am not referring to her partisan incli-
nations, which remained, from the birth of the People's National Party
(PNP) in 1938 until her passing in February 1987, firmly supportive of
that organization.[5] Nor am I using it in the sense of the Greek etymology,
concerned mainly with the business of the *polis*, or the state. Rather, I
am using politics in two ways that carry us beyond this: the first is in
the Aristotelian sense, which is concerned with a political community
whose ultimate aims must be a conversation around how the "good life"
is realized, and how might it be possible and feasible to bring into being
a just society. The second approach, more Foucauldian in character,
approaches politics as being at the heart of all collective social activity,
concluding therefore that all social interaction—whether language,
sexuality, culture, and so forth—is inevitably political, or, as second-wave
feminists would argue with great effect, that even the "personal is
political." From such a perspective, then, the questions to be asked would
encompass a far more extensive spectrum and relate not only to Manley's
overt political predilections but also to an appraisal of her times; her
character; her social formation; the critical junctures and conjunctures
that shifted her focus; and how all of these were reflected and refracted
through her main media of artistic expression—sculpture and drawing—
and in her less heralded but significantly important writing in her diary
entries. To attempt to address these, I want to take us through four stages.
First, I attempt to tease out the foundations of her intellectual formation.
Second, I suggest two significant tensions in her life that followed her
into adulthood and became a sort of muse and energizing impetus for
her entire career. Third, I want to propose five main themes in her politics
that derive from the earlier amalgam. And finally, viewing a selection of
her most outstanding pieces, I want to think about how Edna Manley's
politics was made manifest in her art.

FOUNDATIONS

Edna Swithenbank, born in Bournemouth, England on February 28,
1900, was the fifth child and third daughter of Harvey Swithenbank, a

---

5   David Boxer makes explicit reference to the graphic representation of her
images such as the rising sun and its adaptation by the PNP in its iconography
in the catalogue for a recent exhibition of Edna Manley's work. See David Boxer,
Edna Manley: Into the Sun, The Edna Manley Foundation, Kingston, 2015, 9.

Wesleyan minister, and his Jamaican wife, Ellie Shearer. Swithenbank had married Ellie during a period of residency in Jamaica and then returned to England where, alongside peripatetic work for his church, he sought to raise a large family, eventually numbering nine children. However, he suffered from repeated bouts of ill health and died tragically when Edna was only nine, leaving Ellie the unenviable task of raising nine children by herself. This brief and well-known summary of Edna's origins reveals as much as it obscures. The turn of the century was a world very different from that which would emerge two decades later. It was the domain of European imperial powers that had conquered the globe, with few notable exceptions. Thus, the Berlin conference of 1884–85[6] had divided Africa among the major European powers, ensuring that alongside the usual suspects, the newly emergent German nation, with its powerful economic and military base, had its "fair" share of the spoils.

Following emancipation in 1838, the Sugar Duties Act of 1846 and the institution of Crown Colony government in Jamaica after the 1865 Morant Bay Rebellion, the West Indies, of course, had slipped into the stasis and torpor of a colonial backwater.[7] Loyalty to empire remained largely intact—certainly as an official transcript[8]—and Britannia and her ideology ruled the waves. Central to that ideology was the question of race, and as Stuart Hall has suggested, racism in its sordid history has undergone many transformations.[9] However, by the turn of the century, with the consolidation of European Empire, a new, virulent version based on "scientific" assertions of white superiority was consolidating. It would soon find a pseudoscientific home in the eugenics movement[10] with its heinous notions of racial purification through breeding and separation of the races.

---

6   See, for instance, Muriel Chamberlain, *The Scramble for Africa*, Longman, London [1974] 1999; and Walter Rodney, *How Europe Underdeveloped Africa*, Bogle-L'Ouverture, London, 1983.

7   See Christopher Taylor, *Empire of Neglect: The West Indies in the Wake of British Liberalism*, Duke University Press, Durham, NC, 2018.

8   For a riveting discussion of the unofficial transcripts that questioned and resisted British imperialism and Victorian norms, see Brian Moore and Michele Johnson, *Neither Led nor Driven: Contesting British Cultural Imperialism in Jamaica, 1865–1920*, The University of the West Indies Press, Kingston, 2004.

9   See Stuart Hall, "What Is This 'Black' in Black Popular Culture?" in *Stuart Hall: Critical Dialogues in Cultural Studies*, ed. David Morley and Kuang Hsing Chen, Routledge, London, 1996, 465–83.

10 See Ruth Engs, *The Eugenics Movement: An Encyclopedia*, Greenwood, Westport, CT, 2005.

It is in this historical context that we need to read Harvey's marriage to Ellie, who is variously described by her great-granddaughter Rachel as "mulatto"[11] or by her nephew and later son-in-law Norman, reflecting on his mother Margaret, but equally on her sister and his Aunt Ellie, as an "almost pure white woman."[12] While it is difficult to discern in faded black-and-white prints what exactly Ellie looked like, my own conclusion is that in Jamaica she would have been a fair-skinned "brown" lady, not to be mistaken in polite company for white, but that in the less keen and discerning atmosphere of the Cornish coast, she would have passed quite easily, if no mention were ever made of her "colored" ancestors.

I raise the question of race, an often-uncomfortable matter in polite Jamaican discourse, precisely because it is silenced and muffled today almost as much as it was more than a century ago. What were the hurdles, both psychological and social, that Harvey had to cross to marry Ellie? Or was her phenotype sufficiently "white" that the question was never raised? Certainly, one factor that has to be considered is that the young preacher was not just Methodist but *Wesleyan*, among the more socially conscious of the mainstream churches then, as it remains today. Thus, a popular online post suggests that the Wesleyan church is vigilant in its response to social inequities: "Discrimination and prejudice are key topics of concern, whether applied to race, gender, age, or other areas of life. The foundation … is Galatians 3:28: 'There is neither Jew nor Greek, there is neither bond nor free, there is neither male nor female: for ye are all one in Christ Jesus.'"[13] Yet, whether or not Harvey was enlightened about or, alternatively, ignorant of Ellie's background, she was fully aware, and since the question was unlikely to be asked in Cornwall where they settled, then silence on this matter was for her the default condition. I harp on this because if Wayne Brown's assessment is to be given weight, then it is Edna's public acknowledgment of her "colored" ancestry that leads to seismic waves within her family[14] and suggests the importance of those silences in her own formation as an "English" girl growing up in Cornwall but with these anomalous, shady, connections to the colony of Jamaica.

11   Rachel Manley, *Horses*, 19.
12   Norman Manley, "My Early Years: Fragment of an Autobiography," in *Manley and the New Jamaica: Selected Speeches and Writings, 1938–1968*, ed. Rex Nettleford, Longman Caribbean, London, 1971, xcv.
13   "Who Are the Wesleyans and What Are the Beliefs of the Wesleyan Church?," www.gotquestions.org. For more formal analysis, see Thomas Oden, *Doctrinal Standards in the Wesleyan Tradition*, Abingdon, London, 2008.
14   See Brown, *Edna Manley*, 187–88.

But we are running ahead of our story as we try to trace some of the critical elements in her formation. The silences and hidden tensions of her Jamaican background were accompanied by other critical features of her personality and education to help determine her peculiar formation. Edna was a middle child and, with the caveat of the dangers of my indulging in cheap psychology, she demanded attention. This impulse, assuaged somewhat while her father was alive by his indulgence of arguably his favorite child, increased immeasurably following his untimely death. Described by Rachel as a "defiant, wilful teenager,"[15] Edna was a rebel at nearby Cornwall College, though she gained the respect of the headmistress, a Miss Hanna who wrote her a remarkable character report: "She is original and therefore she sometimes does the unexpected or unsuspected. Conventions are light and airy things to her, capable of destruction at a moment's notice. For anyone who desires not to be dull; to have many subjects on which to ponder; I recommend this youngster as a companion. I understand that she hankers after teaching. May the Lord have mercy on her and them."[16]

It was this definitive feature of her character, a peculiar, independent tomboyishness, an unwillingness to unthinkingly accept authority, that guides her decisions and choices in these early phases and indeed for the rest of her life. It was certainly recognized by her cousin Norman Manley, who, arriving from Jamaica and visiting Ellie's home shortly before taking up the Rhodes at Oxford, is asked by his aunt, "Which one do you like the best?" and answers, without hesitation, "I think the plain one, with the spirit."[17]

Another crucial element for which Hanna was responsible was introducing the impressionable young woman to the work of William Blake (1757–1827). The English painter, poet, and printmaker, largely unheralded in his lifetime, had come by the end of the century to be a leading figure in the Romantic tradition. Blake, like Wordsworth, supported the French Revolution and adopted an attitude of ardent opposition to the abuses of class power in England. However, in his manifest spirituality, he was not by any stretch a typical Enlightenment thinker. While retaining an opposition to the established Church of England—still shocking in its day—he was never opposed to religion in itself. He advocated, instead, a more liberal interpretation of Chris-

15   Rachel Manley, *Horses*, 62.
16   Brown, *Edna Manley*, 45.
17   Rachel Manley, *Horses*, 64.

tianity that railed against the sexual conservatism of the Church as he promoted a doctrine of free love far beyond the conventions of early nineteenth-century Britain. William Blake, often seen as a progenitor of modern anarchism, would, I suggest, become the single most profound influence on young Swithenbank's intellectual and aesthetic growth. One need only look at the subject matter and form of some of Blake's work, such as *The Body of Abel Found by Adam and Eve* (1825) or the synthesis in his poetry of spiritual redemption with political radicalism,[18] to see the patent connections and echoes[19] in Swithenbank's emerging oeuvre.

Two other influences appear to be significant for our purposes. The first is feminism. Her eldest sister, Lena, was a first-wave feminist and campaigned with the suffragettes to give women the vote. While Edna would never herself focus on gender liberation, and repeatedly in her diaries expresses reservations[20] about aspects of the strategy and tactics of the second-wave (1970s) feminists, it is difficult to argue against the fact that in her unconventional (for Jamaica) resistance to female domesticity and her own artistic independence and leadership of the Jamaican arts movement, she was a gender revolutionary in praxis, if not theory. The second is Fabian socialism. The Fabian Society, formed in London in 1884 and named after the Roman general Fabius Maximus who adopted successful gradualist tactics to wear down the power of Hannibal's army, was highly influential in early-twentieth-century England. Supported by influential people such as George Bernard Shaw and H. G. Wells and with the competent leadership of Sidney and Beatrice Webb, the Fabians were

18   See Peter Ackroyd, *Blake*, Sinclair-Stevenson, London, 1995; Boxer, *Edna Manley: Sculptor*, 24; and Boxer, *Edna Manley: Into the Sun*, 7–8, where Boxer elaborates on his 1990 proposal that the principal source for the idea in *Negro Aroused* came from Blake's *Death's Door*, a figure for Robert Blair's poem "The Grave" published in 1808. In the 2015 catalogue, Boxer goes further, however, to propose that there are three earlier works of Blake's, including a plate for his work *America: A Prophecy*, that featured a similar theme and could have served as Edna's inspiration.

19   Or this comment from her after reading a study on Blake by Wickstead in 1974: "It's marvelous to get back to old Blake again, what a man, what a man. Each time I come back, I get deeper into him" (Rachel Manley, *Edna Manley*, 128).

20   Perhaps, on reflection, this is somewhat of an understatement. In an April 1977 entry in her diary, she states, "I simply loathe this 'women's lib' business'" (Rachel Manley, *Edna Manley*, 163). On closer reading, however, she was supportive of the struggle for basic equality, as in the first-wave feminists' fight for the vote, but felt that the doors were now open and too much energy was being wasted destroying their personal relationships. This is certainly an area for further exploration.

central in the formation of the Labour Party, in the same year of Edna's birth, and in forging its subsequent political form. While advocating for social justice beyond the typical liberal reforms and a social welfare system modeled along the German Bismarckian model, the Fabians stopped short of supporting radical revolution. Indeed, early Fabian positions considered the Empire as the right and appropriate framework for development, and as such they could be considered staunch "imperialists,"[21] though it should be recalled that the permanency of empire was very much a part of the zeitgeist of those times. One can, in scouring Edna's reflections, find cohabiting with each other the Fabian binary of both a deep concern for social justice and social reform and a constant refrain of caution of the dangers present in precipitate radical approaches.

What we can then summarize of Edna's early philosophical formation is that it was a heady brew of a rebellious and forthright personality, with an unusual, unresolved connection to the colonies, which had been influenced by Blakeian anarcho-spiritual sentiments, early feminism, and Fabian notions of gradualist social change. This mixture would come to a boil and take on new forms in the next phase, when Edna met and fell in love with her cousin Norman Manley and decided to follow him after marriage to the land of his birth and the place of her imagination, Jamaica.

TWO TENSIONS

The cut and thrust of her unconventional love affair with her cousin is the stuff of Jamaican lore and shall not detain us, except in its most important outlines. Edna met her cousin, six years her senior, when he was on his way to Oxford to take up the Rhodes and she was only fourteen. It would take four more years, the crucial intervention of World War I, Norman's enrollment and fighting in France, the death of both Edna's brother Leslie and Norman's brother Roy in the war, and numerous letters exchanged, for them to know that they were in love. My suggestion at this stage is that the critical hurdle that Edna had to face in entering this new phase was not so much the unconventional relationship between two cousins, but the color question, and caught up in this were the implications as to how she might define herself. Unlike Edna whose phenotype was for all intents and purposes white, Norman's rich mahogany complexion

---

21 See Lisanne Radice, *Beatrice and Sidney Webb: Fabian Socialists*, Macmillan, London, 1984.

clearly revealed his West African genes. In his sliver of a memoir, he makes the point that he was defined by his color in Britain: "As far back as 1914 ... it was impossible to be in England and not be aware of the problem of colour. You were immediately aware in a thousand ways that you belonged elsewhere but not there. You were different."[22] Indeed, Vera Manley, Norman's sister and with whom Edna was corresponding as to how to approach and tell her mother, captured it appropriately in a response to Edna: "You seem to expect a row—so did I at first. I have changed my opinion ... I don't see how there can be a row very well. Aunty Ellie disapproves of cousins marrying or says she does. Frankly, I think it is entirely because of the colour question—and without offending all three of us forever it's a thing she can't bring up. I think she has the good sense always to accept the inevitable."[23] Yet Ellie would try one last time on the eve of the wedding to dissuade them. Wayne Brown writes:

> With a fortnight to go, Ellie Swithenbank, who had vacillated between a reluctant acceptance and fits of anxiety, raised once more the question of the undesirability of children in a mixed marriage. Norman, in barely restrained anger, wrote to Edna asking her permission "to point out (to Edna's family) one or two moral trifles that they don't seem to grasp." To which Edna responded to Norman: "Leave her alone and she'll get accustomed to anything—argue against her and you'll drive her to the wildest extremes—you'll upset the wedding ... and I'll lose my little remnant of a home forever."[24]

Aside from the obvious contradictions in Ellie's assertions—she herself was "mixed" and so by implication were her children—Edna's retreat on frontal confrontation seemed to have been only tactical. More profoundly, she had evidently, in marrying Norman, taken the decision to cross the barrier of psychological denial and silence in her own family and accept wholeheartedly her "colored" heritage. In a memorable letter written to Norman in the heat of the tension with her mother, Edna declares:

> The coloured (i.e., mixed) race can never die out—the coloured race has to go on now—white people are going to be forced to accept them when they see them developing superior intellects—with fine

22 Brown, *Edna Manley*, 64.
23 *Edna Manley*, 104.
24 *Edna Manley*, 115.

physiques—it is a race that is beginning—it has enormous possibilities and with a great tendency towards producing that indefinable person—the genius—I want to do my share towards improving and helping on a new race—we are both intelligent and I have great hopes of what our children will be—I don't want him to be white, I want him to have your own beautiful brown skin—and I want him to grow up proud of his race.[25]

It is this quantum shift toward a new perception of how to define herself that would provide a central tension in the rest of Edna Manley's highly creative career. Phenotypically white and with a mother who had hidden any connection to blackness, Edna, in her self-perception, had acknowledged her Black ancestry. In her wider family, this tension was never resolved, and when, years later, in a London interview she let slip the fact of her colored heritage, it led to splits, some irrevocable, within her family. But for her this moment had been a crossing of the Rubicon, which eventually led to the island of Jamaica and a commitment to its people that permeates her work, from *Beadseller* (1922) through *Eve* (1929) to *Dawn* (1931) and beyond.

Edna and Norman were married in June 1921. Just short of a year later, their first son, Douglas, was born in London, and eleven weeks later, infant in tow, they were on the banana boat *Camita*, headed for Jamaica. Confronting the question of race is something that Edna had done before

---

25   *Edna Manley*, 93. I agree with Maziki Thame's argument that "brownness" and hybridity grew to be a narrative in Jamaican nation-building (indeed, with a heritage harking back to the slave plantation) that positioned itself as superior to "blackness," the color of the vast majority of Jamaicans. This statement from Manley may be understood as part of that narrative, but with two caveats. First, it is made at a moment in which she is breaking with whiteness and is thus positioning herself for the first time as not-white. Second, she is stating it while still in Cornwall, never having set foot in the Jamaican White-Brown-Black matrix and hierarchy of color. It is loaded, therefore, with contradictions, simultaneously the positive recognition of a Black inheritance, an acceptance of who she is (of mixed ancestry), and, potentially, particularly when future events are read into it, a statement on the (false) superiority of hybridity. See Maziki Thame, "Racial Hierarchy and the Elevation of Brownness in Creole Nationalism," *Small Axe* 21:3 (54) (2017): 111–23. It is also useful to consider Colin Palmer's thesis that Jamaica developed her sense of being a Black nation through both popular cultural idioms as well as the intervention of politicians including Garvey, the Manleys, and Bustamante. See Colin Palmer, *Inward Yearnings: Jamaica's Journey to Nationhood*, Kingston, The University of the West Indies Press, 2016.

leaving England. However, Jamaica, with its sharp class differences, persistent though somewhat differently constructed barriers of color and race, along with a stifling parochialism, presented new challenges. Her attempts to negotiate these new hurdles together constitute the second tension that determines her approach to her new home and comes for the remainder of her life to permeate her work.

Jamaica in 1922, even with her sister-in-law Vera's assertion that it would be a better place for Edna and Norman to raise children, retained the unforgiving and unreconstructed color hierarchies of the plantation. Writing with reference to his mother's marriage to Thomas Manley at a somewhat earlier period, Norman noted that when the very fair Margaret married "a near black man,"[26] she was isolated, as nearly all of her friends deserted her. Edna, for her part, faced multiple hostilities. She was visibly white, and married to a dark brown man, which put her in almost the space Margaret had occupied with Thomas. But more peculiarly, she was a young artist, coming out of the school of up-and-coming young sculptors in the active and hectic London scene. In Jamaica not only was there very little art, but that which existed was oriented more toward the decorative than the critical, inquisitive, and avant-garde.[27] And persons, particularly foreigners, not engaged in the traditional professions or in business, much more in the full-time occupation of sculpting, were looked on with suspicion. The social scene, too, was barren,[28] and Edna could not stomach the Jamaican habit of relegating the women to one room while the men gathered to drink and smoke and discuss business and politics in another. Moreover, the couple was poor, arriving in the island with fifty pounds sterling, and there was a child to raise and support without, at first, any domestic help. It would be many years before Norman's success as a barrister would make them relatively comfortable. And then there was the oppressive heat of the Jamaican summer, which triggered Edna's first exodus to the cool hills around Mandeville, where there was some relief from the humidity, but not from the constraints of the society;

26 Nettleford (ed.) *Manley and the New Jamaica*, xcvi.
27 See, in particular, Wayne Brown's rich descriptions in Brown, *Edna Manley*, 124–30.
28 In an interview with Basil McFarlane, Norman Manley reflects on the emptiness of the Jamaican social scene on his return and Edna's arrival: "When I came back to Jamaica, for the first six months I was absolutely appalled—a total barrenness of the mind. Nobody to talk to about anything—Nobody—nobody was interested in anything ... no plays to go to, no concerts to go to ... You talk about books, nobody read any books" (Brown, *Edna Manley*, 124).

leading to her second exit, home with her son to England in October 1923, with no immediate indication of returning.

Photo 1   Edna and Norman Manley in Jamaica c. 1933. Permission Rachel Manley

Indeed, her return the following year, no doubt due to missing Norman with whom she remained deeply in love, was only triggered after his purchase of a run-down house on extensive lands near Four Roads in St. Andrew—what would become the famous Drumblair residence. I mention this sequence to suggest that there was a restlessness surrounding Edna's engagement with Jamaica, in which she never quite came to terms with its social hierarchies. Norman provided her with a nest—Drumblair, and later Nomdmi in the Blue Mountains—in which she could raise a family and engage in her profession of drawing and sculpting. But her engagement with the society was always tentative, critical, and partial. She was *in* the society as Barrister Manley's and much later Premier Manley's wife and companion; but she was never *of* the society, in the sense of fully imbibing and accepting its middle-class structures, norms, and aspirations. This 1985 remark in her *Diaries*, made albeit at a different time of severe economic hardship and following Michael's stinging defeat in 1980, is nonetheless typical of the distances she chose to take as much as the empathies she sought to adopt:

> We wail about the cost of living that goes up and up. The well-off people can still afford to live—so they grumble but they buy. Most of the middle class still cling on to living beyond their means—they don't really give up any of their comforts—but they do more than wail, they protest loudly. But it is the children of the poor in rural areas who leave for school in the mornings with a cup of tea with no milk and a little sugar to make it palatable … there's a whole age group who are going to grow up second-class citizens because they are so underfed—they won't have the health and the stamina to be anything else.[29]

At the same time, as the "white" wife of Barrister Manley, there were the inevitable barriers that existed between her and the majority of Black Jamaican urban and rural people. Wayne Brown describes an experience from that first brief sojourn in Mandeville: "Leaving Douglas with the nurse in the shade, she wandered down to the market place to sit on a wall and sketch, [and] she can hardly have escaped altogether … the resentment of the peasants against her for, as a contemporary English visitor bitterly put it, 'the crime of being white.'"[30] I suggest, then, that the two critical tensions that inhabited Edna's work, distinct, though connected to each other, were, first, the tension inherent in her decision to embrace her Black heritage, and second, the tension arising from the insider/outsider contradiction, in which her growing love for her new country (indeed her mother's country) struggled with her sharp distaste for its sclerotic structures and normative social constructs and cultures.

FIVE CENTRAL THEMES

If we start with these two underlying tensions, related to her encounter with Norman and her subsequent marriage and emigration to Jamaica, and connect these to the formative features that we have previously sketched as critical in her philosophical formation, then we can suggest five distinct political themes deriving from them that are consistent throughout the rest of her life in Jamaica.

---

29   Rachel Manley, *Edna Manley*, 275.
30   Brown, *Edna Manley*, 123.

First, there is a sympathetic and laudatory appraisal and validation of Black people, of poor people, and of democratic majorities. I will return to this in the final part of this chapter, as we look more carefully at some of her work.

Second, there is a nationalism that runs through much of her work, in other words, a positive sense of the possibilities inherent in the ability of the majority of Black people to achieve what they will. This heartfelt outburst two months after the 1983 Grenada invasion expresses that sentiment as much as it does her despair at that low point of Caribbean sovereign expression: "I am old and going out—if I can just make it quickly—as I can't call to the youth of Jamaica to give Jamaica a chance, to give it support, leadership, imagination. To HELL with America and Russia too—why can't WE give our own leadership?"[31]

Third, there is a certain spiritualism, though tinged with agnosticism, perhaps best understood from an appreciation of her Blakeian influences, which pervades her diaries, drawings, and sculpture. She retained a healthy respect for signs, symbols, and the afterlife, and certainly for biblical scripture, while retaining a distinct anti-establishmentarianism toward the formal church.

Fourth, there is a strong social reformist current through much of her work. Edna Manley was undoubtedly socialist, but Fabian moderation was never far from the surface. Thus, she was instinctively hostile to Soviet communism, as she was to what she thought was some of the more precipitate actions of the local Left, whether within the PNP or outside of it.[32]

Finally, closely linked to the fourth point is a spirit of compromise, perhaps the most important legacy of her politics, which pervades her

---

31   Rachel Manley, *Edna Manley*, 267.

32   There is, however, need for further research and thinking around this contention. She repeatedly stated her opposition to communism, but it is often accompanied by a demand for the "people" to play a more prominent role in politics. Thus, in a late 1980 musing on the role of America in the world and in the Caribbean, she asserts: "I hate communism—really hate it—but the voice of the people—with their griefs, their 'no life', the ghetto—the voice of the people must be heard" (Rachel Manley, *Edna Manley*, 220). And there is this comment on the Black Power movement, suggesting sympathies for direct action over passive, incremental resistance: "I'll never forget what the Black Power movement achieved for the Black race in the States. Decent people were shocked and afraid of the direction things were taking—but the Black Power movement did more for the decent people than anything they had been able to achieve for themselves" (*Edna Manley*, 212).

entire life and which is captured most poignantly at the time of Alexander Bustamante's death in 1977. I want to spend a little time on this, because it is difficult to capture it in her art, yet it is so important in understanding the nature of her persona and philosophy. Bustamante, of course, had been the bane of Norman's political life. A founding member of the PNP, he had left it to form his own Jamaica Labour Party when he realized that he no longer needed Manley and the PNP to win elections. A supporter, if tepid, of Federation, he abandoned the idea when he saw that significant local support had shifted for various and differing reasons against the idea and advocated instead single-island independence. The supreme irony is that Manley, who had undoubtedly led the movement against colonialism, was shunted aside by popular mandate, and Bustamante, who had initially been against the idea of independence, became the country's first prime minister. Norman, and indeed Edna, had every reason to disdain Bustamante; yet when Edna heard what she considered as the poor way in which the pro-government media (her son Michael was then in power) had heralded the news of his death, she was livid with anger, and in her diary, gave Bustamante his due: "He did Norman and Jamaica many things which I never forgave—he never saw a new image that was waiting to be born. One couldn't hold him responsible for that, he had never seen it in those terms—but all his life he did look out for the cause of the poor and needy, and in his own vain, arrogant way he was kind."[33]

EXPLORING EDNA'S OEUVRE

In the final part of this chapter, I want to undertake—with some trepidation, particularly as a social and political theorist treading in the den, as it were, of the guardians of aesthetic representation at the Edna Manley College—a brief reading of some of her work, through the lens of our prior three-part discussion of her formation, the two critical and dynamic tensions, and the five central themes identified in her politics.

Six years into her Jamaican sojourn, Manley was already deeply engaged with the African-Jamaican form. *Boy with Reed* both valorizes and romanticizes while working within and beyond the postwar Western European modernist traditions. If the more successful *Eve*, with her African body but more European facial features, is representative of a transitional phase, then *Boy with Reed* is clear evidence of her commitment to a new aesthetic.

---

33 *Edna Manley*, 176.

Photo 2   Boy with Reed (1928). © Maria La Yacona

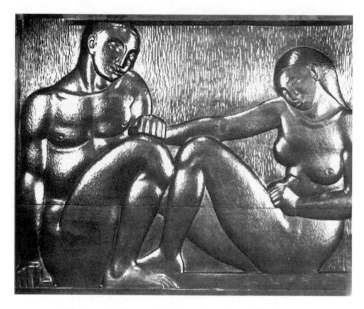

Photo 3   Adam and Eve (1930). © Maria La Yacona

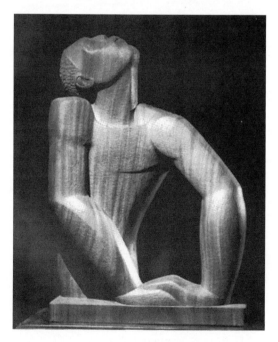

Photo 4   Negro Aroused (1935). © Maria La Yacona

Photo 5   Diggers (1936). © Maria La Yacona

In appreciating *Adam and Eve*, we need to remind ourselves of the context. There is at this moment no tradition of portraying Black people in comfortable intimacy. There is, further, no tradition of portraying biblical characters as Black, more so the two original human beings of the Old Testament. The portrayal itself, in the tenderness of Adam's grasp and the tentativeness of Eve's reaching out to him, leans to equality more than subordination and is thus radical on more than one level: claiming the Bible for Black people, proclaiming the naturalness of Black love, and asserting gender equality. What, for its time, could be more revolutionary?

Much has been written about *Negro Aroused*, as prophecy of the rebellion to come in three years, as proclamation of Black pride and as an awakening. I want to suggest that the heavenly gaze is certainly not one of awe and fear of a transcendent power but rather the fixation on the vision of a New Jerusalem. The hands, out of proportion to the rest of the torso, are the oversized hands of labor and fount of all creativity. It is through the hands of Black labor that the New Jerusalem will be realized. But is there not also, in the silhouette of the statue from base to head, the rugged contours of the Blue Mountains and an implicit statement about the nation and its sheer physical splendor, alongside chants of national liberation and salvation echoing in the peaks and valleys?[34]

The theme of labor is made more explicit and collectivized in *Diggers*. Remember, this is two years before the labor rebellion of 1938, yet here is Manley valorizing the inherent dignity of workers and of their work with an almost Stakhanovite intensity. Critically, though with little surprise, the laborers are unmistakably Afro-Jamaican.

Lest I be accused of andro-centrism, *Market Women* again captures the theme of the dignity of work, but this time with unmistakably Jamaican higglers: hands akimbo, headed to the market, independent, willing to bargain for a fair price, but willing equally to kiss teeth and walk away from the customer if a ridiculous offer is proposed.

Youth is the female version of *Boy with Reed* as it also captures the feistiness (or perhaps the more evocative Jamaican "facetyness," implying arrogance and boldness, might be more appropriate?) explicit in *Market Women*. However, I suggest it goes well beyond both in offering a profound statement of the power of Jamaican womanhood. This—and remember, it appears in the year of the labor rebellion—is a prophetic assertion of the

---

34 Importantly, David Boxer suggests that the title *Negro Aroused* came from the headline of a 1929 edition of Marcus Garvey's paper *The Blackman* (vol. 1, no. 118). See Boxer, *Manley: Into the Sun*, 6.

Photo 6   Market Women (1936). © Maria La Yacona

latent possibilities in Jamaican women, which almost eighty years later is evident in the global statistics where in 2015 the International Labour Organization found that Jamaica, in its percentage of women managers, is at the head of the list of all countries.[35]

35   See "Jamaica Has Highest Percentage of Women Managers Globally," *Jamaica Observer*, January 12, 2015.

Photo 7   Youth (1938). © Maria La Yacona

For me, *Strike* is Edna Manley's single most intriguing sculpture. Like Wayne Brown,[36] but with different conclusions, I am fascinated by the utilization of the image of a young man (purportedly PNP cofounder O. T. Fairclough, observing one of the strikes of 1938) to counterintuitively symbolize the typically kinetic notion of a strike. Instead of picket lines, placards, and all the expected paraphernalia, we have instead a contemplative young Black man, his hand stroking his chin. Yet if one were to

36   See Brown, *Edna Manley*, 254.

Photo 8   Strike (1938). © Maria La Yacona

imagine 1938 as a moment of intellectual awakening, as blinders being opened up on centuries of darkness, then the urgency of thought, to reflect on what has been hidden and obscured, and more critically, on what needs to be imagined and invented, is far more poignant than the mere representation of individuals or masses in action.

Again, context is essential. Rastas were in the 1950s the often feared, rebellious element in the Black underclass; barely understood and,

Photo 9   Brother Man (1961). © Maria La Yacona

certainly before the report udertaken by M. G. Smith, Roy Augier, and Rex Nettleford on the Rastafari movement,[37] barely studied. This bust appears in the year after the Henry rebellion, when Rastafarian leader Claudius Henry's son led a brief and abortive guerrilla insurgency against the still-colonial Jamaican state,[38] with Norman Manley, somewhat ironically,

37   M. G. Smith, Roy Augier, and Rex Nettleford, *The Rastafari Movement in Kingston, Jamaica*, Institute of Social and Economic Research, The University of the West Indies Press, Kingston, 1961.
38   See Barrington Chevannes, "The Repairer of the Breach: Reverend Claudius Henry and Jamaican Society," in *Ethnicity in the Americas*, ed. Frances Henry, Mouton, The Hague, 1976, 263–89; Brian Meeks, "The Henry Rebellion, Counter

Photo 10   The Voice (1980). © Maria La Yacona

as the premier at the time. Three years later and post-independence, with Bustamante in charge, the notorious Coral Gardens events would lead to the death of a number of policemen and Rastafarians, followed by an arbitrary reign of terror and round-up of Rastafarians in the communities surrounding Montego Bay.[39] *Brother Man* is a remarkable assertion of the dignity of Rastafari and a statement of respect coming, we should recall,

Hegemony and Jamaican Democracy," in *Narratives of Resistance: Jamaica, Trinidad, the Caribbean*, The University of the West Indies Press, Kingston, 2000; and Anthony Bogues, *Black Heretics, Black Prophets: Radical Political Intellectuals*, Routledge, New York, 2003, 166–74.

39   See Deborah Thomas, *Exceptional Violence: Embodied Citizenship in Transitional Jamaica*, Duke University Press, Durham, NC, 2011.

from the wife of the premier and soon-to-be leader of the opposition. It should also be compared with *The Voice*.

By 1980 Jamaica is in the turmoil of the long, bloody election campaign, which lasts for most of that year, but on the other hand Rastafari has come into its own. Bob Marley and the Wailers have broken into the world arena and, as Max Romeo sang somewhat earlier, "Everybody join Rasta Bandwagon."[40] But Edna was there before the bandwagon, and managed,

Photo 11   Ghetto Mother (1981). © Maria La Yacona

in both her 1961 piece and this one twenty years later, to capture the stillness, dignity, and dreadness in her iconic images of the Rastaman.

Rachel Manley describes *Ghetto Mother* as "a culture and its people protecting itself and its ground,"[41] and she is right. *Ghetto Mother*, conceived in the cauldron of 1980 when violence was rife and everyone feared for their lives, is also a profoundly nationalist statement of a small

---

40 Max Romeo, "Rasta Bandwagon," Camel, 45 rpm, 1972.
41 Rachel Manley, *Horses*, 320.

country confronted by unimaginable military and economic power. The fright on the faces of the children is invoked not only through the close proximity of the off-stage gunman but also by the entire uncertainty of these unknowable times. There may, however, be some solace in the sheer courage and power of defiant Jamaican motherhood.

CONCLUSION

I conclude with the reminder that I have considered this a preliminary assessment and, indeed, it is a work in progress, only scratching the surface of a rich vein that requires far more investigation. In the balance, there are many unanswered questions: how did Edna's own inherited melting pot of Wesleyan, Blakeian, anarcho-spiritual Fabianism change over time? To what extent was Edna in turn influenced by Norman's own evolving philosophy as he rooted himself in his native land? Undoubtedly, she was, but what, in turn, was her influence on him and how did the two interact over the course of a lifetime? What was the impact of this unique blend on the early PNP and the philosophical course of the national movement? And what profound impact did Edna have on her two sons, Douglas the elder and Michael the younger—in particular, Michael of *The Politics of Change*,[42] of Democratic Socialism, and most pointedly of *Struggle in the Periphery*,[43] certainly his most politically combative work?

None of these closing questions are of course answered, yet they suggest the profound gap, as raised in my opening remarks, on the role Edna Manley has played beyond her enormous artistic contribution to the political formation of modern Jamaica.

I end with a brief excerpt from her diaries that reflects, if nothing else, her dauntless spirit and, despite the tensions and contradictions that I have suggested always persisted, her commitment to the island home of her choice and her mother's birthplace. It is the morning after the bitterly fought 1980 elections. Her husband, Norman, has been dead for some eleven years and her son Michael's party has been ignominiously defeated losing the elections nine seats to fifty-one. So-called "deliverance," the promised but never delivered economic prosperity that the Right prophesied, has come, but for Edna it is a deeply saddening but not unrecognizable moment of reflection but also of recommitment; and

---

42   Michael Manley, *The Politics of Change: A Jamaican Testament*, Andre Deutsch, London, 1974.
43   Michael Manley, *Struggle in the Periphery*, Writers and Readers, London, 1982.

I end with her words: "Another day—last night I was a little bitter, but today that has gone—we have to blame ourselves as well. It's no moment for a post mortem—it's enough to meet a new day. We fought a heroic election. And now what of the future? Where from here? Many will go away but many will stay and life goes on. I think I will stay."[44]

---

44 Rachel Manley, *Edna Manley*, 30.

4

Lamming's Politics and the Radical Caribbean

"Independence is only a freedom to clear the air," said Baako, "to make the abortive life you've known more livable; but it's then the problem of being alive, and trying to be alive in a state of freedom, it's only then the problem begins. And we mustn't postpone the time, Chiki, or the next generation will have to start by first wiping the muck we've left behind out their eyes: the whole muck of suspicion, and distrust, and even hatred, 'cause there's a world of dormant hatred in that crowd you see there!"

George Lamming
Season of Adventure

THE WRITER AS PROPHET

Of the entire powerful school that constituted the postwar generation of Caribbean writers, George Lamming is, with little dissension, the most consciously political.[1] Indeed, it is feasible to argue, as Mary Chamberlain does, that Lamming's literary efforts are simply one component of a broader multi-disciplinary attempt to combat colonialism and its neocolonial successors.[2] If *In the Castle of My Skin*[3] can be considered as one of the great works of childhood autobiography and self-discovery, it is in novels three and four that Lamming, the political analyst, attains his full stride. *Of Age and Innocence*[4] is a classic of late colonialism,

---

1 While this volume was in the early stages of production, George Lamming died at ninety-four, on June 4, 2022, at his home in Bridgetown, Barbados. Many excellent testimonials have already been written and more will appear in the years to come. I have decided, however, to leave this chapter as written in its original form in his lifetime, and not try to artificially reconstruct it as a retrospective.
2 See Mary Chamberlain, "George Lamming," in Bill Schwarz (ed.) *West Indian Intellectuals in Britain*, Manchester University Press, Manchester, 2003, 179.
3 See George Lamming, *In the Castle of My Skin*, Michael Joseph, London, 1953.
4 See George Lamming, *Of Age and Innocence*, Michael Joseph, London, 1958.

the struggle for independence, and the tenuous political alliances that emerge around it. Themes that will recur throughout his still-expanding oeuvre are developed for the first time in *Age*. There is the array of complex characters with multiple narratives and the use of their inner lives to mirror social reality.[5] There is the folding of many Caribbean territories into one—San Cristobal—partly out of economy but also to make a point about social and cultural cohesion. And there is the deep sensitivity, indeed partisanship, on the side of the underdog, particularly the peasantry but also the urban poor.

All these themes created in *Age* are once again deployed, but with even greater effect, in *Season of Adventure*.[6] *Of Age and Innocence* was published first in 1958. At the time, the anti-colonial drift in the Caribbean was well advanced and there were the examples of India and Ghana among others on which to learn from experience and draw inspiration. *Season*, on the other hand, was published only two years later, yet attempts to look at the experience and vicissitudes of San Cristobal after independence. Thus, Lamming, writing before any of the Anglophone territories had gained independence, enters a space of prediction, largely absent in the more retrospective *Age*. The effort, from the perspective of four decades later, can only be considered prophetic.

Season of Adventure traverses the history of San Cristobal from the first republic, created at the time of independence through its self-inflicted travails and ultimate collapse to the establishment of the second republic. The novel ends with the consolidation of the new regime, with Kofi James Williams Baako as its revolutionary leader, though with significant uncertainty as to the direction things will eventually take. Central to the novel is Lamming's concern with the flawed values and culture and the absence of a psychological centeredness of the middle classes. By virtue of training and skills, they have been given the mandate to lead the nation, but they are not the true representatives of the popular will. It is the middle-class adherence to a lifestyle that apes the former colonial masters and their unwillingness to address the dire social and cultural problems of the broad populace that leads, ultimately, to the demise of the first republic. Yet the novel ends with uncertainty, as it is unclear whether

---

5   See Sandra Pouchet Pacquet, *The Novels of George Lamming*, Heinemann, London, 1982, 64.
6   See George Lamming, *Season of Adventure*, Alison and Busby, London, 1979, first published by Michael Joseph, London, 1960.

Baako, despite his closer connections and affinities with the poor, will fully address the evident problems.[7]

Lamming understood the nature of the powerful expectations for improvement and "betterment" that independence would let loose. He also intimately grasped the weaknesses—both social and psychological—of the new generation of Caribbean leaders and how these would ultimately compromise their authority. Even more startlingly, he understood, long before actual history had unfolded, that the replacing of the first generation by new leadership would not decisively address the persistent, undergirding problems. From a reading of *Season of Adventure*, then, with *Of Age and Innocence* as background context, it is evident that Lamming is not only among the most political but also among the most *incisive* intellectuals of his generation that straddled the late colonial and early independence eras.

The proof of this particular pudding is in the eating. Trinidad and Tobago and Jamaica gained independence in 1962. At the head of the Trinidadian government was Eric Williams, who led the popular movement to remove the US naval base at Chaguaramas. Williams, educated at Oxford, was the model colonial scholar. His thesis *Capitalism and Slavery*,[8] despite extensive criticism, remains a classic of West Indian scholarship. Yet when Williams as leader of the People's National Movement (PNM) was first elected in 1956, many felt that his compromises on the timing of the US departure had betrayed the movement. And by 1965 a state of emergency had been declared in the sugar belt, and Williams's erstwhile mentor and ally C.L.R. James was placed under house arrest.[9] The 1965 events were, however, only the dress rehearsal for the greater irony, evident in the Black Power Revolution in 1970. A local student protest against the trial of West Indian students in Montreal

---

7 This is evident in Baako's arrogance when, on taking power, he first addresses the crowd, but more so in Gort's uncertainty surrounding his right to lead. Gort, portrayed by Lamming as the heart and soul of peasant cultural resistance, doesn't trust Baako simply because he is a "doctor." The novel ends with uncertainty: "[Gort] can't say what will happen. He does not know Baako; so he thinks there may be trouble. But he believes the worst is past" (Lamming, *Season of Adventure*, 366–67).

8 See Eric Williams, *Capitalism and Slavery*, Russell and Russell, New York, 1961.

9 For a reasonably accurate narrative of this phase of Trinidad and Tobago's history, see Selwyn Ryan, *Race and Nationalism in Trinidad and Tobago*, Institute of Social and Economic Research, Kingston, 1972.

erupted into massive street demonstrations, the declaration of a national state of emergency and an abortive coup attempt from a section of the regiment.[10] Williams, the anti-colonial hero of Chaguaramas, became the prison warder of 1970. Although Williams never lost control of the state, a guerrilla movement[11] loosely based on Guevaran principles persisted until 1974, when the windfall escalation in petroleum prices—the first oil crisis—poured oil on troubled waters. Trinidad thus experienced social calm for a decade, until 1990 when the Abu Bakr-led Muslimeen movement attempted to overthrow the state by storming the parliament building and the sole television station.[12] Abu Bakr, like the soldiers of 1970, was eventually thwarted, but the recurrence of a coup attempt within the space of two decades underlined the fragility[13] of Trinidadian postcolonial politics.

Jamaica followed its own agenda, though the parallels with Trinidad (and with San Cristobal) are startling. Bustamante's Jamaica Labour Party (JLP) was never a genuine anti-colonial movement. After winning the 1962 pre-independence elections, his first policy statement was to pledge loyalty to the former colonizers by declaring that he was "with the West."[14] In 1968 Bustamante's successor Hugh Shearer banned Guyanese university lecturer and Black Power activist Walter Rodney from returning to the island. In response, students staged a protest march and were tear-gassed by the police. The subsequent riot drew in thousands of unemployed youths from Kingston's inner city and led to a day of burning, looting, and rage. The dramatic events, since then known as the Rodney riots,[15] are generally considered to be the beginning of the end of the JLP regime (Jamaica's first republic) and the catalyst that led to the victory of Michael Manley's People's National Party (PNP) in 1972.

10   See Selwyn Ryan and Taimoon Stewart (eds.) *The Black Power Revolution 1970: A Retrospective*, Institute of Social and Economic Research, St. Augustine, 1995; and Brian Meeks, *The Development of the 1970 Revolution in Trinidad and Tobago*, MSc thesis, The University of the West Indies, Mona, 1976.
11   See Brian Meeks, *Narratives of Resistance: Jamaica, Trinidad, The Caribbean*, The University of the West Indies Press, Kingston, 2000, 48–74.
12   See Selwyn Ryan, *The Muslimeen Grab for Power*, Inprint Caribbean, Port of Spain, 1991.
13   See Brian Meeks, *Radical Caribbean: From Black Power to Abu Bakr*, The University of the West Indies Press, Kingston, 1997, 83–100.
14   Anthony Payne, *Politics in Jamaica, Revised Edition*, Ian Randle Publishers, Kingston, 1994, 11.
15   See Rupert Lewis, *Walter Rodney's Intellectual and Political Thought*, The University of the West Indies Press, 1998, 85–123.

OUT OF EXILE

This was the general political atmosphere when Lamming returned from his "exile" in the United Kingdom in the 1970s. In Trinidad, the radical movement was ebbing under the combined effects of police pressure, the adventurist tactics of the guerrilla movement, and the economic largesse that came from increased oil revenues. In Guyana, after independence in 1966, there was never any hope of a radical alternative from Burnham's People's National Congress (PNC) regime.[16] In the racially polarized climate, Burnham perfected his own template of authoritarian patronage under the deceiving title of "cooperative socialism." Only for a moment in Jamaica, as Michael Manley's Democratic Socialist PNP moved further to the Left, was there the vague possibility of a radical alternative. However, from the very beginning, the Manley regime was hamstrung by a deteriorating economy and a hostile opposition backed by the powerful and entrenched wealthy classes.[17]

Then in 1979, when the writing was already on the wall for Manley, Maurice Bishop and the New Jewel Movement (NJM) seized power and formed the People's Revolutionary Government in the small southeastern Caribbean island of Grenada. For an instant, despite the storm clouds over Jamaica, there was the tenuous hope of an alternative Caribbean politics in the emergence, alongside Cuba, of two revolutionary regimes—Grenada and Nicaragua—where the Frente Sandinista (FSLN) had seized power months ahead of the NJM. This hope, too, was soon to be dashed. The Grenada Revolution imploded in 1983 after the house arrest, freeing, and subsequent killing of Maurice Bishop by his own soldiers and comrades.[18] The Sandinista regime in Nicaragua, battered by subversion and open

---

16   See Percy Hintzen, *The Costs of Regime Survival: Racial Mobilization, Elite Domination and Control of the State in Guyana and Trinidad*, Cambridge University Press, Cambridge, 1989; and Clive Y. Thomas, *The Rise of the Authoritarian State in Peripheral Societies*, Monthly Review Press, New York, 1984. While Thomas's book identifies a general phenomenon, much of its substance is based on his own long engagement with Guyana.

17   For a chronology by Manley himself of the steps taken to destabilize the PNP government, see Michael Manley, *Jamaica: Struggle in the Periphery*, Writers and Readers, London, 1982, 223–37.

18   See Brian Meeks, *Caribbean Revolutions and Revolutionary Theory: An Assessment of Cuba, Nicaragua and Grenada*, The University of the West Indies Press, Kingston, 2001, first edition, Macmillan, London, 1994, 129–86. For a somewhat different perspective on the roots of the 1983 crisis, see Gordon Lewis, *The Jewel Despoiled*, Johns Hopkins University Press, Baltimore, 1987.

war instigated by the United States and executed by the Contras, survived until 1990,[19] when it was defeated in open elections by an alliance of conservative forces.

Lamming's position throughout these turbulent years was less that of the prophet as he had been at the cusp of independence and more the partisan intellectual on the side of progress and revolution. Lamming styled himself a socialist, though of what particular kind is a substantive question that will occupy much of the remainder of this chapter. He was opposed to the intolerable repression and lethal charlatanism of Burnham's pseudo-socialist co-operative republic. When Walter Rodney was assassinated in Georgetown in 1980 after having taken a booby-trapped walkie-talkie from a member of Burnham's army,[20] Lamming traveled to Georgetown and gave one of the most poignant speeches of his career. In his funeral oration, he lauded Rodney in terms that help define his own political ethic:

> What did Rodney represent that was so special? And what is it about his loss to us that has caused so much sorrow? He was, first of all, a serious man; and that, in our territories, does not always make for comfort … he had a rare gift of intellect to which he felt a special duty. It was a tool, a reservoir of power which could only justify itself if it were put into service, and on behalf of social need … Rodney impressed us by a constant struggle to live his view; to bring to his work, as a historian and teacher and political comrade, a certain integrity of commitment.[21]

He supported the Manley regime in Jamaica, though he felt that Manley was ill-prepared[22] for the inevitable destabilization that accompanies any attempt to resist empire. He was a fervent supporter of Maurice Bishop and the Grenada Revolution and spoke often in its defense, both during the revolutionary period and after the US invasion. Nowhere is this defense more passionate, if also highly critical, than in his address "The Plantation Mongrel." In his support of the Guyanese journalist Rickey

19   See Lewis, *Jewel Despoiled*, 84–128.
20   See Lewis, *Walter Rodney's Intellectual and Political Thought*, 243–48.
21   George Lamming, "On the Murder of Walter Rodney," in Richard Drayton and Andaiye (eds.) *Conversations George Lamming: Essays, Addresses and Interviews 1953–1990*, Karia Press, London, 1992, 184.
22   See George Lamming, "Inheritance and Situation: The View from 1986," in Drayton and Andaiye (eds.) *Conversations*, 297.

Singh, who had been viciously attacked by the Barbados government and media for his criticism of Barbadian involvement in the Grenada invasion, Lamming also lambastes the failure of the imagination of the Grenadian revolutionaries:

> Bishop was not only the leader of the revolution. He existed in the popular consciousness of the Grenada people as their most organic link to the revolution. Even those who remained doubtful about the revolutionary process had found in Maurice Bishop a symbol of nationalism with which they could identify. In the context of that political culture the question we ask is this: How do you put such a leader under house arrest without arresting the revolution itself? By what failure of the imagination could such an act be separated from its consequences?"[23]

Above all, he has been a consistent defender of the Cuban Revolution, which he regards in the tradition of C.L.R. James,[24] as the logical continuation of a Caribbean tradition of resistance to empire and power that traces its origin to the Haitian Revolution and the Cuban independence wars of the nineteenth century. In his speech at the Cuban cultural institute Casa de las Americas in 1984, for instance, Lamming, invoking Cuban icon José Marti, weaves together the Cuban independence wars with other processes into one common revolutionary movement, of which the Grenadian defeat is seen as only a momentary setback:

> During these four short years of revolutionary struggle Grenada became a name inseparable from Nicaragua, as Nicaragua is inseparable from Cuba. Fidel had welcomed Bishop in Havana with the same joy that Bishop welcomed Ernesto Cardenal in St. George's, Grenada. This small island, once anonymous and indecipherable on the ocean, created its own ceremony of souls where the spirits of the hemisphere (Cuba, Nicaragua, El Salvador, Jamaica, Trinidad, Guadeloupe, Mexico) met and discovered their own space for reconciling differences of language, history and culture. The defeat of the Grenada revolution has left a wound in the conscience of the hemisphere and a scar of

23   George Lamming, "The Plantation Mongrel," in Drayton and Andaiye (eds.) *Conversations*, 248.
24   See C.L.R. James, "From Toussaint L'Ouverture to Fidel Castro," in *The Black Jacobins: Toussaint L'Ouverture and the San Domingo Revolution*, Vintage Books, New York, 1989, first printing 1963, 391–498.

infamy on all who contributed to its dissolution. But Maurice Bishop and the martyred of Grenada and Cuba who fell with him, survive in our gratitude and esteem. Other armies will arrive in his name.[25]

LAMMING'S POLITICAL THOUGHT

What, then, of Lamming's political thought? His declared position in the 1970s was "socialist," though evidently not adhering to any obvious orthodoxy:

> Politically, I am a socialist, by which I mean that I have a vision of human society in which there would be in fact, the destruction of all classes. I can conceive of a society coming about in which in fact the discussion of problems would not even take this form at all, because we would not in fact be talking about what we mean by middle class or what is the particular role of the middle class. I think that kind of society is very much in view.[26]

He certainly held no romantic view of the still outwardly powerful Soviet Union[27] and roundly condemned what he saw as the USSR's brutal treatment of intellectuals. In this approach, he differed from other Caribbean radicals in the NJM, Cheddi Jagan's People's Progressive Party (PPP) and the Leninist Workers Party of Jamaica (WPJ) headed by Trevor Munroe.[28] He concurred, however, with his close friend and fellow exile C.L.R. James, but despite the significant body of shared views, it would be a stretch to consider Lamming as simply Jamesian in his political outlook. No doubt a central influence was Marx,[29] but it is an unconventional Marxism. Lamming's Marx is viewed through a lens of Caribbean

---

25   George Lamming, "The House of Reconciliation," in Drayton and Andaiye (eds.) *Conversations*, 193–94. Cardenal was minister of culture in the Sandinista government.

26   George Lamming, "Caribbean Politics from the 1930s to the 1970s: An Interview with Robert Lee," in Drayton and Andaiye (eds.) *Conversations*, 269.

27   Drayton and Andaiye (eds.) *Conversations*, 270.

28   For a nuanced analysis of the Caribbean Left of the 1970s, see Perry Mars, *Ideology and Change: The Transformation of the Caribbean Left*, The University of the West Indies Press, Kingston, 1998.

29   Lamming's published speeches and interviews are replete with references and allusions to Marx. See, for instance, "Politics and Culture," in Drayton and Andaiye (eds.) *Conversations*, 77–83, and "The Imperial Encirclement," in *Conversations*, 202–11.

history and culture in ways that are sometimes quite distinct from the Jamesian approach. Indeed, the Caribbean theorist with whom he shared the greatest intellectual kinship would be Walter Rodney, long ahead of C.L.R. James.

We can suggest six interrelated themes that lie at the core of George Lamming's political thought. First, Lamming's outlook is rooted in the centrality of labor. Work is ultimately at the heart of all civilization and the workers who transform nature to make it amenable to human habitation are at the center of human creativity. This is evident in his strong sympathy for Walter Rodney's posthumously published *History of the Guyanese Working People*,[30] for which he wrote the foreword. Rodney stresses the importance of labor in the wresting of Guyanese coastlands from the sea in order to make them available for the planting of sugar cane. Lamming lauds Rodney's success in transforming the way history is researched and studied, from a focus on the rulers of the land to those who actually transform and "humanize the landscape."[31] And, alongside the creativity of their labor, Guyanese working people have struggled for social justice:

> Caribbean scholars have, on the whole, concentrated on the intricate arguments and provisions made by those who ruled the land, those whose concept of social responsibility was confined to their exercise of power and to the protection of their interests as a dominant ruling group. This is an important contribution, but Rodney was engaged in illuminating our understanding from a different perspective. Working people of African and Indian ancestry in Guyana have had a history of active struggle, which it has been our habit to omit in political discourse about the past.[32]

Lamming's concept of labor, importantly, is not narrowly located in any abstract notion of the proletariat but is invested across a broad spectrum of the working people. At the center of this phalanx is the West Indian

30   See Walter Rodney, *A History of the Guyanese Working People: 1881–1905*, Heinemann, Kingston, Port of Spain, London, 1981.
31   See George Lamming, *The Sovereignty of the Imagination*, The Centre for Caribbean Thought and Friedrich Ebert Stiftung, Arawak Publishers, Kingston, 2004, 33.
32   George Lamming, "Foreword," in Walter Rodney, *History of the Guyanese Working People*, xix.

peasant. Lamming has a special place for the peasant, not simply as producer but also as banker for the collective culture. Even when, as in *Of Age and Innocence*, Ma Shephard, the representative of the peasantry, adheres to backward and conservative views, she nonetheless remains the embodiment of the collective memory. Thus, Sandra Pouchet Paquet accurately notes:

> Like Ma and Pa in *In the Castle of My Skin*, Ma Shephard is treated with an understanding and sympathy that are characteristic of Lamming's conception of the West Indian peasant as the creative heart of the community. The character is powerfully and reverentially drawn. Ma's inhibiting religious bias is matched by a love and generosity of spirit that make her a beautiful tragic figure ... She is earth mother, seer, wisdom and age combined, racial memory ... [33]

It is the disconnection from the soil, the desire for modernity, and the purging of "racial memory" that lie at the basis of Lamming's earlier mentioned problems with the Caribbean middle classes.[34]

The second theme, closely connected to labor, is the matter of culture. Lamming has a pronounced view on the question of culture and its importance to the individual psyche as well as the psychic well-being of a people. However, this is not an idealized version of culture, which he sees as rooted in work:

> The original meaning of the word "culture" had to do with the tending of plants and the caring of animals. In other words, this word, and the process it describes, has its roots in the practice of agriculture, and it has never lost this sense of nurturing; of feeding; of cultivating; whether it be a body or a mind that is under consideration. ... The first and essential meaning of culture is, therefore, the means whereby men and women feed themselves; the means whereby they achieve and reproduce their material existence. No food; no life. No food: no book, no religion, no philosophy, no politics, no performing arts.[35]

---

33   Sandra Pouchet Paquet, *Novels of George Lamming*, 51–52.
34   Indeed, if there is a constant refrain in Lamming's oeuvre, it is the recurring critique and dissection of the middle classes from every possible angle. Fola, the young middle-class inductee to the world of the Tonelle, is perhaps the best instance reflecting the ambiguities of the class, but also, its potential for a positive role in a process of radical transformation. See *Novels of George Lamming*, 68–69.
35   Drayton and Andaiye (eds.) *Conversations*, 283.

But neither is it a mechanical view of culture as production. Out of a particular mode of producing, people think and act in ways that are peculiar to them and that give their lives meaning. The dissonance occurs when other cultures seek to impose their normative forms. This was the problem with British colonialism that set Black people against each other in an attempt to compete within the cultural terms of Britain. Colonialism in his generation was "almost wholly without violence," however: "the Caribbean endured a different kind of subjugation: it was a *terror of the mind*, a daily exercise in self mutilation. Black vs. Black in a battle for self-improvement."[36]

A compelling statement on culture is to be found in his metaphoric use of the Ceremony of Souls, which he observed in Haiti and is incorporated in a number of his novels and speeches.[37] For Lamming, the critical thing about the ceremony was that the living had to pay homage to the dead and come to terms with them in order for the dead to rest. This not only created harmony between the living and the dead but also rooted the community in the present, linked it to the past, and located it in a particular physical place.

The third theme, already introduced as an aspect of his thinking on culture, is worthy of a category in its own right and it is the question of the self. The finding of one's inner self as rooted in culture and place are central to Lamming's worldview. In his careful analysis of the causes for the collapse of the Grenada Revolution, Lamming avoids a certain shrill rhetoric that was, at the time, typical of both radical as well as more conservative responses. The frenzied atmosphere of those final days in 1983 that led to Bishop's house arrest and ultimately his murder are not seen as narrowly defined conspiracies but are to be found in that same shredded identity and denial of self that is the heritage of colonialism and slavery. "The crisis is rooted in the persistent legacy of that old colonial experience: the negation of identity and the mutilation of self."[38]

The fourth theme, and again, a recurring one, is the question of place. Everywhere in Lamming's oeuvre is the landscape, and perhaps nowhere is this stated more eloquently and connected to labor and a sense of ownership than in the returning emigrant Mark Kennedy's statement on nationalism:

---

36   Lamming, *Sovereignty*, 7.
37   See for instance, Lamming, "The House of Reconciliation," in Drayton and Andaiye (eds.) *Conversations*, 194.
38   Lamming, "The Plantation Mongrel," in Drayton and Andaiye (eds.) *Conversations*, 248.

Nationalism is not only frenzy and struggle with all its necessary demand for the destruction of those forces which condemn you to the status we call colonial. The national spirit is deeper and enduring than that. It is original and necessary as the root to the body of the tree. It is the source of discovery and creation. It is the private feeling you experience of possessing and being possessed by the whole landscape of the place where you were born, the freedom which helps you to recognize the rhythm of the winds, the silence and aroma of the night, rocks, water, pebble and branch, animal and bird noise, the temper of the sea and the mornings arousing nature everywhere to the silent and sacred communion between you and the roots you have made on this island.[39]

This draws a sharp distinction between Lamming and some trends in contemporary Caribbean Marxism, which consider respect for place, in the throes of the "techno-paradigm shift"[40] to be so much petty bourgeois nostalgia. For Lamming place is what gives texture and meaning to solidarity and provides the foundation for resistance.

The fifth theme is Lamming's regionalism, for his nationalism is really folded into a powerful sense of the Caribbean as a single, if also heterogeneous, cultural space. One need only take a cursory glance at the Contents page of *The Enterprise of the Indies*, that remarkable compendium of Caribbeana edited by Lamming with foreword by Lloyd Best,[41] to appreciate this. There are articles from every language grouping in the region, including a critical essay on Creole and special sections dedicated to Haiti and Cuba. There is an attempt to recognize all the major ethnic groups including those, like the Arawaks, that are no longer

39 Lamming, *Of Age and Innocence*, 174–75.
40 Hilbourne Watson's careful mapping of late twentieth- and early twenty-first-century shifts in technology lead to an unfortunate denial of the importance and persistence of notions such as culture and place, around which people still find purchase for organizing and resisting. See Hilbourne Watson, "Global Neo-liberalism, The Third Technological Revolution and Global 2000: A Perspective on Issues Affecting the Caribbean on the Eve of the 21st Century," in Kenneth Hall and Denis Benn (eds.) *Contending with Destiny: The Caribbean in the 21st Century*, Ian Randle Publishers, Kingston, 2000, 382–446.
41 Best's Trinidad and Tobago Institute of the West Indies published *The Enterprise* along with the *New World* special independence issues for Barbados and Guyana, under the title *On the Canvas of the World*. See George Lamming (ed.) *Enterprise of the Indies*, Trinidad and Tobago Institute of the West Indies, Port of Spain, 1999; and *On the Canvas of the World*, Trinidad and Tobago Institute of the West Indies, Port of Spain, 1999.

visibly present. And there is an attempt to integrate culture, science, politics, and sports into a complex, if equally compelling, quiltwork. Reading *Enterprise* as not only description but political program, it is evident that Lamming's aim is to speak the name of the Caribbean as a prelude to the establishment of a more meaningful sovereignty[42] over its land and seascapes. This, however, is a sovereignty led by the makers of the culture, the peasants, and the broad working people. Lamming is evidently interested not in any abstract notion of resistance to capital but in a very concrete notion of community, of that community finding its existential meaning, and claiming its patrimony, always rooted in a notion of the centrality of labor.

All of this is linked, in the final theme, to a developed notion of the role of the artist in the community. While Lamming has avoided in his novels, essays, and speeches suggesting even the outlines of a new society, he undoubtedly considers his role as not so much a mirror as a refractive lens, focusing and concentrating the rays of popular struggle. In the author's famous entry into the narrative of *Season of Adventure*, when he identifies Powell, the murderer, as his half brother, his purposes are quite evident. As Sandra Pouchet Paquet suggests, the problem is that the privileged few who have benefited from education forget or repudiate their peasant roots.[43] What is necessary is for them to reforge these bonds and put themselves at the service of a genuine national movement.[44] In such an effort, the artist, because (s)he is a mirror of the community, has a very special role to play—a role that can reveal the inner self and ultimately the question of love and passion[45] that should lie at the heart of any movement for liberation.

LAMMING AS PROGENITOR

A close reading of George Lamming's work with an eye to its politics immediately suggests his distance from many of the Marxist movements that inhabited the political landscape of the Caribbean in the 1970s. If

---

42   See for instance, George Lamming, "Coming, Coming Home: Conversations II," House of Nehesi Publishers, St. Martin, 46.
43   See Pouchet Paquet, 1982, 76. See also George Lamming, "The West Indian People: A View from 1965," in Drayton and Andaiye (eds.) *Conversations*, 252–63.
44   See George Lamming, "Culture and Sovereignty," in Drayton and Andaiye (eds.) *Conversations*, 287.
45   See Lamming, "The House of Reconciliation," in Drayton and Andaiye (eds.) *Conversations*, 192.

we think, for instance, of the WPJ in Jamaica, its fairly wooden notions of culture,[46] and the absence of any reference to the psychic self, then there is very little connection to Lamming's sensibilities. In terms of his political economy and developed concept of the primacy of labor, Lamming was closest to Rodney as evinced in his laudatory praise for *History of the Guyanese Working People*. He is certainly close and parallel in many respects to Wilson Harris's sentiments, when Harris calls for a coming together of the artificially separated traditions of the "arts of the imagination" and of history in Caribbean scholarship.[47] While Harris, however, had little time for the intricacies of political economy and socialism, these are very much at the center of Lamming's universe. It is this particular theoretical turn, combining a deep concern for matters of political economy with an equally fixed gaze on matters of culture and the inner self, that makes Lamming unique in his generation.

One has to look to later Caribbean theorists for comparisons and contrasts.[48] David Scott's focus on Foucauldian notions of power and governmentality would probably resonate with Lamming. On the other hand, he might be unhappy with the paucity of reference to labor and political economy in Scott's analysis. Hilbourne Watson's reading of the technological changes in capital might catch Lamming's gaze, but as suggested earlier, the absence of place and the elision of people run counter to his thinking.[49] Far closer in spirit is Paget Henry, who, in his attempt to unveil an existent though embattled Afro-Caribbean philosophy, amplifies ego-systemic themes that were voiced much earlier by Lamming.[50] And Anthony Bogues, in his critical reading of African

---

46   A reading of the 1978 programme of the WPJ, written at the height of the remarkable cultural ferment that delivered artists like Bob Marley, Peter Tosh, and Dennis Brown to the world, reveals not even a cursory reference to these developments as having any relevance to the "national liberation struggle." See *Programme: Workers Party of Jamaica*, WPJ, Kingston, 1978.

47   See Wilson Harris, "History, Fable and Myth in the Caribbean and Guianas," in Andrew Bundy (ed.) *Selected Essays of Wilson Harris: The Unfinished Genesis of the Imagination*, Routledge, London, 1999, 152–66.

48   This chapter first appeared in 2007, when these interlocutors could be, with some imagination, considered among the newer generation of Caribbean scholars. Almost a decade and a half later, they remain among Lamming's successors, but time has now, undoubtedly, relegated them to the older school.

49   For further exploration of Watson, Scott, Henry, and other contemporary Caribbean theorists, see Brian Meeks, *Envisioning Caribbean Futures: Jamaican Perspectives*, The University of the West Indies Press, Kingston, 2007.

50   See Paget Henry, *Caliban's Reason: Introducing Afro-Caribbean Philosophy*, Routledge, London, 2000.

diasporic intellectuals, builds significantly on Lamming's search for epistemic foundations beyond the inheritance of the West.[51] It is still open to debate, however, as to whether either Henry or Bogues in their shift to the episteme retain the fealty to labor that runs throughout Lamming's entire work.

Lamming's special move is to be found in his ambitious attempt to fold together two discourses: one dedicated to understanding epistemic matters and the inner self, and the other simultaneously pitched at the level of a critical analysis of contemporary capitalism. Both, ultimately, are deployed as weapons in the systematic recovery of Caribbean sovereignty. It is thus perhaps appropriate to end this chapter on the work of a man still very much in progress with a quote that encapsulates the specific nature of his unique contribution to Caribbean thought:

> Men and women technically have the means of collaborating with nature in the liberation of man and woman, and yet the paradox of those means is that today, nature is endangered by man. This is to some extent the climate of my preoccupation. In my concrete corner of the world as an organic part of the writing of books, my work is for me really a record of seeing and recording the collective experience of those to whom I am joined in history. That is, I do believe that labour, which is the basis of all culture, must also be the motive force in the humanizing of the working people.[52]

---

51 See Anthony Bogues, *Black Heretics, Black Prophets: Radical Political Intellectuals*, Routledge, London, 2003.
52 George Lamming, "C.L.R. James, Evangelist," in Drayton and Andaiye (eds.) *Conversations*, 210–11.

5

Jamaican Roads Not Taken, or a Big "What If" in Stuart Hall's Life

There is an intriguing quote in Kuan-Hsing Chen's 1996 interview with Stuart Hall, in which Stuart, in response to Chen's question/comment "But you never tried to exercise your intellectual power back home," responds:

> There have been moments when I have intervened in my home parts. At a certain point, before 1968, I was engaged with dialogue with the people I knew in that generation, principally to try to resolve the difference between a black Marxist grouping and a black nationalist tendency. I said, you ought to be talking to one another. The black Marxists were looking for the Jamaican proletariat, but there were no heavy industries in Jamaica; and they were not listening to the cultural revolutionary thrust of the black nationalists and Rastafarians, who were developing a more persuasive cultural, or subjective language. But essentially, I never tried to play a major political role there.[1]

He explains this through his recognition that he had found both a personal space—marriage to Catherine—and a political space, as a collaborator in the British New Left and that Jamaica herself, in the transition to independence, had become a somewhat different society, breaking with the past, making it somewhat easier for him to leave and coincident with the changes in his own life.

This conscious sense of not seeking to intervene in a changed political space with which he no longer felt intimately familiar was captured when

---

1   Kuan-Hsing Chen, "The Formation of a Diasporic Intellectual: An Interview with Stuart Hall," in David Morley and Kuan-Hsing Chen (eds.) *Stuart Hall: Critical Dialogues in Cultural Studies*, Routledge, London, 1996, 501–2. See also Colin MacCabe, "An Interview with Stuart Hall: December 2007," *Critical Quarterly* 50, nos. 1–2 (2008): 17.

both I and Tony Bogues met with Stuart separately in 2003 to invite him to attend the Centre for Caribbean Thought's conference that we were planning in his honor the following year. His response to both of us was that, yes, he was born in Jamaica, but it would be difficult to describe himself as a "Caribbean intellectual" and, therefore, was it appropriate to include him in a series of conferences honoring key contributors to Caribbean thought? In the end we managed to convince him to attend, and the 2004 conference turned out to be a remarkable event[2] in which Hall "came home" and found, as it were, his Jamaican and Caribbean audience. The truth is, though, that beyond the cognoscenti, Hall's work was in the period after 1968 to which he referred—the period of the popular upsurge of radical politics in the region—right up until the moment of our conference, virtually unknown. I knew of Stuart as a brilliant Jamaican because he had been my dad's classmate at Jamaica College, and as he was one of the school's Rhodes Scholars, I recognized his name inscribed along with that of Norman Manley and others on the long blackboards outside the neo-Gothic Simms Building at school. But it was not until the mid-1980s that I had heard anything about his work, and I read my first Hall article long after finishing my PhD thesis in 1988.

Thus, aside from the tantalizing intervention quoted above, his name and more so his thinking were largely unknown to the generation of '68, those who were tossed into politics after the infamous exclusion of Walter Rodney on his return home to Kingston from the 1968 Montreal Black Writers Conference. The intense, one-day Black Power riots, which followed the police tear-gassing of the student protest in support of Rodney, signaled the beginning of a decade and a half process of radicalization which led to the 1970 Black Power Revolution in Trinidad and Tobago, the election of the Michael Manley government in Jamaica in 1972, and the Grenada Revolution of 1979–83.[3]

THE GENERATION OF '68

Another famous Anglo-Caribbean expatriate thinker of the Left—C.L.R. James—was certainly better known and influenced a generation of

---

2   See Brian Meeks (ed.) *Culture, Politics, Race and Diaspora: The Thought of Stuart Hall*, Ian Randle Publishers, Kingston, 2007.

3   See Kate Quinn (ed.) *Black Power in the Caribbean*, University Press of Florida, Gainesville, 2014; and Selwyn Ryan and Taimoon Stewart (eds.) *The Black Power Revolution 1970: A Retrospective*, Institute of Social and Economic Research, Trinidad, 1995.

Caribbean scholars,[4] but in terms of a substantial impact on the theoretical orientation, form, strategy, and tactics of the burgeoning movement, Jamesian ideas were at best marginal.[5] There was the Antigua Caribbean Liberation Movement (ACLM) in Antigua, under the leadership of the Jamesian Tim Hector and the Working People's Alliance (WPA) in Guyana, where Rodney himself, before his assassination (in 1980) along with Rupert Roopnarine, Eusi Kwayana, and others, sought to build a more independent Left. Other Jamesian tendencies included the Revolutionary Marxist Collective (RMC) in Jamaica, the New Beginning Movement (NBM) in Trinidad,[6] and the Movement for Assemblies of the People (MAP) in Grenada. Only MAP would emerge to play a central role in the evolving political landscape, but only after its merger with JEWEL to form the Marxist-Leninist New Jewel Movement (NJM), later the vanguard party of the Grenadian Revolution.

---

4   See Norman Girvan, "New World and Its Critics," in Brian Meeks and Norman Girvan (eds.) *The Thought of New World: The Quest for Decolonisation*, Ian Randle Publishers, Kingston, 2010, 4.

5   See, in particular, Perry Mars, *Ideology and Change: The Transformation of the Caribbean Left*, The University of the West Indies Press, Kingston, 1998, 39–61. James's notions of a non-vanguardist, spontaneous movement of the people had some initial influence, particularly through the Antiguan, Grenadian, and Trinidadian movements, but as I have argued elsewhere, James had no developed strategy for insurrection, beyond the advocacy of popular spontaneous uprising. When an insurrectionary situation arose, as in Grenada between 1974 and 1979, the NJM therefore turned to the old playbook of the underground vanguard, which turned out to be an effective tool for overthrowing the Gairy regime but not for popular rule in the aftermath. The other factor was the clearly compelling international situation—in which Cuba in the 1970s, based on booming sugar prices, seemed to be thriving, the Vietnamese had liberated their country, and the liberation movements had achieved independence through guerrilla warfare in Angola, Guinea Bissau, and Mozambique. All were led by Marxist-Leninist parties, significantly raising the cachet of this trend. See Brian Meeks, *Radical Caribbean: From Black Power to Abu Bakr*, The University of the West Indies Press, Kingston, 1996, 72; and Brian Meeks, *Caribbean Revolutions and Revolutionary Theory: An Assessment of Cuba, Nicaragua and Grenada*, Macmillan Caribbean, London, 1993, 178.

6   On the New Beginning Movement and Jamesian influences generally, see Matthew Quest, "New Beginning Movement Coordinating Council for Revolutionary Alternatives in Trinidad and the Caribbean," *CLR James Journal* 23, nos. 1/2 (Fall 2017): 267–305; and, for the importance of the 1968 Congress of Black Writers in Montreal as a gathering point for global Black radicalism and the Caribbean contingents, see David Austin, *Moving against the System: The 1968 Congress of Black Writers and the Making of Global Consciousness*, Pluto Press, London, 2018.

Thus, by the mid-1970s, most of the independent, radical trends had either been eclipsed by or converted to one or another variant of what I refer to here as "Caribbean Marxism-Leninism." I use this notion in order both to avoid a simplistic reductionism and to identify the specific characteristics of the parties and movements that came to dominate the Caribbean Left. These parties included the Cheddi Jagan–led People's Progressive Party (PPP) of Guyana, which had held office and been excluded from power twice by the British but remained bedeviled by the ethnic question and its partisan rootedness in the East Indian bloc;[7] the Movement for National Liberation (MONALI) in Barbados; the Youlou Liberation Movement (YULIMO) in St. Vincent; the Workers Revolutionary Movement (WRM) in St. Lucia; and the Dominica Liberation Movement (DLM). However, the two most significant, aside from the PPP, were the Workers Party of Jamaica (WPJ) and the NJM.

The WPJ, despite dominating the Jamaican Left outside of the Manley's governing People's National Party (PNP), failed to gain any significant electoral support in the elections-driven Jamaican political system. It nonetheless accumulated significant influence through its almost hegemonic control over a generation of students and scholars at the University of the West Indies Mona campus; its linkages to the PNP regime; and most importantly and in the end most damagingly, its close connections and influence within the NJM. The NJM, for its part, became not only part of the opposition alliance following the 1976 elections but also the leader of the party, Maurice Bishop became Leader of the Opposition. Three years later, with the successful overthrow of the Eric Gairy regime, Bishop would become prime minister of the People's Revolutionary Government (PRG) of Grenada for the next four and a half years. The Grenadian Revolution, of course, ended tragically, with open divisions surrounding questions of leadership in the party leading to the October 1983 arrest of Bishop; his release by an incensed crowd of supporters; his attempt to wrest control of the military fort; a clash with the military; and his execution, along with some of his closest supporters, at the hands of his own soldiers.[8]

---

7   See Colin Palmer, *Cheddi Jagan and the Politics of Power: British Guyana's Struggle for Independence*, University of North Carolina Press, Chapel Hill, 2010.
8   See Meeks, *Caribbean Revolutions and Revolutionary Theory*, 1993; Gordon K. Lewis, *Grenada: The Jewel Despoiled*, Johns Hopkins University Press, Baltimore, 1987; Manning Marable, *African and Caribbean Politics: From Kwame Nkrumah to Maurice Bishop*, Verso, London, 1987; and Shalini Puri (ed.) *The Legacies of Caribbean Radical Politics*, Routledge, London, 2011.

This tragic and unprecedented end to the Grenadian Revolution, which also signaled the demise of an organized and vibrant Caribbean Left, has led to heated, often recriminatory interventions seeking to explain and understand how it could have happened. Most analyses, including, I admit, my own, focus more on personalities, leadership, structures, and the supporting or denying of purported conspiracies. For instance, Bobby Clarke, not untypically, blames Bernard Coard, Bishop's deputy prime minister, whom he argues had been influenced by the "Stalinist" Trevor Munroe,[9] without further elaboration of this emotive notion and its applicability in this context. In one of the more thoughtful attempts to come to terms with the tragic sequence of events, G. K. Lewis, however, along with recognizing the dangers inherent in military overthrows and "the mixture of revolution and armed force,"[10] also raises warnings about the danger of mechanically applying Leninist approaches to party organization in entirely different historical contexts to that of Russia in 1917.[11]

It is in the spirit of Lewis's attempt to understand the theoretical weaknesses and lacunae in the NJM and by implication in Caribbean Marxism-Leninism[12] that I want to proceed with the following hypothetical exercise, by counterpoising critical features of Caribbean Marxism-Leninism with Stuart Hall's career-long and profoundly humanist engagement with Marxism through the avenue of the conjuncture. I want to suggest that it was precisely a perspective like Hall's that might have provided an effective counterpoint to the damaging, authoritarian features of Carib-

---

9 Robert "Bobby" Clarke, "Statement on Grenada by Robert 'Bobby' Clarke" (email document), October 14, 2009, in Brian Meeks, *Critical Interventions in Caribbean Politics and Theory*, University Press of Mississippi, Jackson, 2014, 113.

10 Lewis, *Grenada*, 162.

11 *Grenada*, 167.

12 I want to nuance Perry Mars's argument in which he suggests that the weaknesses that led to the demise of the Caribbean Left lay more in questions of leadership than ideology. There is much truth, and indeed I am invested in the argument that it was the leadership and its failures that contributed immeasurably to the crisis in Grenada with its debilitating impact on the Left in general. However, the role of ideology has been underplayed, or presented as a stock word or phrase, such as "Leninism" or sometimes even "Pol-Potism," which unfortunately is a lazy alternative to more careful analysis. Ideology in the end informed the leadership and shaped the framework and boundaries of their decision-making. It thus needs far more careful scrutiny in the new round of scholarship that will eventually appear on this period (Mars, *Ideology*, 162). For a more recent perspective closer to mine, see David Austin, "Vanguards and Masses: Global Lessons from the Grenada Revolution," in Aziz Choudry and Dip Kapoor (eds.) *Learning from the Ground Up: Global Perspectives on Social Movements and Knowledge Production*, Palgrave Macmillan, New York, 2020, 173–89.

bean Marxism-Leninism. An approach like his was missing in Jamaica, and this absence contributed to the de facto emergence of particularly wooden and dogmatic theories that came to dominate the Caribbean Left and contributed in no small measure to the tragedy of the Grenada Revolution.

HALL'S CORE

I begin by suggesting that unlike positions taken by Chris Rojek and certainly Charles Mills in his critique of Hall's approach to race,[13] and despite recognizing an evolution, particularly a shift from an earlier more Gramscian inflection to a later, more discursive approach, there is an evident and consistent[14] core to Hall's oeuvre that includes the following elements.

1. Unlike some post-Marxian perspectives, Hall continues to place critical importance on capital and of "material conditions" generally, in the shaping of the contemporary world. Thus in his 1988 essay "The Toad in the Garden: Thatcherism among the Theorists," while recognizing that there is no "univocal" way in which class interests are expressed, Hall nonetheless underlines that "class interest, class position, and material factors are useful, even necessary, starting points in the analysis of any ideological formation."[15] And in his

---

13   See Chris Rojek, *Stuart Hall*, Polity, Cambridge, 2003; and Charles Mills, "Stuart Hall's Changing Representation of 'Race,'" in Meeks (ed.) *Culture, Politics, Race and Diaspora*, 120–48.

14   Both Chris Rojek (2003) and Charles Mills (2007) can be considered as among Hall's more respectful critics, acknowledging what they consider his important theoretical advances yet remaining weary as to whether, in the case of Rojek, his emphases on difference and anti-essentialism have not undercut the ability of his project to have an impact on real political life. Rojek asks, "Can difference be the basis for effective political agency?" (*Stuart Hall*, 187). Charles Mills's misgivings include the suggestion that Hall's fabled eclecticism, in seeking, for instance, to utilize both Gramscian notions of hegemony with its implications of a dominant class/bloc and Foucauldian notions of dispersed power, may in the end be incompatible. He pleads, "How could it be possible to test and verify or falsify a theoretical mélange with so many conflicting components?" (*Culture, Politics, Race and Diaspora*, 141). The detailed exploration of these genuine questions certainly remains legitimate but goes somewhat beyond the purposes of this short exercise.

15   Stuart Hall, "The Toad in the Garden: Thatcherism among the Theorists," in Carey Nelson and Lawrence Grossberg (eds.) *Marxism and the Interpretation of Culture*, University of Illinois Press, Urbana, 1988, 45.

2007 interview with Colin MacCabe, Hall reminds him of the importance of the tendencies in capital to concentrate wealth and shape intellectual expression: "global capitalism is an incredibly dynamic system. And it's capable of destroying one whole set of industries in order to create another set. Incredible. This is capitalism in its most global, dynamic form, but it is not all that secure. It's standing on the top of huge debt and financial problems. And I can't believe those problems won't come eventually to find their political, critical, countercultural, intellectual expression. We're just in the bad half of the Kondratiev cycle!"[16]

2. Nonetheless, he discounts the mechanical notion of any direct cause-and-effect relationship between material conditions and so-called superstructural spheres. Social and cultural life, Hall has consistently argued, is not only mediated and articulated away from the "forces of production," but particularly in the contemporary era of intensified media engagement, the internet, and the image, this autonomy is even more enhanced. "This approach replaces the notion of fixed ideological meanings and class-ascribed ideologies with the concepts of ideological terrains of struggle and the task of ideological transformation. It is the general movement in this direction, away from an abstract general theory of ideology, and towards the more concrete analysis of how, in particular historical situations, ideas 'organize human masses, and create the terrain on which men move, acquire consciousness of their position, struggle etc.'"[17]

3. Specifically, in relation to classes and organized systems of domination, he opposes the mechanical approach inherent in certain Marxisms, which assume an automatic connection, for instance, between working classes and socialist ideas, or ruling classes and ruling ideas. Hegemony, Hall insists, emerges through complex processes of articulation and interpellation:

Ideas only become effective if they do, in the end, connect with a particular constellation of social forces. In that sense, ideological struggle is part of the general social struggle for mastery and leadership—in short for hegemony. But "hegemony" in Gramsci's

16 MacCabe, "Interview," 42.
17 Stuart Hall, "The Problem of Ideology: Marxism without Guarantees," in Morley and Chen (eds.) *Stuart Hall*, 41.

sense requires, not the simple escalation of a whole class to power, with its fully formed "philosophy", but the *process* by which a historical bloc is constructed and the ascendancy of that bloc is secured. So, the way we conceptualize the relationship between "ruling ideas" and "ruling classes" is best thought in terms of the processes of "hegemonic domination."[18]

4. He is fully appreciative of and utilizes effectively Gramsci's notion of organic philosophy as the contradictory yet critically important way of thinking utilized by "ordinary" people. This philosophy or common sense, he asserts, has within it elements of conservatism and of progress toward something new, and by implication must be engaged with from an approach of critical respect. "But what exactly is common sense? It is a form of 'everyday thinking' which offers us frameworks of meaning with which to make sense of the world. It is a form of popular, easily-available knowledge which contains no complicated ideas. ... It works intuitively, without forethought or reflection. It is pragmatic and empirical."[19] This approach, I suggest, is at the heart of Hall's outlook, because it not only suggests his deep respect for ordinary people and their perspectives, but also underwrites his open, non-hierarchical approach to politics.

5. Closely wedded to this and elaborated in more detail in his iconic essay "What Is This 'Black' in Black Popular Culture?" is a consistent anti-essentialist grain. The essay is itself a paean against the elevating of racial or cultural blackness as a bulwark against racism. Hall first argues that we need to deconstruct racism itself and appreciate that it is not static in order to also appreciate that anti-racist thinking cannot afford to become a victim of the same essentialist thinking that makes racism abhorrent: "The moment the signifier 'black' is torn from its historical, cultural and political embedding and lodged in a biologically constituted racial category, we valorize, by inversion, the very ground of the racism we are trying to deconstruct."[20]

6. Hall's perspective is always developed through an approach that can be called "thinking through the conjuncture." Again, he usefully

---

18   Hall, "Problem," 43–44.
19   Stuart Hall and Alan O'Shea, "Common Sense Neoliberalism," *Soundings* 55 (Winter 2013): 8.
20   Stuart Hall, "What Is This 'Black' in Black Popular Culture?" in Morley and Chen (eds.) *Stuart Hall*, 472.

adopts Gramsci's notion of the social conjuncture as the array of articulated social forces, ideas, and cultural tendencies in a given moment as a particularly effective and robust lens through which to view and understand contemporary reality. It allowed him, captured most famously with Martin Jacques in his characterization of "New Times," to appreciate the changing social relations in Britain in the 1980s and to theorize and predict the rise of Thatcherism and neoliberalism:

> If "post-Fordism" exists then it is as much a description of cultural as of economic change. Indeed, that distinction is now quite useless. Culture has ceased (if ever it was-which I doubt) to be a decorative addendum to the "hard world" of production and things, the icing on the cake of the material world. The word is now as "material" as the world. Through design, technology and styling, "aesthetics" has already penetrated the world of modern production. Through marketing, layout and style, the "image" provides the mode of representation and fictional narrativization of the body on which so much of modern consumption depends. Modern culture is relentlessly material in its practices and modes of production.[21]

7. I end with Hall's far less referenced perspectives on international politics, which are critically important for our purposes. These were forged at the time of the crushing by the Soviet Army of the Hungarian Revolution[22] and the Khrushchev revelations concerning the brutal, authoritarian nature of Stalin's rule. These, I suggest, inoculated Hall against any romantic view of the Soviet Union as the fountainhead of "really existing socialism" and any illusion that the USSR was the automatic bulwark of defense against imperialism for the newly independent countries. It also forced him, along with many of his generation who formed the British New Left, on to the back foot in order to rethink Marxism from the ground up, without a set of already successful prescriptions just

---

21   Stuart Hall, "The Meaning of New Times," in Morley and Chen (eds.) *Stuart Hall*, 233.
22   See Robin Blackburn, "Stuart Hall: 1932–2014," *New Left Review* 86 (March–April 2014): 77; and Jonathan Derbyshire, "Stuart Hall: We Need to Talk about Englishness," *New Statesman*, August 23, 2012, http://www.newstatesman.com/print/188526.

waiting to be applied and with a willing and able physician standing ready in the wings.

We can best summarize the heart and essence of Hall's work through the words of one of his critics. Despite his expressed reservations as to whether his academic preoccupations could ever be converted into a genuine praxis, Chris Rojek nonetheless generously proposes that "Hall's politics favours widening access, exercising compassion, encouraging collaboration and achieving social inclusion."[23] Many of these features were either absent or incorporated into hierarchies of authority and exclusion in both the theoretical approaches and application of 1970s Caribbean Marxism-Leninism.

CARIBBEAN MARXISM-LENINISM

To begin with Hall's international perspectives first, it is fair to say that Caribbean Marxism-Leninism, if nothing else, held a remarkably unhistoric view of the Soviet Union, leaping across time from the glory moments of the 1917 October Revolution, via the Red Army's heroic defense and victories against Nazi Germany, to the contemporary (1970s–1980s) period. Elided entirely is mention of the brutality of collectivization, the Stalin show trials, Trotsky's assassination, or any reference to Khrushchev's revelations about Stalin after his death. No mention, of course, is made of the Hungarian events or of the much more contemporary Czechoslovakian Spring and Soviet invasion of 1968. Two excerpts from Trevor Munroe's booklet *Social Classes and National Liberation*, derived from a series of "socialism lectures" given to students in the early 1970s, suggest the tone and tenor of the times. In relation to the significance of the Soviet Union:

> The Russian Revolution, therefore, did these three things: mash down the colonial system, mash down feudal exploitation and mash down capitalist exploitation in one-sixth of the world in October of 1917; and on those foundations began to build a new life, a new society in which no class lived on the backs of the labor of any other class. ... The great October Socialist Revolution broke forever and ever the monopoly of the capitalist class on power and when I say power, I mean every kind of power.[24]

---

23   Rojek, *Stuart Hall*, 193.
24   Trevor Munroe, *Social Classes and National Liberation in Jamaica*, Workers Party of Jamaica, Kingston, 1983, 29–30. A thorough and critical history of the

And on the relationship between "socialism" (i.e., the Soviet Union and its allied countries) and the National Liberation Movement:

> The very existence of socialism is the biggest help to the National Liberation Movement, even when the leaders of particular countries under imperialism completely reject and are totally against socialism, it is still the biggest help to the whole area of National Liberation. ... Therefore, we say that the alliance between socialism and National Liberation is a natural thing because socialism is the biggest force against imperialism and imperialism is the block to National Liberation.[25]

Looking back now on this simplistic, severely edited version of history to which many young, otherwise thoughtful students and young people were so easily won, the search for the reasons as to why is not easily answered, but among them I suggest the following.

1. The decisive defeat of the Left in Jamaica in the 1950s with the expulsion of the four leaders of that tendency (the Four H's)[26] from the PNP. This effectively silenced debates around Marxism and its role in national liberation for two decades, and particularly around that time in the 1950s when Hall and many others were forging a radical perspective but in the full glare of Hungary and of Khrushchev's speech.

2. The banning of left-wing literature in Jamaica in the 1960s, which made virtually all radical literature contraband, along with the

Workers Party of Jamaica, capturing both its dogmatic features and its uplifting role in community building, medical and legal support, as well as its central involvement in trade union and gender struggles, is yet to be written. Important insights, however, are to be found in Rupert Lewis, "The Jamaican Left: Dogmas, Theories, and Politics, 1974–1980," *Small Axe* 58, no. 23:1 (2019): 97–111; and David Scott, "The Dialectic of Defeat: An Interview with Rupert Lewis," *Small Axe* 10, no. 5:2 (September 2001): 85–177.

25 Munroe, *Social Classes and National Liberation in Jamaica*, 33.

26 The "Four H's" were the leading members of the left wing of the PNP who were expelled in 1952 as the PNP moved away, as the Cold War consolidated, from its earlier, more radical positions. See Richard Hart, *The Ouster of the 4Hs from the People's National Party in 1952*, Caribbean Labour Solidarity, London, 2000. Hart, a solicitor and prolific historian, would in later years play a prominent role in politics in Guyana, revolutionary Grenada, and Britain. For a critical survey of his life and times, see Rupert Lewis (ed.) *Caribbean Political Activist: Essays in Honour of Richard Hart*, Ian Randle Publishers, Kingston, 2012.

emerging Black Power literature (and, bizarrely, Anna Sewell's novel *Black Beauty*).[27]

3. The reemergence of legal Marxist literature in the 1970s, following the election of Manley to power in 1972, but with titles almost exclusively from the Soviet presses, Novosti and Progress. Thus, titles by Brutents, Ulyanovsky,[28] and others on national liberation and the role of the Socialist countries, which were written precisely to eliminate swaths of contemporary history, became the dominant sources of information for this eager and thirsty generation.

4. The example of neighboring Cuba in which the Soviet Union had given generous support was interpreted as an exemplary instance of "proletarian internationalism" and in which it was assumed that the Soviet Union would replicate this assistance in each and every instance in which there was a revolution against imperialism.

The overall effect of this was the emergence of an intellectual mindset that was less concerned with the fine-grained understanding of the local situation, the broad, terrains of ideological struggle, and how these interacted with the international (indeed a Hallian, conjunctural approach) as it was convinced that the arrow of history had already been launched and was on its straight and accurate flight. Events were already overdetermined by the revealing truths of Marxism-Leninism, and what was required was to make the local revolution, if a revolutionary situation emerged, and join the victorious worldwide socialist and national liberation movements.

In contrast to Hall's conception of organic philosophy and the need to respectfully engage in a conversation, with the inevitable elements of give and take, Caribbean Marxism-Leninism overtly adopted the notion that the majority of the working class is "backward," both culturally and ideologically, and thus needs to be taught and guided by the advanced elements. So, in the WPJ booklet *The Working Class Party*, the following conclusion is drawn: "So, the first thing we need to understand about the position of the working class in capitalist society and the effects of

---

27 See Rupert Lewis, "Jamaican Black Power in the 1960s," in Kate Quinn (ed.) *Black Power in the Caribbean*, University Press of Florida, Gainesville, 2014, 53–75.

28 See, for instance, K. N. Brutents, *National Liberation Revolutions Today*, Progress, Moscow, 1977; and R. Ulyanovsky, *Socialism and the Newly Independent Nations*, Progress, Moscow, 1975.

capitalism on the working class and on the working people is that the system itself makes the vast sections of the working class backward at the same time as it makes a small section advanced."[29]

This leads inevitably to the corollary that the party, the vanguard, must be the instrument to bring consciousness to the majority of backward workers, as exemplified in Maurice Bishop's 1982 speech to NJM cadres, called "Line of March of the Party":

And the fifth point, the building of the Party, because again it is the Party that has to be at the head of the process, acting as representatives of the working people and in particular, the working class. That is the only way it can be because the working class does not have the ideological development or experience to build socialism on its own. The Party has to be there to ensure that the necessary steps and measures are taken. And it is our primary responsibility to prepare and train the working class for what their historic mission will be later on down the road. That is why the Party has to be built and built rapidly, through the bringing in of the first sons and daughters of the working class.[30]

Reading this speech again after many years, its deeply patronizing essence is even more evident. Indeed, Bishop's invocation here goes beyond the typical vanguardist argument, in the suggestion that the party in this instance is not just the vehicle of the advanced workers but a substitute for them, until such time as they are sufficiently fit to be brought into the organization and educated up to the required advanced standing. If there is any central feature, then, of Caribbean Marxism-Leninism that might be teased out for closer scrutiny, it is this hierarchical structuring of levels of consciousness[31] with its implications of the necessity for tutelage and guidance, not only from the advanced workers—the more "Leninist" formulation—but in the absence altogether of "advanced workers" from the

---

29   Trevor Munroe, *The Working Class Party: Principles and Standards*, Workers Party of Jamaica, Kingston, 1983, 15.
30   Maurice Bishop, "Line of March for the Party," in Paul Seabury and Walter A. McDougall (eds.) *The Grenada Papers*, Institute for Contemporary Studies, San Francisco, 1984, 73.
31   Charles Mills, effectively utilizing Plato's Cave allegory, makes this point effectively in one of the earlier, more insightful reflections on the crisis and collapse of the revolution. See Charles Mills, "Getting Out of the Cave: Tension Between Democracy and Elitism in Marx's Theory of Cognitive Liberation," *Social and Economic Studies* 39, no. 1 (March 1990): 1–50.

party, that is the undisguised tutelage of the intellectual stratum. Surely, this leads, as night follows day, to the Grenada crisis of 1983. The party derogated the right to modify its leadership structure at will, including the effective demoting of the leader and prime minister to joint leader, without any reference to the population and to what it might think. This led to a series of events that have been adequately discussed elsewhere and need not be repeated, leading, in lockstep fashion, to Bishop's death, the US-led invasion, and the end of radical Caribbean politics for a generation.

WHAT IF?

As this chapter began, somewhere during the 1960s, Stuart Hall made a decision to lay his bed permanently in the United Kingdom, where he helped build the formidable discipline of cultural studies at Birmingham, thereby influencing a generation of scholars in the UK and worldwide, and contributed immeasurably to critical political discourse in Britain, Europe, the United States, and beyond. The enigmatic question, of course, which can never be answered, is: What would have the outcome been had he brought his formidable intellect and his remarkably fluid and democratic approach to theorizing to bear on his own Jamaica of the 1960s, the very country in which a popular upheaval with region-wide consequences was ignited in 1968? What would the radical movement of the 1970s have looked like with Stuart Hall contending with some of the more dogmatic, hierarchical, and wooden perspectives that came to dominate? Perhaps it might have made little difference (as indeed was the case with C.L.R. James and his supporters), as the international environment may well have weighed decisively in favor of pro-Soviet, Marxist-Leninist tendencies that did, in fact, briefly gain momentum and enjoyed their moment in the sun. Perhaps we need altogether to move beyond the narrative of great men being the decisive engines of history. But perhaps with his prestige and fluency and his possessing the undoubted, if ironic, cachet of being a Rhodes Scholar, returning from the United Kingdom, Stuart Hall might have been taken seriously and might have influenced the emergence of a more flexible, open, radical, and popular movement in Jamaica. What would this have meant for the course of events in that country and more so for the entire Caribbean, including, most of all, Grenada, where the groundwork had already been laid for more insurrectionary forms? History evidently did not follow this course, but it is worthwhile to muse about the far-reaching consequences if it had.

PART II

Imagining

6

Beyond Neoliberalism's Dead End: Thinking Caribbean Futures through Stuart Hall and *The Kilburn Manifesto*

In 2013, five years after the onset of the worst financial crisis since the Great Depression, a gathering of British scholars calling themselves the Soundings group, and including in their ranks Stuart Hall, Doreen Massey, and Michael Rustin, launched *The Kilburn Manifesto*,[1] named after the London community in which at least three of the collective members lived. It was the cumulative result of a series of interventions that Soundings had engaged in over the previous years, seeking, inter alia, to provide a robust and thorough exploration of the causes and character of the 2008 crisis and what it meant for the continued dominance of the hegemonic neoliberal project. Even more importantly, it sought, running against the grain of much contemporary social science theorizing, to propose a framework and direction for the future, to move beyond what they considered the paucity of creative ideas in the mainstream British Labour Party and to put on the table a series of questions, interventions, and actual policy proposals that might lead to an invigorated Left agenda for the medium and long term.

To this end, not only was *Kilburn* startlingly original, but it served as a riposte and decisive response to critics of Stuart Hall and those close to him who have been associated with the "cultural studies" label. While *Kilburn* is self-consciously a collaborative enterprise (a method of intervention that defines almost all of Hall's work), Hall's fingerprints and lasting influence are all over the document, and while Hall died, sadly, in 2014, *Kilburn* is a convincing response to his critics like Rojek, Morley,[2]

---

1 Stuart Hall, Doreen Massey and Michael Rustin (eds.) *After Neoliberalism? The Kilburn Manifesto*, Lawrence and Wishart, London, 2015.
2 See Chris Rojek, *Stuart Hall*, Cambridge, Polity, 2003; and David Morley, "So-Called Cultural Studies: Dead-Ends and Reinvented Wheels," *Cultural Studies* 12, no. 4 (1998): 476–38.

and others who have argued variously that cultural studies—and by extension, his work—is too eclectic, too much under the sway of post-modernist abstraction, is obscurantist, depoliticized, and unable to have any real application to politics and policy.

Quite to the contrary, *Kilburn*, in compact, cogent, and easily accessible fashion, addresses a range of critical questions and topics beginning with an introduction that assesses the post-2008 conjunctural moment, through Doreen Massey's astute discussion of the power of language in shaping, influencing, and helping to consolidate the neoliberal ascendancy[3] and to Hall's and O'Shea's Gramscian-inflected discussion of the ambivalent role of common sense, as both agent of and potential source of disruption to the neoliberal agenda.[4] These essays lay the foundation for a series of interventions around gender, youth, race, class and generation, the state, the economy, and the international order, all with concrete insights, questions, and proposals that are far too many to summarize in any comprehensive manner in this short paper. Far from opaque abstractionism, then, this is a concerted and accessible path, if not program, for a new progressive politics of the British future, though with many insights beyond it that demand engagement, critique, and further elaboration.

If one were to try to elaborate the pivotal discussions, they would include, as suggested, the separate chapters by Massey and Hall and O'Shea, which in different ways attempt to map the discursive space and suggest its importance in the consolidation and continued, if contested, dominance of neoliberal ideas. The antithesis is also advanced by them, in that it will be vital to deploy the discursive—the "good sense" embedded in "common sense"—in the long, possibly drawn out "war of position" that will have to be waged if neoliberalism is ultimately to be transcended.[5] Mention must also be made of the chapter "States of

---

3   See Doreen Massey, "Vocabularies of the Economy," in *After Neoliberalism?*, 24–36.

4   See Stuart Hall and Allan O'Shea, "Common-Sense Neoliberalism," in *After Neoliberalism?*, 52–68.

5   It is Hall's interpretation and adaptation of Gramsci's notion of hegemony as building on popular common sense that is of interest here. Gramsci starts with the assertion that "ordinary" people generate their own ideas as to good and bad and that ruling blocs incorporate, reposition, and weave these ideas into ways of interpreting the world that conform to their hegemonic project and lead to the acceptance of their authority. Equally, the revolutionary challenge to and transformation of existing hegemonies will require radical movements

Imagination" by Janet Newman and John Clarke, which argues plaintively for the continued importance of the much-maligned state, but one that is redeployed to share its power geographically, through local devolution, as well as socially, through the involvement and incorporation of new interests clustered around gender, race, generation, and class. Newman and Clarke are also assertive that while the old form of centralized, bureaucratic state must go, some kind of state will nonetheless continue to play a necessary centripetal role of holding things together, but, they insist, it should be a "dialogic state," constantly involved in conversations with its citizens and deeply democratic in its institutional form.[6]

A further central conversation requiring greater elaboration is Massey's and Michael Rustin's chapter on the economy, the title of which, "Whose Economy? Reframing the Debate," suggests its main thrust. In the introduction, they describe Britain's contemporary economy, in the very recognizable form it took in the period immediately before the 2016 Brexit Referendum as one dominated by speculation and the financial sector, with widening inequality, the gutting of the middle and working classes, and the hollowing out of the state sector in all its dimensions. This segues into the aforementioned question: "What is the economy and who is it for?"[7] The deceptively simple answer they propose is that the economy should contribute to the enabling of decent lives for everyone and the flourishing of human potential in a way that is sustainable. In addition, there is the sketch of an alternative that includes the following elements.

First, the authors reassert the importance of the state in production and economic life. Starting with the assumption made by Newman and Clarke, they agree that even under neoliberalism's minimalist version, it is self-evident that the state is deeply committed in guaranteeing and bolstering the market, confirming, even as this is denied, its pivotal importance. The question they propose, therefore, is not whether the state should be engaged more actively in the economy, but rather where and how should this engagement be focused.

---

to understand and incorporate notions of common sense, though differently inflected, for projects with opposing social foundations. See Jennifer Daryl Slack and Lawrence Grossberg (eds.) *Stuart Hall: Cultural Studies 1983*, Duke University Press, Durham, NC, 2016, 172–73.

6 See Janet Newman and John Clarke, "States of Imagination," in *After Neoliberalism?*, 99–115.

7 *After Neoliberalism?*, 119.

Second, there is a call for the questioning of the dangerous dominance of the financial sector alongside the contestation of financialized "common sense"—the entire apparatus of budgetary austerity and its language that over time has come to be seen as natural and God-given. Alongside this, concrete steps are proposed to regulate and reduce the rampant profitability of the sector as well as—possibly through public-sector banking—to reintroduce the public interest into the financial sphere.

Third, the authors call for a move away from a speculative economy by dampening the attractiveness of assets in order to divert investment to more productive enterprises. And in conclusion, they propose a series of priorities that include a new systematic investment in green infrastructure—a Green New Deal. This must be read along with the chapter on energy policy—"Energy beyond Neoliberalism"—which includes the proposal of creating a series of "energy commons";[8] with all of the above undergirded by the assumption that any new, innovative economy must be informed by a systematically deeper democracy.[9]

I find *Kilburn* compelling first of all because it draws and accurately captures the peculiar feature of the contemporary conjunctural moment, in which we can suggest that neoliberalism—despite the global disaster of 2008–2010 and the evident failure of OECD governments to frontally address the causes of the crisis—continues to hold sway as the globally dominant approach to economic policy. Though the arrival in November 2016 of the Trumpian moment and the subsequent Brexit decision in the United Kingdom both suggest a growing reaction to globalization and a shift to more nationalist agendas, it is too early to suggest that neoliberalism as ideology and guide to policy is dead. Indeed, if we think of the world that is reconsolidating since 2010, the powerful forces advancing the neoliberal agenda and seeking to reassert their main policies of structural adjustment, privatization, state constriction, and increased austerity remain the dominant voices, even in the face of numerous instances of evident failure.

Opposed to this, there is a growing global resistance, evident in the arc of southern Europe from Greece to the Iberian Peninsula, the Corbyn ascendancy to the leadership of the Labour Party and its remarkable

---

8 See Platform, "Energy beyond Neoliberalism," in *After Neoliberalism?*, 156–75.
9 See Doreen Massey and Michael Rustin, "Whose Economy? Reframing the Debate," in *After Neoliberalism?*, 116–35.

return to competitiveness in the 2017 general elections,[10] and through the Latin American battles for electoral dominance, in which the Left, once in ascendancy, is now on the defensive.[11] Most notably, in the 2016 US presidential primaries, the Bernie Sanders campaign proved remarkably popular, and many still suggest that, had he gotten the nomination, his left-wing populism would have won him the presidency.[12] Perhaps even more fascinating to note is that Sanders's candidacy seems to have helped shatter the long-existent American taboo of discussing socialism in any form in polite company, with polls both during that period and since, suggesting that large pluralities of millennials were favorable to "socialism," however ill-defined the notion.[13] In moments of systemic crises, however, it is not the populism of the left alone that emerges. The shadow of fascism and various modalities of authoritarianism are resurgent once again in Poland, Turkey, the Philippines, and Latin America,[14] to mention outstanding instances. Most urgently, Donald Trump, an unpredictable, deeply undemocratic, and authoritarian character was elected in 2016 and in his four years in office repeatedly encouraged and gave succor to

10   See Jonathan Freedland, "Jeremy Corbyn Didn't Win: But He Has Rewritten All the Rules," *Guardian*, June 10, 2017, https://www.theguardian.com/comment isfree/2017/jun/10/jeremy-corbyn-general-election—labour-rewrites-rules.
11   See Dawisson Belem Lopes, "Is Populism Really Retreating in Latin America?" *Aljazeera*, March 4, 2017, http://www.aljazeera.com/indepth/opinion/2017/03/populism-retreating-latin-america-170303043908269.html; and M. R., "Why Populism Is in Retreat across Latin America," *The Economist*, November 21, 2016, https://www.economist.com/blogs/economist-explains/2016/11/economist-explains-12.
12   See Lucy Pasha-Robinson, "Bernie Sanders Would Have Won the Election If He Had Got Democratic Nomination, Says Trump Pollster," *The Independent*, October 31, 2017, http://www.independent.co.uk/news/world/americas/us-politics/bernie-sanders-us-presidential-election-win-donald-trump-won-democratic-nomination-hillary-clinton-a8029926.html.
13   A 2011 Pew poll found 47 percent of millennials having negative views of capitalism, while 49 percent held positive views of socialism. A later Harvard University poll of 2016 found 51 percent not in support of capitalism and 33 percent in favor of socialism. Significantly different results on support for socialism, to be sure, but even the lower figure of 33 percent in favor is remarkable by any measure. See Max Ehrenfreund, "A Majority of Millennials Now Reject Capitalism, Poll Shows," *Washington Post*, April 26, 2016.
14   See, for instance, Peter Baker, "Rise of Donald Trump Tracks Growing Debate over Global Fascism," *New York Times*, May 28, 2016, https://www.nytimes.com/2016/05/29/world/europe/rise-of-donald-trump-tracks-growing-debate-over-global-fascism.html.

the Far Right.[15] This radicalization led inexorably to his refusal to accept the loss of the 2020 elections, the January 2021 failed insurrection, and lingering fears as to the future of American democracy.

I am convinced that the eminently Hallian style of the *Kilburn* intervention, working through a conjunctural[16] analysis with a rigorous reading of the political and economic moment, parallel to a detailed exploration of the impact of words, ideas, and the discursive on bringing this moment into being and facilitating its consolidation through appeals to people's sense of right, wrong, and morality,[17] is highly relevant. It helps to explain that which is inexplicable, that is, the continued sway of neoliberalism, despite its evident bankruptcy in the sphere of practical policy and solutions to the worsening evidence of crisis, including widening global inequality, slow, anemic economic growth following the recession, and increasing evidence of global environmental collapse. This is what George Monbiot colorfully and accurately describes as the "zombie doctrine"[18] of neoliberalism—its ability to continue walking as a framework for economic analysis and policy long after it should be dead.

15   See for instance, Rosie Gray, "Trump Defends White Nationalist Protesters: 'Some Very Fine People on Both Sides,'" *The Atlantic*, August 15, 2017, https://www.theatlantic.com/politics/archive/2017/08/trump-defends-white-nationalist-protesters-some-very-fine-people-on-both-sides/537012/.

16   In his reflective 2007 essay "Through the Prism of an Intellectual Life," Hall outlined the significance of conjunctural analysis: "contingency is the sign of this effort to think determinacy without a closed form of determination. In the same way people say 'you are a conjuncturalist'. 'You want to analyse, not long, epochal sweeps of history, but specific conjunctures'. Why the emphasis on the conjunctures? Why the emphasis on what is historically specific? Well it has exactly to do with the conception of the conjuncture. The fact that very dissimilar currents, some of a long duration, some of a relatively short duration, tend to fuse or condense at particular moments into a particular configuration. It is that configuration, with its balance of forces, which is the object of one's analysis or intellectual inquiry." Brian Meeks (ed.) *Culture, Politics, Race and Society: The Thought of Stuart Hall*, Ian Randle Publishers, Kingston, 2007, 280.

17   Hall, in an important essay on "Domination and Hegemony," stresses that hegemony is the establishment of the leadership of ideas across a range of sites and critically of the moral dimension: "Anybody who wants to command the space of common sense, or popular consciousness, and practical reasoning has to pay attention to the domain of the moral, since it is the language within which vast numbers of people actually set about their political calculations. The Left has rarely talked about that space in which the difference between 'good' and 'bad' is defined; it has rarely attempted to establish the language of socialist morality." Stuart Hall, "Domination and Hegemony," in Slack and Grossberg (eds.) *Stuart Hall*, 173.

18   George Monbiot, "The Zombie Doctrine," http://www.monbiot.com/2016/04/15/the-zombie-doctrine/.

Certainly from the perspective of a scholar who has closely observed and studied Jamaica[19] over the past four decades in the long interregnum since the collapse of the radical initiatives of the 1970s, it is evident that the only kind of analysis that is worthwhile is one that might explain how, despite the failure of more than forty years of structural adjustment, with accompanying devaluations and the ravaging of the poor and middle classes, without any significant spurts of growth[20] (controversial as that term is), there has been an almost hermetic closure around intellectual conversations, much less policy interventions that might diverge from the devaluation, privatization, and austerity prescriptions of the International Monetary Fund (IMF) and World Bank. Equally, there is a need to explore how it is that socialism, a sharply contested but nonetheless acceptable notion for debate in the 1970s, came to be verboten and beyond sensible discussion and why the market as the only viable solution to almost everything came, as though it was always naturally understood as such, to be seen as common sense.

The Antillean Caribbean, aside from the anomalous instance of Cuba, can be characterized as one of the more compliant regions that has, since the 1983 collapse of the Grenadian Revolution, provided less open and overt resistance to the neoliberal agenda, with Jamaica being among the most noteworthy instances. Since 1980 both the nominally progressive People's National Party (PNP) government and the Right-leaning Jamaica Labour Party (JLP) have served terms in office, though the PNP dominated for a long stretch of eighteen years through the 1990s and into the first decade of the twenty-first century. Neither, however, has radically departed from the playbook. While it would be overly simplistic to suggest that their policies were the same, it is reasonable to propose that they have led to similar results. Jamaica's economy over this entire period has been generally listless, with little growth, growing inequality, increasing incidences of crime and corruption, and the catastrophic emigration of a generation of highly motivated and skilled citizens.

---

19   See for instance the chapter "Jamaica in a Time of Neoliberal Infatuation," in Brian Meeks, *Envisioning Caribbean Futures: Jamaican Perspectives*, The University of the West Indies Press, Kingston, 2007, 1–107.

20   Jamaica over the past four decades has been among the most anemic countries in the World in terms of the typical growth rate measurements. See, for instance, Rose Mary Garcia, *Jamaica Economic Performance Assessment*, USAID, May 2008, http://pdf.usaid.gov/pdf_docs/Pnadl775.pdf.

Following in the wake of the parlous Jamaican experience, the Caribbean, generally, is in an extraordinary moment of stasis and uncertainty in which there are simply no longer any success stories. Most graphically, the American affiliated "Commonwealth" of Puerto Rico, which in the 1950s and 1960s was presented as a model of growth and development with its Operation Bootstrap initiative of "industrialization by Invitation," has been in a spiral of fiscal collapse even before the damage wrought to its infrastructure and productive capacity by the apocalyptic Hurricane Maria in 2017. The disregard for whatever could pass for Puerto Rican sovereignty in the appointment by Congress of an "Oversight Board"[21] to manage the economic affairs of the territory—an effective retrogression to virtual colonial status—is only matched by the limited response to the hurricane's damage, underlining the view that the island's American citizens were at best second class. Puerto Ricans have responded with what is turning out to be the largest wave of migration to the mainland, reshaping electoral possibilities in the cities of their concentration[22] and undermining, as in Jamaica, the pool of skilled and qualified persons able to build a viable economy at home.

Other models, proposed at various moments as exemplary, are in tatters. Thus, in Trinidad and Tobago the claim that their strategy of diversification away from pure petroleum dependency to an economy linked to petrochemicals and other industries has, alongside an unsustainable and rampant consumerism, proven incapable of withstanding the current calamitous fall in the price of oil and gas. Trinidad, as it burns through its precious foreign exchange reserves at unsustainable rates, is evidence that diversification, however laudable a goal, has not slayed the beast of petroleum reliance.[23]

The small, remaining dependencies of the United Kingdom, among them the Turks and Caicos, the Cayman Islands and the British Virgin

21   See Stephen Mufson, "White House Names Seven to Puerto Rico Oversight Board," *Washington Post*, August 31, 2016, https://www.washingtonpost.com/business/economy/white-house-names-seven-to-puerto-rico-oversight-board/2016/08/31/9cee9376-6f8b-11e6-9705-23e51a2f424d_story.html.
22   See Lizette Alvarez, "A Great Migration from Puerto Rico Is Set to Transform Orlando," *New York Times*, November 17, 2017, https://www.nytimes.com/2017/11/17/us/puerto-ricans-orlando.html.
23   See Robert Looney, "Once a Caribbean Success Story, Trinidad and Tobago Faces an Uncertain Future," *World Politics Review*, January 13, 2017, https://www.worldpoliticsreview.com/articles/20904/once-a-caribbean-success-story-trinidad-and-tobago-faces-an-uncertain-future.

Islands, once touted for the success of their offshore banking initiatives, now face gravely uncertain futures in the light of EU and US investigations and crackdowns aimed at undermining tax havens. And the devastating blows, occurring in quick succession, to both the British and US Virgin Islands from both Hurricanes Maria and Irma,[24] underline the sheer precariousness of the very smallest states.

Even Barbados, which since independence in 1966 has been the most stable of the Anglophone economies with internationally outstanding indices of human development, faces grave challenges.[25] The short-term policy of selling limited land to rich expatriates has served to escalate the price of available housing, making it unaffordable for working people. Alongside this, revenues from the tourism industry have been slow to recover from the recession, adversely affecting the entire economy and leaving vulnerable the expenditure side of the budget, especially the historically admirable provisions for education as well as health and social services. Barbados is now in danger of losing its relative autonomy to dictate its own policy and could, in the near future, be forced to adopt the typical IMF structural adjustment policies, with known and potentially damaging effects.

The French *Departements* of Martinique, Guadeloupe, and Guiane, since the popular 2009 demonstrations for greater autonomy,[26] now exist in an uncomfortable political limbo with the metropole, in which their politics is increasingly in favor of greater sovereignty and deeper connections with their neighbors, while practicalities dictate that they must suppress these motivations in favor of the substantial subsidies and freedom of movement to and from Paris (and the EU) that French affiliation allows. This, of course, is also the critical factor that has exercised the imagination of Puerto Ricans as they chafe under the post-Maria second-class treatment meted out by the Trump regime. The short-run answer to these newly emerging hostilities to metropolitan dominance may be to stick with the known power, whose resources, even when scantily deployed, far outweigh those available in the independent

---

24   See Jeremy W. Peters, "In the Virgin Islands Hurricane Maria Drowned What Irma Didn't Destroy," *New York Times*, September 27, 2017, https://www. nytimes.com/2017/09/27/us/hurricane-maria-virgin-islands.html.

25   See Thomas Dowling, Nkunde Mwase, and Judith Gold, *Barbados: Selected Issues*, International Monetary Fund Publications, July 13, 2016, http://www.imf. org.

26   See Yarimar Bonilla, *Non-Sovereign Futures: French Caribbean Politics in the Wake of Disenchantment*, University of Chicago Press, Chicago, 2015.

islands; yet the fact that questions of sovereignty and allegiance are even on the agenda underlines the fragile, marginal, and tenuous state of the region's political economy, the absence of clear solutions, and the search for alternatives in the present conjuncture.

The regional anomaly, as for the past six decades, is Cuba, which, despite blockade and isolation from its northern neighbor, retains a degree of autonomy unsurpassed in contemporary small states but has paid the price for this with an embattled and shortages-driven fortress economy. It is perhaps too soon to determine future directions for Cuba, given the dramatic 180-degree turns in US foreign policy, from diplomatic recognition under Obama to frostiness and once again a return to partial quarantine under Trump. An increased diplomatic and economic isolation will, given the previous history, almost certainly lead to a closing of ranks and delay experimentation with new, less centralist, more democratic, socialist policies that might conceivably have followed Fidel Castro's passing in 2016. A further opening, however, if viewed from the perspective of the Communist Party (PCC) is also risky, coming at a time when vast numbers of the youth in Cuba are tuned into the global streams of consumerism and inspired by a hip-hop culture that contains both streams of misogynistic materialism alongside counter-vailing narratives of resistance to the hegemonic order. If, again, there is an opening, would the inevitable deluge of US/Western goods, images, and lifestyles serve to undermine the economic underpinnings of the Revolution, leading to the hemorrhage of its support base? Or would the party find the wherewithal to survive the onslaught and reinvigorate the Revolution with a new generation of supporters, based on the tangible benefits delivered in education, health, and social welfare alongside the psychic advantages of living in an independent homeland?

The chances for survival of the political system in its present architecture are, at best, difficult.[27] While influential sections of the PCC are still speaking in the language of embattled sacrifice and fortitude of the Special Period, such an approach may rapidly be losing credibility among the young. Unless a generation of new thinkers emerges that is able to draw selectively from Cuban experience but also appreciate and incorporate new thinking similar to that captured in *Kilburn*, then the PCC in its present monolithic and monopolistic form will be increas-

---

27 See, for instance, William M. Leogrande, "The Trouble with Cuba's New Economy," *America's Quarterly*, October 11, 2017, http://www.americasquarterly. org/content/trouble-cubas-new-economy.

ingly unsuited to address the more complex and multifaceted social and political interests and demands of the twenty-first century. The Cuban Revolution has, in its history, however, endured crises far more severe than this present one and survived.[28]

My interests in *The Kilburn Manifesto*, however, extend beyond thinking through its methods and proposals and their relevance, however modified, to the Caribbean context. Nine years ago, I wrote my own "manifesto," *Envisioning Caribbean Futures*,[29] which sought to achieve somewhat similar objectives. By working through a critique of leading contemporary Caribbean social theorists and presenting an analysis of the global and regional moment of the early 2000s, it suggested a possible radical direction for Jamaica and the Caribbean in the "mid-term." *Envisioning*, which came out in 2007, was prescient—though not the only instance like this[30]—in that it recognized the dangers of financial globalization and predicted the possibility of a crash, which did indeed come a year later. This at the time, of course, was not entirely novel as discussions on the dangers of deregulated and financialized economies were rife, it mainly confined to the Left. It is interesting, though they evidently refer to vastly different contexts, to compare the proposals made in that volume for radical reform of the state and economy of a small, distorted, post-plantation economy and to suggest how they agreed or differed with the *Kilburn* proposals made almost a decade after. Those are clearly focused on an advanced Western capitalist country, but by counterpoising them, we might think through new approaches to imagine mid-term futures for the Caribbean and beyond it.

Envisioning, in summary, argued that while the Westminster parliamentary model in Jamaica allowed for relatively peaceful transitions of power and a reasonably stable political environment, it also contributed to sharp, violent contestations for power and, when these were linked to a virulent patron/client system, created a dangerous history of tribal politics, dividing communities and ultimately breeding a system of quasi-autonomous garrison enclaves led by armed dons or

28   See, for instance, Susan Eckstein, "From Communist Solidarity to Communist Solitary," in Aviva Chomsky, Barry Carr, and Pamela Maria Smorkaloff (eds.) *The Cuba Reader: History, Culture, Politics*, Duke University Press, Durham, NC, 2003, 607–22.

29   See Meeks, *Envisioning*, 2007.

30   See, for instance, Andrew Glyn, "Imbalances of the Global Economy," *New Left Review* 34 (July–August 2005): 14.

local warlords. The tribalization of politics and the "winner takes all"[31] provisions of the Westminster system also led to the calamitous need to win power and retain it at any cost. Thus, fiscal propriety was often sacrificed at the altar of electoral necessity, leading to an untenable spiral of debt, followed by bail outs and the punishment of structural adjustment from the international financial institutions. Based on these assessments, the proposal for a way out of this morass was not to entirely abandon the Caribbean Westminster electoral system, which carried with it a history of credible (if flawed) democratic institutions, but to deepen democracy by a variety of measures that would undermine the power of the wealthy, the political class, and the state bureaucracy. The sheer embedded power of dominant classes and the entrenched nature of the state apparatus needed, in order to allow popular expression, to be curbed through a series of measures—most notably, popular involvement in the drafting of the annual budget, greater devolving of power to local government, legislated gender equality, and the possible consideration of voting rights for the large Jamaican diaspora population. All these proposals were predicated on the invoking of an original moment in the convening of a "Constituent Assembly of the Jamaican People at Home and Abroad,"[32] which, as its name suggests, would provide an unprecedented democratic intervention in the drafting of a new constitution and would, importantly, reconvene every generation to rethink its statutes, thus undermining the entrenching of permanent generational paternity to the founding drafters of the new arrangements.

At the specific level of the economy, the proposals advanced were somewhat more modest, including a creative adaptation of the developmental state model—though with the emphasis on democratic intervention in decision-making and transparency in the construction of its leading institutions—and a set of possible cutting-edge industries that the new model might advance, including popular music and entertainment as an integrated, Caribbean-wide industry as the leading arm of a dynamic service-oriented economy.

---

31 See Selwyn Ryan, *Winner Takes All: The Westminster Experience in the Caribbean*, Institute for Social and Economic Research, St. Augustine, Trinidad and Tobago, 1999; and Brian Meeks and Kate Quinn (eds.) *Beyond Westminster in the Caribbean: Critiques, Challenges and Reform*, Ian Randle Publishers, Kingston, 2018.

32 Meeks, *Envisioning*, 129–30.

In hindsight, both political and economic proposals in *Envisioning*, while specifically identified as interim measures and specifically as "not socialism"[33] but rather crafted as an avenue out of decades of stasis, fell short in a number of ways that *The Kilburn Manifesto* makes apparent.

First, they did not sufficiently appreciate and address in a decisive way the discursive development of neoliberalism and the unavoidable necessity to engage in combat with it at the formative level of its ideas. While the second chapter, titled "Jamaica in a Time of Neoliberal Infatuation,"[34] sought to chart the history of the rise of the structures and shape of the neoliberal era, it fell short in not sufficiently interrogating the discursive dimensions. How was socialism, which dominated among the young in the form of Michael Manley's "Democratic Socialism" in the 1970s, exorcised? What were the avenues and the specific moments in which the notion of "the magic of the marketplace" gained acceptance and ascendancy? What were the mechanisms by which a variety of effervescent, collectivist, and self-help notions from the 1970s—such as "each one teach one," "t'un yu han' mek Fashion," Livity,[35] or "Social Living"—ruled out of court and relegated to the basement of ideas? This requires much more consideration as we recognize that it is the hegemony of the deeply flawed ideas of the supremacy of the pure market, of the infallibility of rational choice theory, and of the primacy of the selfish individual as the only important unit of economic analysis that has brought the world to this sorry and dangerous moment.

Second, in its political proposals, while *Envisioning* certainly sought to push the possibility of change within the existent modified Westminster model of governance, it fell short of proposing, as I think is done with great effect in *Kilburn*, a new kind of state, cognizant of the varied interests of the twenty-first century and willing to concede entire spheres of power to the people in novel ways. Thus, what I think *Kilburn* accomplishes with great effect, and better, is to propose not an increase of the role of the state in society, as twentieth-century socialism imagined, but, critically, an increase of the role of society in the state.[36]

---

33 *Envisioning*, 97.
34 *Envisioning*, 61–107.
35 "T'un yu han' ... " means effectively to use one's own (if limited) resources to invent novel ways to survive. "Livity" is a Rastafarian word for "a decent, moral, clean, environmentally friendly way to live the good life."
36 See Newman and Clark in *After Neoliberalism?*, 104–6.

With reference to the economic proposals, beyond the sketching and outlining of new sectors and the advancing of the idea of deeper democratic engagement, the larger problem of how to confront global wealth and finance is also left silent in *Envisioning*. This is perhaps inevitable in the context that the real power in these matters resides in places like the city of London, just down the road from Kilburn and therefore of immediate concern to the drafters of that manifesto. Yet, beyond drawing a picture of the dangers in late capitalism, it was remiss of me in *Envisioning* not to incorporate a conversation on possible future directions for the global economy writ large but rather to focus primarily on how a small state might, even under seriously adverse conditions, maneuver in its interstices. The two levels of analysis and accompanying proposals—the local and the global—are inevitably intertwined, and discussion of one without the other will weaken both conclusions.[37]

Finally, the failure to raise and substantially explore the simple question at the cornerstone of *The Kilburn Manifesto*—"What and who is the economy for?"—is cause for reflection and critique. Without a concerted attempt to answer this question and to place on the table (as Kilburn effectively does) a set of irreducible conditions for human flourishing that the economy must provide, and from this, to elaborate further proposals, there is the always present danger of lapsing into the default condition of "letting the market determine," the failure of which is where both *Kilburn*, in its own way, and *Envisioning* began and is the moment of crisis we are now living in.

CONCLUSION

The Kilburn Manifesto is a powerful retort to those who have argued that Stuart Hall and his eclectic, sometimes apparently contradictory, efforts to read culture and politics through the lens of the conjunctural moment is depoliticized and abstract. Starting with a rigorous appreciation of a particular moment (the aftermath of the crash of 2008–2010) and reading it through both an understanding of global and local political and economic movements as well as an understanding of how ideas and language work to consolidate power, Hall and his allies take us through

---

37   For a broader discussion of *Envisioning*, see the book discussion in *New West Indian Guide* with Jay Mandle, "The New Argonauts and Brian Meeks's *Envisioning Caribbean Futures*"; Rivke Jaffe, "Notes on the State of Chronic: Democracy and Difference after Dudus"; Brian Meeks, "Response to the New Argonauts"; and Jay Mandle's "Response ... ," *New West Indian Guide* 85, nos. 1 and 2 (2011): 53–78.

a set of proposals that, while ultimately only testable in the real world of political engagement, go significantly beyond the conventional routines and raise important questions and proposals for both theory and praxis.

I suggest, however, that there are a few further questions that are either silent or muted in *Kilburn* that certainly demand further consideration. The first relates to the absence of any serious discussion around the meta-theoretical question whether market mechanisms can be viewed as the primary means of organizing the economy. While *The Kilburn Manifesto* points to the limitations of the market and the historic and recurring role of the state as intervener in keeping it afloat and functioning, there deserves to be a more thorough discussion on the efficacy of the market itself. I suggest that among the appropriate questions that need to be resuscitated are those around its fraught and violent formation—what Marx discussed at length as "primitive accumulation"[38] and the birth of what should, following Cedric Robinson, be considered "racial capitalism."[39] The implications of Robinson's argument that race is imbricated in the very marrow of capitalism leads to the conclusion that in order to move beyond it, the evident and hidden structures of race also need to be thoroughly dismantled. This, among many other conclusions, brings to the fore the question of reparations from those who benefited from slavery, for the peoples and regions that suffered from it. This must be accompanied by a sustained critique of its historic dependence on the public purse and public institutions as in the US bailout of the banks in 2009–2010—in other words, the extent to which late capitalism has normalized the socialization of risk. Compounded with this is its evident tendency to breed inequality, most recently discussed in arguments around Thomas Piketty's[40] work, leading to the logical question whether it remains a suitable vehicle, indeed, central mechanism, for the sort of human-based economy that is urgently required for the future. Surely, there is an extended debate from Marx through Karl Polanyi[41] down to Alec Nove's *Feasible Socialism*

---

38   See Karl Marx, "The So-Called Primitive Accumulation," in *Das Kapital: A Critique of Political Economy*, Chicago, Gateway, 1970, 349–52.

39   See Cedric Robinson, *Black Marxism: The Making of the Black Radical Tradition*, London, Zed Books, 1991.

40   See Thomas Piketty, *Capital in the Twenty-First Century*, Belknap Press of Harvard University Press, Cambridge, MA, 2014; and Heather Boushey, J. Bradford Delong, and Marshall Steinbaum, *After Piketty: The Agenda for Economics and Inequality*, Harvard University Press, Cambridge, MA, 2017.

41   See Karl Polanyi, *The Great Transformation: The Political and Economic Origins of Our Time*, Beacon Press, Boston, 1957.

and Michael Albert's *Parecon*[42] that demands further consideration of this burning question. In the many narratives that describe the egregious failures of Soviet-style central planning, its successes, in providing the basics for survival and for a significant measure of social well-being for tens of millions of people, often go unmentioned. The specter of Soviet Communism needs to be laid to rest, but socialism as a profoundly humanist and moral enterprise needs to be disinterred, looked at, and spoken about once again, in the light of day.

The questions that need to be asked include: How might a new, democratic, multi-polar, and devolved (Kilburnesque) state adapt novel methods of planning informed by advances in cyber democracy, crowd-sourcing,[43] social networking, and as yet unimagined advances of the digital era? How might a new socialism, or what I have called elsewhere, borrowing from the Jamaican reggae great Burning Spear, a new approach to "social living,"[44] build on the profoundly egalitarian essence of the old socialism with its universal access to health care, education, and social protection while consolidating and expanding social freedom as well as enabling constant experimentation in politics and the social sphere?[45] These would explore various permutations of market and state integration in addition to entirely new and unprecedented modalities of exchange and production, all accompanied by transparency and popular engagement. If, however, the experience of our recent sordid infatuation with market orthodoxy is any measure, it is an exploration that is impatient of debate.[46]

---

42   See Alec Nove, *Feasible Socialism*, Unwin Hyman, London, 1983; and Michael Albert, *Parecon: Life after Capitalism*, Verso, London, 2003.
43   While the 2012 Icelandic experience in drafting a new constitution might not be considered a model of crowdsourcing and popular consultation, it is nonetheless a pilot. Future instances might learn from both its successes in utilizing the internet for collating new ideas, as well as its weaknesses in not allowing sufficient time for consultation and not sufficiently disconnecting the exercise from partisan structures. See Giulia Dessi, "The Icelandic Constitutional Experiment," October 23, 2012, *Open Democracy*, http://www.opendemocracy.net.
44   This refers to his 1976 hit "Social Living," in which he chants hypnotically: "Do you know Social Living is the best?" See Burning Spear (Winston Rodney), "Social Living," *Reggae Greats: Burning Spear*, Mango Records, 1984.
45   For a useful discussion along these lines, see Axel Honneth, *The Idea of Socialism*, Polity, Cambridge, 2017.
46   Fortunately, a new debate on the relevance of socialism and non-capitalist forms in the Caribbean has developed with the appearance of the fall 2016 *CLR James Journal* special issue in honor of the Guyanese economist C. Y. Thomas.

The final concern surrounds the question of growth and the possibilities for new economic approaches based on "degrowth."[47] In *Kilburn* this is skirted around with, among others, notions of the Green Economy, popular energy initiatives, and so on, but the frontal debate as to whether economies can continue interminably on paths of growth is not pursued. This is more an instance of omission than commission, but one that nonetheless needs to be mentioned as we contemplate the growing inequality within and between states; the global overproduction of goods; the growing structural unemployment due to both "globalization" as well as the present and immanent disappearance of jobs to new robotic engineering;[48] and the rapidly deteriorating state of the global environment, with consensual wisdom suggesting that we are deeply embedded within the Anthropocene era[49] with grave consequences for the future of humanity and life, writ large.

Matt Lundahl, in particular, in his review of Thomas's proposals for a socialist path, critiques his proposals for a centralized state-planned model of socialist development in Thomas's 1974 volume *Dependence and Transformation*. See C. Y. Thomas, *Dependence and Transformation: The Economics of the Transformation to Socialism*, Monthly Review Press, New York, 1974. Lundahl traces the familiar failures of state planning as captured famously in Janos Kornai's study of Hungary—and more broadly speaking, the Soviet Union and "really existing socialism"—to arrive at the predictable conclusion that such a model led to known distortions, shortages, and failures of production. See Janos Kornai, *The Socialist System: The Political Economy of Capitalism*, Princeton University Press, Princeton, NJ, 1992. Where Lundahl fails to direct our thinking is to consider that the dominant, indeed hegemonic, path that the world is now all on board with is leading at its own pace to environmental destruction, widening inequality, systemic unemployment, and political and social malaise. A feasible path may not be Soviet-styled state planning, but neither can it be business as usual with the neoliberal market economy. See Matt Lundahl, "Utopia in the Caribbean: The Transformational World of C.Y. Thomas," *CLR James Journal* 22, nos. 1 and 2 (Fall 2016): 35–86.

47 See, for instance, Riccardo Mastini, "Degrowth: The Case for a New Economic Paradigm," *Open Democracy*, June 8, 2017, https://www.opendemocracy.net/riccardo-mastini/degrowth-case-for-constructing-new-economic-paradigm.

48 These point to a confluence of events that give substance and urgency to arguments like those of Wolfgang Streeck, who argues that whether or not there are alternative modes of production on the horizon, capitalism as we know it may be approaching its end. See Wolfgang Streeck, *How Will Capitalism End?*, Verso, London, 2016.

49 See, for instance, Jeremy Davies, *The Birth of the Anthropocene*, University of California Press, Oakland, 2016; and Ian Angus, *Facing the Anthropocene: Fossil Capitalism and the Crisis of the Earth System*, Monthly Review Press, New York, 2016.

The discussion, therefore, as to whether growth can continue interminably is urgent, and particularly so for small, vulnerable islands like Barbuda, from which every living inhabitant was forced to evacuate following the ravages of Hurricane Irma in 2017[50] and those among the Pacific Islanders who are already being submerged by rising sea levels. Growth, then, needs to be disrupted from its normal, natural precedence as the object of economics and the purpose of the global economy; it must instead be seen as an urgent and central problem in itself in any coherent conversation about possibly more human, more environmentally sensible, and more radical alternatives for the mid- to long-term future, if there is to be one.

---

50 Barbuda is the smaller of the two islands in the eastern Caribbean state of Antigua and Barbuda. See Marshall Shepherd, "Are Hurricanes Creating Climate Refugees in the Caribbean?" *Forbes*, September 21, 2017, https://www.forbes.com/sites/marshallshepherd/2017/09/21/are-hurricanes-creating-climate-refugees-in-the-caribbean/.

7

Hegemony and the
Trumpian Moment

I have been thinking about hegemony in the Caribbean for more than two decades,[1] utilizing the Gramscian notion that social formations are structured in dominance, but that domination is often not primarily executed through force; rather, the social bloc in charge is able to produce and reproduce discourses and sets of ideas that give structure and shape to its apparent right to rule. Hegemony, in this sense, implies the weaving of a network of first-, second-, and third-order ideas, beliefs, myths, gestures, and styles that come together to constitute a skein of common sense that provides justification for domination and the rightness to rule, laying the foundation for consent through the assumption that the governmental project, its methods and effects, makes sense.[2] Some corollaries to this

---

1   See, for instance, Brian Meeks, "The Political Moment in Jamaica: The Dimensions of Hegemonic Dissolution," in Manning Marable (ed.) *Dispatches from the Ebony Tower*, Columbia University Press, New York, 2000, 32–52, Brian Meeks, *Envisioning Caribbean Futures: Jamaican Perspectives*, The University of the West Indies Press, Kingston, 2007; and Brian Meeks, *Critical Interventions in Caribbean Politics and Theory*, University Press of Mississippi, Jackson, 2014.
2   Gramsci's approach to Marxian analysis is often seen as the moment of a qualitative break with a certain mode of Marxism that sees immediate and evident causalities between the material base of social life (the economic and classes that emerge within it) and the so-called superstructural realm of ideas, culture, and other "secondary" effects. There is, however, evidence in Marx's own work of a far less schematically driven approach to understanding political moments and many traditions beyond Gramsci that erode or sever the tenuous connections to "the economic" that he, in the last instance, maintains. See, for instance, Ernesto Laclau and Chantal Mouffe, *Hegemony and Socialist Strategy: Towards a Radical Democratic Politics*, Verso, New York, 1989. From a very different foundation, see Cedric Robinson, *Black Marxism: The Making of the Black Radical Tradition*, Zed Books, London, 1983; and Ranajit Guha, *Dominance without Hegemony: History and Power in Colonial India*, Cambridge, MA, Harvard University Press, 1997. The late Jamaican/British scholar Stuart Hall, whose work is referenced extensively here, charts a tortuous middle ground that argues for the autonomy of the cultural sphere but not an abandonment of the Marxian notion of more than

include, first, that the netting of consent is always unraveling, always in dire need of patching and repair; and second, that it is permeable and that light invariably escapes from its confines. Yet, to shift metaphors, as with a fisherman's net, some fish escape, but the net still serves its purpose of retaining a significant part of the catch within its confines. Or as Stuart Hall, in capturing the tentative, unfinished character along with the moral imperatives of the notion, suggests:

> It follows that hegemony can only be conceived as a historical process, not a thing achieved. But on the other hand, it is not merely the ongoing maintenance of rule and domination. It has to be specified "empirically" if the power of the ruling class or dominant bloc is in fact a moment of hegemony. Additionally, because hegemony is the establishment of the leading position on a variety of sites of social and political struggle, it includes domains that are usually ignored by Marxists, like the discourses of morality. Anybody who wants to command the space of common sense or popular consciousness and practical reasoning, has to pay attention to the domain of the moral, since it is the language within which vast numbers of people actually set about their calculations.[3]

I moved to the United States, to Brown University, in the late summer of 2015. In the following summer of 2016, Donald Trump was selected by the Republican Party as its presidential candidate, and I noted this strong sense of familiarity in the dissonance, antagonisms, and often sheer bad behavior that accompanied his campaign and that reprised for me the social crisis of Jamaica as it approached what is often described as

---

vestigial linkages to the sphere of the economic. See Stuart Hall, "The Toad in the Garden: Thatcherism among the Theorists," in *Marxism and the Interpretation of Culture*, eds. Cary Nelson and Lawrence Grossberg, University of Illinois Press, Urbana, 1988, 35–57. And Perry Anderson, in his short, critical survey of the notion, is consistent in searching for the hidden and often ignored connections between hegemony used in reference to dominance within a state and between states in the international sphere. If nothing else, Anderson concludes that the discussion of one without the other is inadequate, as is his assertion that hegemony, while suggesting acceptance and acquiescence, is inevitably tied on a sliding scale to coercion or its threat. See Perry Anderson, *The H-Word: The Peripeteia of Hegemony*, Verso, London, 2017.

3 Jennifer Darryl Slack and Lawrence Grossberg (eds.) *Stuart Hall, Cultural Studies 1983: A Theoretical History*, Duke University Press, Durham, NC, 2016, 173.

a near civil war situation before the 1980 general elections.[4] I thought it worthwhile, therefore, to review the tools and methods that I have used to try to explain the recent history of Jamaica and to experiment with their applicability in what might be termed the Trumpian moment, which has consolidated with his unanticipated electoral victory in November 2016.

In the Jamaican case, I used this notion to suggest that the social pact between, on the one hand, middle-class politicians and their social base and, on the other hand, insurgent workers and the poor that encrypted this particular structure in dominance, operated within a very time-specific framework, bracketed by the popular labor riots of 1938 and their aftermath; of the bankruptcy of British colonialism coming out of World War II and the pressure on the United Kingdom—significantly greater after Suez—to relinquish her colonies; of the social democratic impulses for economic welfare that had grown after the rebellion and were intersecting with the postwar political ascendancy of the Labour Party; of the "glorious thirty years" of economic boom after the war, which provided, even in the constricted/distorted economic space of the post colonies, an opportunity for rapid growth and an accompanying, if limited, social welfare experiment. This social pact meant that in exchange for the subaltern classes granting their acquiescence and ceding political power and the direction of society to the middle classes, the two main political parties, together, initiated important social policies, including universal free basic and subsidized secondary education, improved though severely flawed social services and health services as well as limited low-income housing solutions. This pact took the country into independence with an ideology of Creole nationalism effectively captured in the Jamaican national motto "Out of many, one people." This on the surface reflected an admirable notion of racial harmony, but on closer investigation, in a country with more than 90 percent of its population of African descent, seemed to obfuscate this essential reality and the long history of racial and colorist subordination of people of African descent, by veiling the country's distinct character and history under the notion that the country was constituted of "many people" of which the African majority was

---

4   In October 1980, the democratic socialist government of Michael Manley, which forged close ties with Fidel Castro's Cuba and supported the principles of the Non-Aligned Movement, was defeated by the pro-free market, pro-Ronald Reagan Jamaica Labour Party, led by Edward Seaga. The figure of eight hundred deaths in the internecine fighting leading up to the elections is now generally considered conservative but nonetheless supports the case for a pre-civil war moment.

simply just one of no special significance.[5] To the extent that the pact was successful, I suggest that it was for a very brief moment, primarily in the immediate pre-independence decades from the 1940s until 1962, when the most favorable global economic conditions—including open migration to the United Kingdom and the growth of the new bauxite/alumina industry—provided the possibility of the dominant social bloc fulfilling, at least partially, some of its side of the bargain.

However, by independence things had already begun to fall apart. The closure of the safety valve of migration to the United Kingdom and the failure of the chosen strategy of "industrialization by invitation" to generate sufficient employment alongside the continuation of some of the most egregious features of colonialism, in race and color barriers to employment and upward mobility, had, by the late 1960s, fostered deep social unrest. Accompanying this was the collapse of Creole nationalism and its replacement among the young of counter-hegemonic tendencies that forged different worldviews and explanatory frameworks, of which the most evident were the Black Power movement and closely allied to it Rastafarianism,[6] which would acquire globally iconic status with the prominence of its musicians as vocalizers of what would become an international counter-hegemonic discourse in the 1970s and beyond.

The Democratic Socialist interregnum of Michael Manley from 1972–1980 witnessed a confluence of these new counter-hegemonic notions with a popular movement that surrounded and inhabited the institutional structure of the People's National Party (PNP), one of the established, middle-class-led parties. The new discourses departed in large measure from the conservative boundaries of the earlier social pact and gave wind to the sails of a movement that significantly undermined the laws, institutional structures, and social norms of colonial Jamaica. Manley's PNP, however, was defeated in the 1980 elections by a combination of a new global economic situation that was unfavorable to small mineral-exporting states and a determined resistance from the local wealthy, who feared that their social and economic dominance was threatened and they were fully supported by the United States, as the global guardian of world capitalism.

---

5   See Meeks, *Critical Interventions*, 192.
6   See Meeks, *Critical Interventions*, 75–85; Horace Campbell, *Rasta and Resistance: From Marcus Garvey to Walter Rodney*, Africa World Press, Trenton, NJ, 1987; and Deborah Thomas, *Exceptional Violence: Embodied Citizenship in Transitional Jamaica*, Duke University Press, Durham, NC, 2011.

Manley's defeat in 1980, however, did not return the island to a new equilibrium. Instead, it has endured four decades of what I have suggested is "hegemonic dissolution," in which counter-hegemonic discourses have continued to proliferate and in which the weakening of the state under pressure from neoliberal structural adjustment policies has provided space for the emergence of novel, quasi-statal criminal/political fiefdoms, which, until recently, have grown in strength and morphed into new and unprecedented forms.[7] Yet despite these threats to its survival, the institutional framework of two-party governance, inherited from independence, remains, though it has lost its gloss and "natural" right to rule.

This impasse, underlined by the failure of the movement of the 1970s and popular resentment from the poor over persistent economic stagnation, is manifest in cultural resistance and an unwillingness of the subaltern to live within the "decent" cultural markers of official society. But equally and critical in understanding the present moment in Jamaica is to grasp the failure of the subaltern majority to forge a new project of social emancipation from below. It is at this juncture of social incapacity on both sides, and its implications for sclerosis and stasis, that hegemonic dissolution is to be located.[8]

In summary, the postwar social pact, forged at the juncture of a favorable international moment, provided a period of relative stability, but its structure in dominance was threatened in the 1970s by a popular insurgency which itself failed. The successor period of neoliberal dominance, which has lasted for close to four decades, has not been able to forge a new pact, but rather there has been a long hiatus of stagnation, anomie, and limited economic growth—all punctuated by violence, uncertainty, and an unprecedented migration, especially of the skilled and the capable. I pause here to suggest a distinction between political crisis and hegemonic dissolution. We can imagine a political crisis emerging in the Jamaica of the late 1970s as a coalition of urban and rural poor, gathered behind a small and fraying middle-class intellectual leadership

---

7   See Meeks, *Critical Interventions*, 169–82.

8   I am conscious here of James Scott's notion developed in *Domination and the Arts of Resistance* and elsewhere that there is never a hermetic hegemony and that there is in a sense always rebellion among the subaltern; however, the danger in this formulation is that in elevating all forms of resistance to incipient rebellion, it becomes difficult to predict and distinguish genuine open rebellion because of its prior conclusion that the subaltern are always in revolt. See James C. Scott, *Domination and the Arts of Resistance: Hidden Transcripts*, Yale University Press, New Haven, CT, 1990.

to implement a popular and broadly democratic project of national "progress." However, it confronted a powerful alliance of the local business and commercial strata, supported by a viable coalition of traditionally oriented popular support and a disenchanted majority of the middle class. This counterrevolutionary alliance gained significant backing from the local hegemon, the United States, and the radical project was decisively defeated in a bloody but legitimately accepted electoral exercise. It was the seemingly irresolvable face-off between these sharply divided social coalitions that defined the political crisis. Hegemonic dissolution, on the other hand, is the process that has meandered along since then, in which none of the existing coalitions (no new ones have emerged) has been able to decisively stamp its legitimacy on the national conversation and shape the agenda for social and political development.

Before suggesting how these insights might contribute to an appreciation of this Trumpian moment, it is perhaps worthwhile to think about how Stuart Hall sought to explain and understand an earlier British conjuncture that witnessed, parallel to Manley's demise in Jamaica, the consolidation of Thatcherism and the breaking up of the Keynesian, welfarist consensus.[9] First, in looking at the growth of Thatcherism, with its anti-union, anti-collectivist essence, Hall sought to avoid both economistic and historically flattened readings of the process. He attacked the notion that every economic crisis invariably led to the same set of responses and outcomes as occurred in previous crises. Thus, he argued, the stock response to the shift in Britain to the Right, which proposed that Thatcherism was essentially fascism, was entirely misguided. History, he offered, was not a "series of repeats."[10] Rather, he suggested that what was emerging as the Far (Thatcherite) Right's response to the crisis of the 1970s was an authoritarian populism, which, unlike classical fascism, "had retained most (though not all) of the formal representative institutions in place and which at the same time has been able to construct around itself a popular consent."[11] This popular consent, he suggests, was

9   See Stuart Hall, "The Great Moving Right Show," in *Stuart Hall, Selected Political Writings*, eds. Sally Davison, David Featherstone, Michael Rustin, and Bill Schwarz, Duke University Press, Durham, NC, 2017, 172–86.
10   Hall, "Great Moving Right Show," 173. This also prompts the reminder that the Thatcherite/Reaganite/Hayekian project of the limited state and the deregulated economy is markedly different in significant ways from that of Trumpian economic nationalism and nativism, though it should be added that both anchor their projects in police and military expansionism.
11   "Great Moving Right Show," 174.

shaped out of existing commonsensical notions—values of "Englishness" and the rights of the Englishman as an individual—as well as darker, racist notions of white, British superiority and the assumed "dangers" of immigration. These, he argued, were now repurposed to weigh in against social welfare, socialized health, public education, and collectivism in general:

> It works on the ground of already constituted social practices and lived ideologies. It wins space there by constantly drawing on these elements which have secured over time a traditional resonance and left their traces in popular inventories. At the same time it changes the field of struggle by changing the place, position, the relative weight of the condensations within any one discourse and constructing them according to an alternative logic.[12]

Thus, Hall concluded that it is through the massaging of multiple discourses that Thatcherism forged a new hegemonic initiative that strove to build and consolidate consensus around the unassailability and natural rightness of the marketplace and captured in the now, forty years later, well-battered but still surprisingly standing notion that "there is no alternative."

In returning to the contemporary moment in the United States, it is useful to reassert that there is never a single hegemony, with a single set of narratives and linguistic markers. Hegemony is sutured, sewn, and incomplete. Yet this leaves space for the lesser assertion that dominant hegemonies do exist for a time. There is also never a single insurgent counter-hegemonic narrative; rather, these are multiple, fractured, and require, precisely, significant suturing to present themselves as coherent, robust alternatives to their dominant protagonists.

What is the economic conjuncture that undergirds all of this? As Wolfgang Streeck suggests, there has not been one since the thirty years of the great postwar boom, but we should recall at least three crises: the crisis of global inflation of the 1970s; closely followed by the explosion of public debt of the 1990s; and most recently the crisis of private debt and the collapse of financial institutions in the Great Recession of 2008.[13] Recovery from the Recession was slow and more than a decade later it is

---

12 "Great Moving Right Show," 186.
13 See Wolfgang Streeck, *How Will Capitalism End?*, Verso, London, 2016.

evident that large swaths of the population remain mired in poverty and hopelessness. This, more than anything else, is the economic foundation for Trump's white, rural, rustbelt, male support, which was critical in his razor-thin victories in Pennsylvania and the Midwest and his 2016 Electoral College majority.

Explanations for this are well-rehearsed though worth repeating and are inevitably to be found in the dramatic restructuring of the world economy. First, and perhaps most profoundly, is the sharp rise in the use of robots, which explains in part the present sluggishness in employment, but certainly will have greater impact in the mid to long term.[14] Second and more commonly understood are the continuing effects of globalization, with jobs shifting from Michigan, Ohio, and Kentucky south of the border (Mexico, Central America, the Caribbean) and the racing to the bottom of ever cheaper labor markets (Vietnam, Bangladesh, China). Many of the new jobs emerging in this environment are in non-unionized service sectors, like fast food, retail, and self-employed urban transport, and carry none of the security and benefits of earlier unionized positions. Then, in turn, the crash of many of these lower-paid jobs is already occurring, as large-scale disruptive technologies utilizing social media and instant internet communication (Amazon in retail and Uber in transport) assume sectoral leaderships, requiring far fewer workers, even as they offer cheaper costs to the (often unemployed or underemployed) consumer.

Persistent and entrenched unemployment in redundant sectors contributes to a third factor, which is the growth of inequality. In 2016, inequality in America reached new extremes, with the top 1 percent controlling 38.6 percent of the wealth and the bottom 90 percent holding only 22.8 percent, down from close to a third, when tracking of these statistics first began by the Fed in 1989.[15] A fourth consideration is the shift over the past twenty years to rapid product differentiation in financial markets and more recently their quantum digitization, which

14 Samantha Masumaga, "Robots Could Take Over 38% of US Jobs within about 15 Years," *Los Angeles Times*, March 24, 2017, www.latimes.com/business/la-fi-pwc-robotics-jobs-20170324-story.html/; Darrell M. West, "What Happens If Robots Take Jobs? The Impact of Emerging Technologies on Employment and Public Policy," Center for Technology Innovation at Brookings, October 2015.
15 Matt Egan, "Record Inequality: The Top 1% Controls 38.6% of America's Wealth," accessed November 2017, http://money.cnn.com/2017/09/27/news/economy/inequality-record-top-1-percent-wealth/index.html.

has increased the flow and efficiency of trading, leading to vast new accumulations of wealth, harvested at the margins of financial transactions and fast-trading digital futures markets.

Streeck, employing some of these tendencies in his bleak prophecy for the future of capitalism, proposes that the present moment is defined by the compounding of intersecting crises: first, he proposes that growth is giving way to stagnation; second, in instances where there is economic "progress" it is less shared; third, the long interregnum of neoliberalism has starved the public space, leading to damaged infrastructure across the board; fourth, corruption, held at the margins in the first postwar decades, has now become rife; and fifth, the capitalist system, held together by the Cold War and US dominance in the West, is now adrift with the potential for increasing anarchy.[16] Streeck, in developing each of these themes, argues that capitalism as we presently understand it will probably soon collapse but will not necessarily be replaced by something coherent (or better) for a long time. Further discussion around each of these themes before arriving at his precipitous conclusions is, of course, urgently necessary. What is apparent, though, is that the sense that it is not business as usual, that government is not serving its purpose and that the wealthy and powerful set the rules and run the system for themselves, is palpable and driving narratives across the political spectrum in what I suggest is the American equivalent of a moment of hegemonic dissolution.

Was there ever a coherent meta-narrative that brought together significant sections of America under one netting? While avoiding some imaginary, original moment, we can suggest that perhaps in the postwar (1945–1974) context of unprecedented economic growth and accompanied by Cold War anti-communism, consolidating notions of American exceptionalism, and unreconstructed masculinism, there was a framework that dominated among some sectors and for a while, particularly if we were to exclude much of the Black population, particularly those in the segregated South, from the picture.[17] This somewhat coherent hegemony—white and male in its structuring of dominance—

16   Streeck, *How Will Capitalism End?*, 72.
17   I am sensitive here to W.E.B. Du Bois's insightful use of "double consciousness" as recognition of an entire Black subaltern space of resistance occupied by Black people who have never fully bought into the dominant framework of power and of American exceptionalism. See W.E.B. Du Bois, "Of Our Spiritual Strivings," in David Levering Lewis (ed.) *W.E.B. Du Bois: A Reader*, Henry Holt, New York, 1995, 29.

hasn't existed for some time. Indeed, we can suggest that if we think about the impact of the countercultural movements of the 1960s, the civil rights movement, Black Power, and the anti-war movement, its collapse has been evident in phases, associated with both the three major economic crises of the last thirty years and the popular movements that have grown in response to them, in addition to other factors.

A sufficiently thorough approach to understanding currents and counter-currents in the present conjuncture would have to necessarily explore numerous discursive records, including the speeches of politicians, both during electoral exercises and while in office; a variety of carefully selected literature, both fiction and nonfiction; alongside popular cultural manifestations, such as recorded music, art, and theater, and styles in order to begin sifting, triangulating, and assessing dominant cultural trends and emergent countercultural initiatives. A start, however, can be made by going straight to the ubiquitous polls that provide a shortcut to the ebb and flow of popular thinking.

A useful place to begin, particularly in light of the purported resurgence of the religious Right in the ranks of the Republican Party and thus in the country's decision-making structure, is the extent to which there is belief in religion. A 2017 Pew poll asking whether it was necessary to believe in God to be moral found that 56 percent felt it was not necessary, increasing by 7 percent from 2011 when some 49 percent in that poll felt the same way.[18] On the attitude to same-sex marriage, in 2001 Americans opposed same-sex marriage by 57 percent to 35 percent. In 2017, this had shifted significantly to support for same-sex marriage by 62 percent in favor to 32 percent opposed.[19]

On the attitude as to whether interracial marriage was a good thing, in 2010 24.5 percent of another Pew poll had signaled yes, it was, but by 2017 this had increased to 39 percent. On the other hand, as to whether it was a bad thing, in 2010 13 percent thought so, and by 2017 this had fallen by four points to 9 percent.[20] On the central question of the nature

18 Gregory A. Smith, "A Growing Share of Americans Say It's Not Necessary to Believe in God to Be Moral," accessed October 2017, www.pewresearch.org/fact-tank/2017/10/16/a-growing-share-of-americans-say-its-not-necessary-to-believe-in-god-to-be-moral/.
19 Pew Research Center, "Changing Attitudes on Gay Marriage," June 26, 2017, www.pewforum.org.fact-sheet/changing-attitudes-on-gay-marriage/.
20 Gretchen Livingston and Anna Brown, "Public Views on Intermarriage," accessed November 2017, www.pewsocialtrends.org/2017/05/18/2-public-views-on-intermarriage/.

of the economic system, a 2016 Harvard University poll asked whether there was support for capitalism and found that a slight majority of 51 percent of millennials did not support capitalism with only 42 percent supportive of it. When asked about favorability to socialism, the same poll found some 33 percent supportive of socialism. Only among the cohort of respondents more than fifty years old were the majority in favor of capitalism.[21] In its report on the Harvard study, the *Washington Post* compares it with a 2011 Pew poll, which found a similar figure of 47 percent having negative views of capitalism, but that poll found that in relation to a positive perception of socialism, 49 percent held positive views while 42 percent were negative.[22]

On general questions of people's attitudes to politics and the state of the country, seven in ten persons in a 2017 *Washington Post* poll concluded that politics had reached a dangerous new low point. The same poll found that there was deep and growing distrust for the political sphere. In 2017, only 14 percent of those polled felt that politicians were ethical and honest. In a 1987 poll, that figure was 39 percent, declining to 25 percent in 1997. On the open-ended question as to what the causes for dysfunction in the political system were, the largest cohort, some 65 percent, responded that it was the undue influence of money in politics; this was followed by 56 percent asserting that it was due to the influence of wealthy political donors. A similar percentile said it was because of the influence of people with extreme political views, while 51 percent concluded that it was due to one man, that being Donald Trump. When asked whether divisions in the country were as bad as during the Vietnam War, a significant majority of 70 percent concluded that they were at least as bad.[23]

What do these admittedly somewhat randomly selected polls tell us when read through the lens of hegemony? First, and self-evident to anyone who lived through or observed the two years after Trump's 2016 victory in the United States, is that there is a sharply, perhaps irreconcilably divided polity. On the one hand, there is a large minority of entrenched adherents to the hoary constellation of white, masculinist

21   Max Ehrenfreund, "A Majority of Millennials Now Reject Capitalism, Poll Shows," *Washington Post*, April 26, 2016. https://www.washingtonpost.com/news/wonk/wp/2016/04/26/a-majority-of-millennials-now-reject-capitalism-poll-shows/.
22   Ehrenfreund, "Majority of Millennials."
23   John Wagner and Scott Clement, "'It's Just Messed Up': Most Think Political Divisions as Bad as Vietnam Era, New Poll Shows," *Washington Post*, October 29, 2017, www.washingtonpost.com/graphics/2017/national/democracy-poll/.

hegemonic narratives. This central core of racist, homophobic, and xenophobic[24] perspectives dominates, guessing roughly from the various polls cited, among anywhere from a quarter to more than a third of the adult population. True adherents are more rural, older, white, and male, but any notion that they are therefore isolated in the American political landscape was dispelled with Trump's election and the consolidation of Republican majorities in both houses, brought about by, in different measures, gerrymandering, the natural biases of the electoral system to rural areas and less-populous states, as well as the deeply undemocratic peculiarity of the Electoral College. Opposed to this, there is a growing counter-hegemonic insurgency, which already constitutes a clear majority of the population. What is most striking—despite the schisms, fractures, degrees of commitment, and tentativeness among many sectors of this majority—is the evident and quite dramatic growth of racial, sexual, and religious tolerance, which is amplified even further when broken down into age groups to show the swing and consolidating numbers in favor of openness, diversity, and inclusion among younger cohorts. There is finally, as a corollary of this, no consolidated social bloc or consensual understanding among the dominant elements of American society on the way forward for either the short- or medium-term futures.

Equally striking is the deep disillusionment with capitalism, perhaps the inevitable result of the 2008 recession, and, accompanying this, the growing attractiveness of alternatives, though we should be careful as to what is meant when people declare in favor of socialism in the polls. While, therefore, this is a period of what we can consider as the early phases of hegemonic dissolution, or a particular moment in which a clear majority—perhaps among the young an overwhelming majority—is open to a radically different image of American society and faced with a sclerotic economic system is questioning capitalism itself, they are confronted with a regime elected and supported by a minority of the voting population that is anti-immigrant; is willing to impose Jim Crow–like measures to deprive voting rights and gerrymander electoral seats; is climate-, science-, and truth-denying; is homophobic in both rhetoric and policy measures; and is willing to dismantle anything reeking of collective social responsibility, most notably the relatively conservative Obamacare health system.

---

24   See, for instance, Adam Serwer, "The Nationalist's Delusion," *The Atlantic*, November 20, 2017, www.theatlantic.com/politics/archive/2017/11/the-nationalists-delusion/546356/.

Does the Trumpian moment therefore herald the arrival of a new, virile insurgency in the way in which Thatcherism (while significantly different in social context, strategy, and tactics), building on popular notions of individual freedom and wielding them to crush and sideline trade unions and a collectivist agenda, managed to negate and supersede state-led Keynesianism in the 1980s? While there were certainly gestures from both Trump's campaign and the first year of governing that suggest there was a recognition that perhaps new people needed to be won to the project, the evidence as a whole leans away from this being the primary objective.[25] Thus, the campaign statements on a more national industrial policy and a revamping of national infrastructure, while fraught with huge fiscal and logistic roadblocks, suggested at least an impulse to win broader constituencies through employment and economic growth, if on a course of development built on narrow notions of nationalism, American greatness, and exceptionalism.

What, however, seems to be the dominant trend since the January 2017 inauguration is a far darker three-pronged strategy predicated, first, not on winning over new converts by skillfully undermining the intellectual foundations of the opposition, but rather on a determined attempt at consolidating base support among the entrenched minority of the mainly white voting population that is wedded to Trumpism.[26] This is, I think, self-evident through his appeals to the worst racist and chauvinist tropes, even when the regime could have avoided alienating everybody else, as in Trump's favorable, coddling response to the Charlottesville Alt-Right, neo-Nazi rally.[27] The second is to continue using the power of the executive and existent Republican majorities at the state level to rig the electoral system through a combination of gerrymandering and

---

25 See, for instance, Henry Olsen, "Whatever Happened to Trump's Populist Agenda?" *New York Times*, November 20, 2017, www.nytimes.com/2017/11/20/opinion/trump-populism-republicans.html.

26 Shamus Khan defines this, I think accurately, as an "Unholy Alliance" between elite interests and white nationalist sentiments, between billionaires and the "left behind" white working-class population. It requires, he suggests, a countermovement that can forge egalitarian, class-based messages that breach the racial appeal of Trump and the Alt-Right. See Shamus Khan, "The Big Picture: Unholy Alliances," *Public Books*, November 3, 2017, www.publicbooks.org/the-big-picture-unholy-alliances/.

27 See, for instance, Michael D. Shear and Maggie Haberman, "Trump Defends Initial Remarks on Charlottesville: Again Blames 'Both Sides,'" *New York Times*, August 15, 2017, www.nytimes.com/2017/08/15/us/politics/trump-press-conference-charlottesville.html.

voter restriction, in order to ensure unassailable Republican majorities at both the state level and the national/presidential level, via the Electoral College.[28] Third, and perhaps the most effective measure for the mid to long term, is the policy of stacking the judicial system with a raft of right-wing judges at all levels to assure the passage of supportive legislation and forestall any Democratic reversals of the system in the near future.[29] This is a very different and far more insidious option than, in another era, the Thatcherite approach of populist authoritarianism,[30] because it assumes that genuine populism is out of reach, that the majority is already lost to all reason. Its path to dominance, therefore, is underwritten by sleight of hand and ruse—in boldest terms, it is the framework for a soft, judicial coup.

The critical factor here is that older, dominant hegemonic constructs are compromised. Clinton and Obama liberalism—while it shouldn't be forgotten that Hillary Clinton clearly won the popular national vote—is seen by many as wedded to Wall Street and ultimately to the frayed and largely discredited neoliberal Washington Consensus. It still has not been able to provide a credible explanation for the 2008 crisis that captures the predatory policies of the banks and financial institutions, leading to the housing market bubble that brought the cards tumbling down. Its complicity is perhaps most evident in the failure of the Obama administration to convict any of the leading players. The counter-recessionary strategy of 2009–2011 worked to forestall collapse but was never followed by a long-term state-led strategy of economic restructuring, employment generation, and environmentally sustainable policies that might have captured the popular imagination and short-stopped the rise of Trump. The alternative and contending narrative on the Left, evident in the Bernie Sanders candidacy and the upsurge of popular support in his favor, alongside popular protest movements such as Black Lives Matter

28   Drew Desilver, "Trump's Victory Another Example of How Electoral College Wins Are Bigger Than Popular Vote Ones," *Pew Research Center*, December 20, 2016, http://www.pewresearch.org/fact-tank/2016/12/20/why-electoral-college-landslides-are-easier-to-win-than-popular-vote-ones/.
29   See Jeffrey Toobin, "Trump's Real Personnel Victory: More Conservative Judges," *New Yorker*, August 2, 2017, www.newyorker.com/news/daily-comment/trumps-real-personnel-victory-more-conservative-judges.
30   See, for comparison, Kenneth Surin, "Authoritarian Populism: Viewing Trump, Reviewing Thatcher," *Counterpunch*, February 7, 2017, www.counterpunch.org/2017/02/07/authoritarian-populism-viewing-trump-reviewing-thatcher/.

and the movement against the Dakota Access Pipeline, remains relatively vibrant and attracts significant attention through both traditional and social media, but hasn't yet gelled into a viable and believable framework.

Take, for instance, the reemergence of socialism as an increasingly popular vision, as reflected in some of the polls mentioned above. The disastrous collapse of "really existing socialism" in the 1990s, and the detritus of racist and xenophobic ideas, movements, and states that have been left in its wake, should by any estimate have led to the death of socialism as a viable notion of liberation for a generation or more. Yet, despite all of this and against the overwhelming odds, socialism has reemerged as an idea with significant support. But what is it really? Does it have power that, say, Thatcherite neoliberalism possessed in the early phases of its brief but influential life? My assessment would be that it doesn't, at least not yet,[31] and this is due in part to the shabby legacy of "really existing socialism" but also to the fact that there has been a failure to elaborate a convincing set of rigorously argued ideas that might then be popularized into commonsensical notions of its rightness—a twenty-first-century socialist vision—that would rival, for instance, the 1980s commonsense certitudes of TINA, that there is no alternative to market-led capitalism.

Socialism has at least six hurdles to cross before it might begin to approach that moment. The first would have to be to work toward an approach that shatters the assumption—rooted in twentieth-century history—that social solidarity is inevitably wedded to state domination over the individual. The second would be to elaborate a theory of social freedom that extends beyond the liberal assertion of minimal negative freedom but yet incorporates it as an essential part of its platform.[32] The third would be to abandon the notion that markets are welded to capitalism and to begin to imagine the possibility of functioning markets beyond the boundaries of capitalism. For if there is any notion that history has discarded, it is that a centralized command state can assume control of an entire economy without doing severe damage to

31 Though in recent decades there have been important contributors to such a conversation. See, especially, Alec Nove, *The Economics of Feasible Socialism*, Unwin Hyman, London, 1983; Michael Albert, *Parecon: Life after Capitalism; Participatory Economics*, Verso, London, 2003; and Eric Olin Wright, *Envisioning Real Utopias*, Verso, London, 2010.

32 See Axel Honneth, *The Idea of Socialism: Towards a Renewal*, Polity Press, Cambridge, 2017.

both people's economic lives and any expansive notion of freedom.[33] The fourth would be to continue and develop the critical debates surrounding the limits to economic growth and to think through its policy implications for consumption, energy, and, more broadly speaking, the purposes of living. The fifth would have to be a new internationalism, conscious of the inevitability of migration in an increasingly mobile world and willing to recognize the historical responsibility in the Global North for social, economic, and political crises in the Global South that in both the long and short frames are the catalysts for mass movement. The sixth would be that socialist theorists must recognize that white racism is not a secondary phenomenon of capitalism but is deeply embedded in its history and contemporary structure, and that any strategy of economic socialism that does not at the same time exorcise in its policy and praxis institutional racism will end up falling short and probably losing the support of Black people and other people of color, even before it is able to attain national prominence.[34] All of these conversations need to be moved out of the stifling, often arcane halls of academia and brought into the popular domain, where they can be subjected to critique, modified, discarded in some instances, and re-presented as new articulations of common sense—a vibrant, new, hegemonic project, for a moment of social transformation.

Trumpian racism, chauvinism, and revanchism is institutionally in charge, but has no program nor interest in winning over a working majority of the population. The liberal center, while equivocating at best on the distinct struggles of important movements in the majority coalition, has very little that is new to offer as a broad platform for addressing imminent economic disruption and its social implications. Radical alternatives from the Left, meanwhile, remain fragmented, are often at the margins of debate, and have yet to devise a concerted strategy for the near future.

Gramsci describes this moment, in which old hegemonies are on the retreat and new ones are still in infancy and there is at the same time no

---

33   Janos Kornai, *The Socialist System: The Political Economy of Communism*, Princeton University Press, Princeton, NJ, 1992.
34   I have elsewhere used the notion of "social living" to refer generally to a hybrid approach that moves beyond the economic parameters of twentieth-century socialism, exorcises Eurocentrism, and incorporates popular social thinking and praxis in its framework, while retaining the central concern for community and the social. See Brian Meeks, *Envisioning Caribbean Futures*.

consolidated (if always temporary) hegemonic narrative (what we refer to here as hegemonic dissolution), as a dangerous one:

> At a certain point in their historical life, social groups detach themselves from their traditional parties in that given organizational form, when the men who constitute, represent and lead them, are no longer recognized as the proper representation of their class or fraction of a class. When these crises occur the immediate situation becomes delicate and dangerous, since the field is open to solutions of force, to the activity of obscure powers represented by "men of destiny" or "divine men."[35]

Sadly, there are precedents for times like this in relatively recent world history. Thus, it might be useful to refer to Hannah Arendt at length, who in *The Origins of Totalitarianism* reflects on the critical importance of a battle for ideas in winning the public away from potential totalitarian leaders:

> Under conditions of constitutional government and freedom of opinion, totalitarian movements struggling for power can use terror to a limited extent only and share with other parties the necessity of winning adherents and of appearing plausible to a public which is as yet not rigorously isolated from all other sources of opinion. Only the Mob and the elite can be attracted by the moment of Totalitarianism itself. The masses have to be won by Propaganda.[36]

It is the methods of totalitarians-in-waiting, however, that is cause for closer scrutiny. Thus, Arendt points to their propensity for the "re-writing of history,"[37] the need to give the "appearance of infallibility (never admitting to wrongdoings),"[38] the fact that their propaganda is "marked by its extreme contempt for facts as such,"[39] and, poignantly, in light of prior discussion in this chapter, that "totalitarian propaganda can

35   Antonio Gramsci, *The Modern Prince and Other Writings*, International, New York, 1970, 124.
36   Hannah Arendt, *The Origins of Totalitarianism*, Harcourt, Brace, Jovanovich, New York, 1976, 341.
37   Arendt, *Origins*, 341.
38   *Origins*, 348.
39   *Origins*, 350.

outrageously insult common sense only where common sense has lost its validity."[40] Or, even more ominously, her warning of

> the possibility that gigantic lies and monstrous falsehoods can eventually be established as unquestioned facts, that man may be free to change his own past at will, and that the difference between truth and falsehood may cease to be objective and become a mere matter of power and cleverness, of pressure and infinite repetition.[41]

Totalitarianism arises, she suggests, not in a moment of the dominance of the intellectual notions of the potential totalitarian party, but at the juncture of a battle for ideas, in which the deeply untrue arguments are at first dismissed as bombastic and laughable, yet unwaveringly persist to be amplified, steadfast in the face of facts, until a crisis allows for power to be consolidated, at which point they are asserted by force as the only, unassailable truth.

The alarming reality today is that a regime reflecting many of these traits in its daily praxis is already in charge of the executive power of the most powerful country in the world, with its soft power through policy and diplomatic channels and unrivaled array of weapons of mass destruction that could lead to the end of life as we know it. The failure of the liberal and Left majority of the American people to elaborate and consolidate a vibrant new set of ideas—redefining the possibilities for social change that would address the sharp and growing inequalities of financial capitalism, the seemingly irresolvable likelihood of systemic unemployment in a robotic/cybernetic future, and the demands for popular inclusion from a multiracial, multiethnic society—leaves the field open for the domination of dangerous men with messianic messages. The time for a new conversation and the patient building of persuasive discourses around a new social living is now, and is urgently necessary.

---

40   *Origins*, 352.
41   *Origins*, 333.

8

Roadblock on Hope Road:
The End of Imagination and
Capital's Late Afternoon

The title of this chapter is admittedly somewhat enigmatic. I will, however, leave you with the enigma for the time being, in the hope that it will be self-evident at the end. I want to begin by locating and appreciating the significance of Walter Rodney, of 1968, and of my generation. I like to think of my "generation" as a distinct subset of those who were students at the University of the West Indies in October 1968, with many of them thus being active participants in the street phase of the one-day rebellion, supported by those of us who were still in high school and therefore only enthusiastic watchers. The knowledge that those who were on the streets and facing tear gas and police batons included our immediate seniors had a profound effect. The violent response to the peaceful protest, closely linked with the original act of injustice in banning Rodney from returning home to his young family and the subsequent vilification of the student participants by the Jamaican government, sparked a flame of indignation directed against injustice and calumny that, certainly for me and many others who witnessed those events, has lasted a lifetime. In this sense, I like to think of October 16, 1968, as the beginning of what I and Geri Augusto, who teaches with me a course at Brown University called "Global Black Radicalism,"[1] refer to as "the Long Seventies"—the period from Rodney's 1968 banning, via Trinidad's Black Power Revolution in 1970, to Jamaica's era of popular upsurge and cultural revolution, between the 1972 election and the bloody defeat of 1980 and ending with the rise and tragic fall of the Grenada Revolution, from 1979 to 1983.

This peculiar Caribbean narrative was, of course, only part of a broader, global one, that included the Tet Offensive in Vietnam that led

---

1 For a brief description of the course "Global Black Radicalism," see https://www.brown.edu/academics/africana-studies/COURSES/detail?term= 201610&crn=16566.

almost immediately to the burgeoning of the peace movement in the United States; the Prague Spring that attempted to define a different, more democratic mode of socialism in Czechoslovakia; the "May '68" strikes and demonstrations in France, which threatened the existence of the French state, initiated new freedom movements, and questioned old bureaucracies; the radicalization of the US civil rights movement and the turn to Black Power, particularly after the assassination of Dr. Martin Luther King Jr.; the Mexico student protests that preceded the 1968 Olympics and the brazen massacre of hundreds by the Mexican state; the symbolic Black Power salute by the US athletes Tommy Smith and John Carlos in the Olympic stadium in Mexico on the medal podium of the 200-meter event; anti-dictatorial uprisings in Greece, Brazil, and elsewhere; the birth of the South African Students Organization under Steve Biko's leadership, signaling the rise of the Black consciousness phase of the anti-apartheid struggle; and much more.[2]

The uprisings of 1968 did not "succeed"; indeed, captured poignantly in the election of Richard Nixon to office at the end of a year of unprecedented protests in the United States, it could be argued that 1968, if conceived as a global movement against capital, hierarchical domination, and bureaucracy, lost decisively. But if we think through the lens of the longue durée, then 1968 stamped indelibly on global thought new boundaries for freedom, new visions of democracy, new philosophical perspectives on the meaning of life and what it means to be human, that persist, have grown, and continue to flourish and expand today.

What inspired us? We young Jamaicans were no doubt influenced in that moment by what was happening globally, but there was enough injustice in our own little island to gestate a movement. The disappointments of independence, in which hopes for a vastly better economic future were soon dashed; persistent and glaring poverty; huge and burgeoning disparities of wealth; a general alienation from conventional two-party politics, which seemed to have run its course as an avenue for social improvement; and, last but not least, the persistent urgency of the aesthetic question—the cruel irony of the denigration of blackness in an

---

2 Through 2018, the Department of Africana Studies/Rites and Reason Theatre, Brown University, sought to remember, commemorate and critically engage with the year 1968 and its legacies through a series of cultural interventions, a play, a dedicated undergraduate course and a symposium, among other events. See the archive at https://www.brown.edu/academics/africana-studies/events-programs/events-archive.

overwhelmingly Black country—all provided grist for the radicalization of the young, along with many others. Much of this energy of audacious resistance was captured symbolically in the Rastafari movement, which encapsulated many of these sentiments in its strident opposition to "Babylon" while retaining fealty and cultural credibility to the Jamaican and African diasporic sensibility for the spiritual. But all of this is prelude. I would like to think of this chapter as, if not a "grounding" as in Rodney's formulation, then, hopefully a collective "reasoning" in the Rastafari tradition.

Rodney's most trenchant and lasting contribution to a rethinking of the praxis for the Caribbean scholar/intellectual was his ability to combine critical theory together with activism. The activity of "grounding," or meeting regularly with people in their communities, on the ground,[3] was his clear approach and method of raising awareness, and that meant, in the short time he was in Jamaica, leaving the safety and confines of the Mona campus and reaching out to groups all over the island.[4] This "dangerous" practice immediately revealed, if nothing else, the distance that had been very self-consciously cultivated between town and gown, in the way in which the University of the West Indies had been safely sequestered from the city, in anticipation of a cross-fertilization of radical ideas between students and "the masses." This, by the way, was the very opposite of the approach to higher education that was initially proposed for the University of Guyana, in which the founders envisioned an institution intimately involved in the life of the working people. That, however, is a story for another time.

The other outstanding feature of his career, and the one that we will spend some time unpacking, is that Walter Rodney considered himself a Marxist. I should probably amend that somewhat by saying that for Rodney, Marxism provided a credible historical explanation of exploitation and a useful time sequence that recognized that capitalism was transient, only a moment in global history that would pass, and Marx's schema

---

3   See, for his own explanation, Walter Rodney, *The Groundings with My Brothers*, Bogle L'Ouverture, London, 1969.
4   See Rupert Lewis, *Walter Rodney's Intellectual and Political Thought*, The University of the West Indies Press, Kingston, 1998; Fragano Ledgister, "'Intellectual Murder': Walter Rodney's Groundings in the Jamaican Context," *Commonwealth and Comparative Politics* 46, no. 1 (2008): 79–100; Horace Campbell, *Rasta and Resistance: From Marcus Garvey to Walter Rodney*, Africa World Press, Trenton, NJ, 1987; and Jerome Teelucksingh, *Ideology, Politics and Radicalism of the Afro-Caribbean*, Palgrave Macmillan, New York, 2016.

was a useful methodological frame to help explain this sordid history.[5] More so, and this is often overlooked, Marx recognized the importance of the cruel exploitation of peoples from the African continent in the crucial, particularly violent phase of "primitive accumulation," without which there could be no "modern" capitalism, as captured famously in his morbidly lyrical portent: "The turning of Africa into a warren for the commercial hunting of black skins, signaled the rosy dawn of the era of capitalist production."[6] However, beyond the acknowledgment of this original brutality, there is very limited exploration of the place and role of Africans and of Black people in the West, beyond the recognition of their objectification and subordination in bringing the system up to full speed.

It was left to a generation of Black thinkers, among them the Trinidadians C.L.R. James and Eric Williams, both progenitors of the contemporary Black radical tradition, to attempt to shift the focus and make Black people the central subjects of their own history. James in *The Black Jacobins*[7] sought to shift the story of African captives in the West from that of mere factors of production to revolutionary subjects of their own glorious history, defeating in St. Domingue the formidable military might of Napoleon, the Spanish, and the British, and claiming freedom. Williams in *Capitalism and Slavery*[8] attempted to shift the geography of reason, by proposing that Emancipation was not, as British scholars often portrayed, an act of altruism in which the slave owners suddenly saw the light; it resulted out of both a necessary step in the changing structural requirements of capital as well as a defensive response that was urgently precipitated by the militant resistance of the captives.

Walter Rodney took this line of thinking one logical step further by returning to the continent to suggest how contemporary Africa was in a dire state of underdevelopment precisely because of a history of slavery and colonialism. Rodney's conclusions followed and advanced a tradition

---

5   Rodney's careful reading of the Russian revolution provides insights into his critical interpretation of Marxism and his Pan-Africanist core. See Robin D. G. Kelley and Jesse Benjamin (eds.) *Walter Rodney, the Russian Revolution: A View from the Third World*, Verso, London, 2018.
6   This oft-quoted sentence is from Karl Marx, *Capital*, vol. 1: *The Process of Production of Capital*, Ch. 31: "Genesis of the Industrial Capitalist," https://www.marxists.org/archive/marx/works/1867-c1/ch31.htm.
7   C.L.R. James, *The Black Jacobins: Toussaint L'Ouverture and the San Domingo Revolution*, Secker and Warburg, London, 1938.
8   Eric Williams, *Capitalism and Slavery*, University of North Carolina Press, Chapel Hill, 1994.

developed by Aimé Césaire, C.L.R. James, George Padmore, Claude McKay, Claudia Jones, Oliver Cox, and many others who sought to use Marx's underlying methodology and assumptions and apply them to the service of the people of the African diaspora. I am not suggesting that Rodney or any of these other interlocutors did not have flaws and gaps in their analysis. Angela Davis, in a recent review of the new Verso edition of Rodney's *How Europe Underdeveloped Africa*, points to the insufficient attention placed on questions of gender and how with a gendered lens we can better understand how capitalist exploitation operates through multiple avenues of engagement. However, to be fair to Rodney, Davis notes that he, more than others of that period, refers repeatedly to the specific exploitation of African women; and to appreciate its context, it was written shortly before the flowering of the contemporary feminist movement and could not therefore benefit from its novel and profound insights.[9] There is also, with the focus on the political economy dimensions of African incorporation, far less attention placed on the hugely and equally critical psychological sphere of Atlantic slavery, and the emergence of anti-blackness as an insidiously durable vehicle for mental slavery and incapacitation.

Thus, to return to our thread, while Marx's *Capital* goes far beyond the ahistorical certitudes of neoclassical economics in his recognition that capital has a history, an arc that rises and will ultimately fall, there have always been—as invoking the names of the Black thinkers mentioned before suggests—significant lacunae in Marx. He does, as I have suggested, recognize the origins of capital in primitive accumulation, of indigenous capture and slavery, but fails to see or elaborate on what the racial embeddedness of this implies both historically and for the present moment. This leaves the room open for many "Marxists" to conclude, if we might employ a somewhat simplistic caricature, that "over here we have capitalist exploitation while, on the other hand, over there we have slavery leading to racism." Capitalism from such a mechanical approach is rooted in economic, foundational causes, while racism is merely its super-structural effect. Not enough in this simplistic characterization is made of the recognition that the two (capitalism and racism) were always wedded, indeed welded, from their very formative stages. Thus, systems of racial ordering and hierarchy-making, philosophies of anti-blackness,

---

9   See Angela Davis, "Walter Rodney's Legacy," foreword to Walter Rodney, *How Europe Underdeveloped Africa*, Verso, London, 2019.

and tropes of self-hatred are not only interconnected with capital but integral to it and cannot really escape from its orbit.[10] While, as Stuart Hall suggests in his notion that there were many racisms,[11] the rules of interpretation and organization may have been modified over time, the basic structure of a racialized order is a necessary requirement for both the super exploitation of proscribed demographic cohorts and also, importantly, the political management of rebellious majorities within the capitalist order. In other words, what Marx could not understand and was therefore unable to elaborate on[12] is that racial—and, closely connected to it, national—ordering and othering is a necessary component of the circulation of value and not a limited question or an ephemeral matter to be relegated to the super-structural (and secondary) tier of capitalist relations.[13]

This is the space we are in as we contemplate the world of the first quarter of the twenty-first century. This is what I prefer to consider as "the late afternoon of capital"—not yet at twilight but a point when the arc of the sun is definitely shifting toward the horizon.[14] And such a shift, as we know, at certain latitudes can and will lead to an earlier-than-expected setting of the sun.

Why would I want to make this claim? First, let us consider the growth of financial capital[15] and, on its sheer scale and concurrent independence,

---

10   For her classical approach to this question, which shifts the foundation away from the Marxian narrative on the material foundations of history, see Sylvia Wynter, "On How We Mistook the Map for the Territory and Re-imprisoned Ourselves in the Wrongness of Being, of Desêtre: Black Studies Towards the Human Project," in *Not Only the Master's Tools: African American Studies in Theory and Practice*, ed. Lewis R. Gordon and Jane Anna Gordon, Paradigm, Boulder, 2006, 107–69.

11   See, for instance, Stuart Hall, "New Ethnicities," in *Stuart Hall: Critical Dialogues in Cultural Studies*, ed. David Morley and Kuan-Hsing Chen, Routledge, London, 1996, 441–63.

12   I wish to give special recognition here to Cedric Robinson, particularly regarding his study *Black Marxism: The Making of the Black Radical Tradition*, University of North Carolina Press, Chapel Hill, 2000.

13   Interestingly and as an aside, my friend and colleague Anthony Bogues, as we speak, is deep in the Amsterdam archives, working on this question as to how capital came to be and its convoluted but steady and certain emergence as a racialized order. I look forward with anticipation to his findings.

14   For a useful discussion that argues that capitalism will end, see Wolfgang Streeck, *Will Capitalism End?* Verso, London, 2016.

15   For his extensive and widely discussed treatise on the changing structure of capital and its impact on inequality, see Thomas Piketty, *Capital in the Twenty-*

the growing disconnection from the concerns of ordinary people. Factory owners, we can propose, must have some minimal concern for their workers, who need to be sufficiently healthy, well fed, and motivated to appear at the factory door each morning. Financial capitalists, on the contrary, are divorced from this human connection and, certainly from the perspective of their profit-taking, are disconnected from the conditions and considerations of ordinary working people. This distancing has been further exacerbated as a result of dramatic shifts in wealth arising in part from rapid product differentiation in financial markets and the digitization of trading, which has increased the flow and efficiency of financial markets and exponentially enhanced the profit margins of financial elites. Second, I want us to think about the environmental disaster that is already upon us, with the consensus that we are already in a new archaeological era—the Anthropocene[16]—defined by humanity's insertion into the future strata of geological memory by the destructive impact on the environment of the last five centuries of racial capitalism. The recent Intergovernmental Panel for Climate Change[17] is suggesting that we are facing widespread disaster when average global temperatures exceed an increase of 1.5 degrees, which could be as early as 2030 if the misuse and abuse of planetary resources continues on its present path. The third marker I wish to underline is the gradual and now more rapid decline in available jobs due to robotization. Some estimates suggest that 38 percent of contemporary jobs will be assumed by robots in fifteen years.[18] Entire

---

First Century, Belknap Press of Harvard University Press, Cambridge, MA, 2014. Some of the salient points of Piketty's complex study are captured by Robert Solow: "slower growth of population and productivity, a rate of return on capital distinctly higher than the growth rate, the wealth-income ratio rising back to nineteenth-century heights, probably a somewhat higher capital share in national income, an increasing dominance of inherited wealth over earned wealth, and a still wider gap between the top incomes and all the others." See Robert M. Solow, "Thomas Piketty Is Right," in After Piketty: The Agenda for Economics and Inequality, ed. Heather Boushey, J. Bradford DeLong, and Marshall Steinbaum, Harvard University Press, Cambridge, MA, 2017.

16 See Jeremy Davies, The Birth of the Anthropocene, University of North Carolina Press, Chapel Hill, 2016, 58. Françoise Vergès, however, argues that predominant discussions of the Anthropocene as the fallout of humanity, writ large, obscures its lineage as the inevitable outcome of the specific history of racial capitalism. See Francoise Verges, "Racial Capitalocene," in Gaye Theresa Johnson and Alex Lubin, Futures of Black Radicalism, Verso, London, 2017, 72–82.

17 See the 2018 Intergovernmental Panel for Climate Change Report and updates at https://www.ipcc.ch/.

18 See Samantha Masumaga, "Robots Could Take Over 38% of US Jobs within about 15 Years," Los Angeles Times, March 24, 2017; and Darrell M. West, "What

industries, such as taxis and traditional store- and mall-based retail sales, are already shrinking and likely to virtually disappear, with dire implications for global employment rates. For those who assume that the jobs lost will generate new ones in the manufacture of robots, the probable answer is very few, as increasingly it will be robots that will be engaged in the manufacturing of robots, therefore permanently limiting the pool of available jobs. My fourth point, derived especially from the first and third above, is that there is steadily growing inequality.[19]

All the above are facilitated and enhanced by the consolidation over the past four decades of the neoliberal counterrevolution, which trumpeted privatization, divestment of state enterprises, austerity, the small state, and the unfettered market as the sure prescriptions to overcome the rise of militant trade unionism, the limited advances that working people had made in the post–World War II years, and the real bottlenecks that had emerged in Keynesian, state-led capitalism. Keynesian policies, ironically, had come to be portrayed as the enemy of free enterprise when, implemented before and particularly during the war, they had rescued capitalism from the global crisis of the Great Depression. Now, however, the documentation supporting the utter disaster of neoliberalism is rapidly accumulating, including, among all unexpected places, a study published recently by the International Monetary Fund. It concludes, inter alia, that among a group of thirty-one countries in a study of comparative fiscal policies, the United Kingdom (which in many respects has been ground zero for privatization and "magic of the market" policies, beginning with Margaret Thatcher but followed by subsequent Labour and Tory governments) was second to worst in terms of its performance and long-term financial prospects. The causes, the study damagingly concludes, stem from an overly financialized economy operating under the "fiscal illusion" that cutting taxes to the wealthy and privatizing public

---

Happens If Robots Take the Jobs? The Impact of Emerging Technologies on Employment and Public Policy," Center for Technology Innovation at Brookings, October 26, 2015. For a somewhat more skeptical reading of the impact of contemporary technology, see Devash Raval, "What's Wrong with Capital in the Twenty-First Century's Model," in Boushey, DeLong, and Steinbaum (eds.) *After Piketty*, 75–98.

19 See earlier reference in chapter 7. Matt Egan, "Record Inequality: The Top 1% Controls 38.6% of America's Wealth," *CNN*, September 27, 2017. For a rich discussion around Thomas Piketty's popular exploration of contemporary inequality in *Capital in the Twenty-First Century*, see Boushey, DeLong, and Steinbaum (eds.) *After Piketty*.

enterprises would lead to growth and prosperity. Instead, the results have been huge, unsustainable deficits, poorly performing and collapsing public-sector services, and the greater likelihood of economic crises in the short to midterm.[20]

I should add that none of these conclusions, suggesting that capitalism in all its historical complexity is nonetheless transitory, is necessarily novel. Karl Polanyi, for instance, in his prescient classic *The Great Transformation*,[21] certainly appreciated the tenuousness of capital as a system as he was sensitive to its fragility. Perhaps more surprising is Joseph Schumpeter, whose work *Capitalism, Socialism and Democracy*[22] and notion of capitalism's "creative destruction" is usually quoted in defense of the market. While remaining critical of Marx's prediction as to how capitalism would break down, Schumpeter concludes that eventually it would collapse. In summary, then, the shifting structure of capital toward financial capital, the seeming incapacity of contemporary manufacturing and service capacity, driven, by technological revolution, to absorb labor, and the exhaustion of the global environment as an infinite garbage dump for human waste all suggest that an existential moment for capitalism is closer than many of us imagine.

What, then, are the political effects engendered by the state of capital in this moment? Shifting focus for the moment to the United States, the exponential accumulation of financial wealth in the past three decades has profound implications for the sustenance of an open, even if from the start highly limited, democracy. Think, for a moment, of the sheer power of the Koch brothers, and other hyper-wealthy conservative individuals and groups,[23] to determine elections through legal and illegal means, elect judges, and set new restrictive parameters for voting and modifying the terms for campaign contributions. Their signature effort, the Citizens United[24] legislation, perpetuates the use of dark money in campaigns

20 See the International Monetary Fund, *Fiscal Monitor: Managing Public Wealth*, International Monetary Fund, Washington, DC, October 2018.
21 Karl Polanyi, *The Great Transformation: The Political and Economic Origins of Our Time*, Beacon Press, Boston, 1944.
22 Joseph Schumpeter, *Capitalism, Socialism and Democracy*, Harper and Brothers, New York, 1947.
23 Whose vastly increased power is a direct product of the financialization of the global economy with all its implications for burgeoning inequality alongside unimaginable wealth.
24 See, for instance, Matt Bai, "How Much Has Citizens United Changed the Political Game?" *New York Times*, July 17, 2012.

for the further consolidation of the conservative agenda through voter suppression, gerrymandering, and various permutations of legal and illegal persuasion. Think also of the implications of the breakdown of the US-led global consensus of the recent past that centered on a common Western consensus on globalization and WTO rules, undergirded by the Washington Consensus of balanced budgets, austerity, privatization, free trade, and its retinue. Emerging in the wake of their failures are dangerous offspring: Trumpism, Brexit, narrow nationalist policies, draconian and increasingly inhuman blockades against immigration, unsustainable militarist budget deficits, and, lurking not too far in the shadows, a new authoritarianism with fascist tinges.

Closely connected to these is the decline of the American state due to sharpening differences around basic consensual questions, evident in a variety of battles, crisscrossing cultural, legislative, and judicial spheres, both before and continuing with a vengeance after Trump's election. The global rise of the authoritarian Right, now ensconced in office in Russia, Poland, Italy, Austria, the Philippines, Turkey, Egypt, and now Brazil, to name some of the most heralded instances, is evidence that these developments are not peculiarly American or British. This moment can be understood as both a response to the perceived damages to national interests from globalization and a fearful reaction to the proliferation of popular democratic initiatives, among them, the Black Lives Matter and #MeToo movements, and myriad global counterparts, which represent the tangible evidence of popular resistance to global disaster.

This particular inflection point is, however, frightening, because, while the Far Right possesses a certain international momentum and is consolidating power in critical nodal points, the popular forces are disorganized and without a common agenda, much less a program. Such a program, were it to emerge, might form the basis of a coalition of the liberal center with the multiple contingents of a new Left, for positional struggles around questions of peace, democracy, and social, racial, and gender equality for positional battles for survival in the short to medium term.

I turn now to the Caribbean, where my first comment is that after decades of looking for and identifying "successful" models, there are no longer any clear and evident narratives of success. Barbados, the remaining British colonies, Puerto Rico, Trinidad and Tobago, Martinique, and Guadeloupe, have all appeared from time to time as potential models for the rest of the region to emulate. What is new is that they have all lost their luster and preferred status. The case of Barbados is instructive.

Careful fiscal policies, combined with a significant social redistribution of wealth, primarily through the avenues of education and health, led to three critical decades in which both production levels and standards of living improved, outpacing, on all indicators, most of her neighbors. This was facilitated by a social pact in which the wealthy, in exchange for limited interference in their social and economic status, agreed implicitly and explicitly to invest a significant part of their resources at home. But Barbados always remained close to the margins and demanded a buoyant world economy that would keep tourism, light manufacturing, services, and other sectors afloat. Once the world economy went into decline in 2007–2008, tourism rapidly declined and the already stressed economy, which had cut corners by failing to invest in depreciating tourism capital, went into freefall. This was exacerbated by a policy of the selling of scarce beachside land to rich foreigners, severely increasing the average cost for the purchase and rental of all housing stock, which added to the general cost of living and significantly impacted the deteriorating economic situation of the poor and middle classes.[25]

Jamaica, despite modest ups and downs, has remained in stagnation and crisis for four decades. The government in the 1970s took baby steps in attempting some actual, if modest, redistributive measures.[26] The most substantial gains were made in improving access to education, addressing long-postponed matters of basic human welfare, and (not to be underestimated) combating, through policy and rhetoric, the psychic welfare of its historically battered people, as well as real efforts to institute genuine citizenship—a prerequisite, I suggest, for any successful national project.[27] However, the Manley regime faced implacable hostility from local interests who saw their historical advantages and privileges threatened. When, however, the dominant hegemon entered the fray, particularly after the regime's principled support for Cuban intervention to help save Angola from South African invasion,[28] violence grew, and

25   For a partial discussion of Barbados' recent economic path, see Thomas Dowling, Nkunde Mwase, and Judith Gold, "Barbados: Selected Issues," International Monetary Fund, accessed September 20, 2018, https://www.imf.org/external/pubs/ft/scr/2016/cr16280.pdf.

26   See Evelyn Huber Stephens and John D. Stephens, *Democratic Socialism in Jamaica: The Political Movement and Social Transformation in Dependent Capitalism*, Princeton University Press, Princeton, NJ, 1986.

27   See Rachel Mordecai, *Citizenship under Pressure: The 1970s in Jamaican Literature and Culture*, The University of the West Indies Press, Kingston, 2014.

28   See Michael Manley, *Jamaica: Struggle in the Periphery*, Writers and Readers, London, 1982.

middle-class support was lost, as the country appeared increasingly to be ungovernable. This was worsened by the economic contractions that accompanied both the crisis of the global economy, following the 1973 oil crisis, and the obvious attempt, to quote Richard Nixon in reference to the Allende regime in Chile, to "make the economy scream."[29] The subsequent IMF agreement to purportedly return fiscal balance to the economy exacerbated the political pressure on the government and initiated policies that, some forty years later, are being questioned from the bottom up by the officers of the very IMF.

In thinking about the Caribbean region with more long-distance lenses, it is clearer to me now that first there are systemic, inevitable problems faced by small states that need to be identified and understood. However, accompanying these, there are very conscious actions taken by hegemonic powers to consolidate power, secure narrow economic advantage, and maintain their hegemony.

Socioeconomic crises of huge proportions, like those faced by Allende in Chile in 1973, Manley in Jamaica particularly between 1976 and 1980, and Maduro in Venezuela today, need to be seen through these multiple lenses and not reduced to a crude and narrow reading of the inevitable failure of populist, Marxist, or socialist policies and approaches. I add the necessary caveat and rider that, at least in part,[30] all these regimes have in different ways engaged in policies that often included serious

29   See Peter Kornbluh, "Chile and the United States: Declassified Documents Related to the Military Coup, September 11, 1973," accessed June 5, 2017, https://nsarchive2.gwu.edu/NSAEBB/NSAEBB8/nsaebb8i.htm.
30   Orlando Patterson suggests an alternative approach to understanding Jamaica's trajectory that contrasts her postcolonial economic failures with Barbados' relative economic successes across a range of human development indices. Patterson's central argument suggests that Barbados' better performance is to be located in the presence of state builders who "captured and mastered" the administrative and governmental structures and cultures of the British, allowing that country to better withstand the vicissitudes of postcolonial economic storms. There is much to this argument that demands closer scrutiny and attention, but it falls short in that it elides both the scale of social upheaval in post-independence Jamaica that demanded a radical program and the magnitude of the subsequent imperial opposition to Manley's Democratic Socialism that crushed the momentum for social change for at least a generation. There is no sense of either the historical movement of capitalism or the Caribbean's place in it, particularly at this moment of evident crisis. See Orlando Patterson, "Why Has Jamaica Trailed Barbados on the Path to Sustained Growth?" in *The Confounding Island: Jamaica and the Postcolonial Predicament*, The Belknap Press of Harvard University Press, Cambridge, MA, 2019, 21–119.

errors of judgment and instances of unforgivable naiveté that ultimately contributed to their loss of support. We need, therefore, to understand from a very sober and critical perspective the internal philosophical and political reasons why the leadership of these popular, nationalist regimes failed to forge durable consensuses that were able to transcend their base and forge working, national majorities around programs of democracy, economic improvement, and justice. I think it is important to begin a conversation that recognizes not only the continuing brutal, predatory reality of imperial hegemony and how it works to strangle progressive movements, but also the way it concentrates on the only too real strategic missteps of regimes that have sought to "storm heaven" and break the cycle of dependency and persistent poverty.

In summary, the Caribbean territories are like flotsam and jetsam on the riptide of a capitalist system in existential crisis. Let me allude to what might be another useful metaphor. Imagine leaky lifeboats slung over the side of a sinking mother ship and faced with an inexorable and violent sea. What are the resources that we, survivors in these tenuous lifeboats, possess to prevent ourselves from being overwhelmed by the tempestuous ocean? The most important, of course, concern the character and vitality of the people on board—our survivors. If the people are healthy and able to row, we have a better chance. If they find the wherewithal to overcome bickering and differences, they have the greater possibility of pulling together and their chances improve. If those who survive on the individual boats possess specific skills—the technology as to how to patch potential leaks and repair broken oars or damaged motors—then these skills will assist the process, and chances of survival will be further enhanced. If the boats stay together and coordinate navigation, share limited resources, and take on board the survivors of those boats that are fatally damaged, then, again, chances of survival are increased. The overarching reality, however, is that the cards are pretty much stacked against any of these leaky lifeboats surviving to shore. Some will sink immediately. Others, mired in the water, unable to go forward or backward, may survive for a little longer. But very few will find that combination of fortuitous luck, unity of purpose, and technological savvy to stay afloat, row together against the perilous surf, and make it to shore.

Let us now return to the wider, global picture. Where have there been "success" stories? I use quotation marks to remind us that growth, the inevitable marker for success, needs a long and thorough overhaul. What is successful growth? A hotel on every available meter of coastline?[31] Dense, low-wage factories belching pollutants? When—particularly for small islands with very limited space, bleached white coral reefs, and overfished waters—is enough *enough*? What are the implications in all of this for a new and radical conversation around the hidden but important counterfactual question of "degrowth"?[32]

However, if we are to consider success in the traditional sense of growth and improved living standards, then these have almost invariably occurred where specific political exigencies forced states to compromise away from predominantly market-led approaches and to initiate substantial state intervention and social reform. These occurred due to sharp internal popular resistance or the perception and reality of external threat. Thus, to use a European instance, the Scandinavian countries were able to implement social democratic regimes where internal battles between labor and capital forced capitalists to make historic compromises and reforms with labor in order to survive and in fear of the likelihood of Sovietization.[33] In the case of the Four Asian Tigers, especially South Korea, Taiwan, and Singapore, the primary threats were perceived as coming from Communist North Korea and China. States and local capital, in these contexts, were compelled to forge alliances with popular sectors and initiated extensive land reforms, established socialized systems of health, education, and welfare, in exchange for the loyalty of citizens and in opposition to the "communist menace."[34] This shifting of

31 See Polly Patulo, *Last Resorts: The Cost of Tourism in the Caribbean*, Monthly Review Press, London, 2005.
32 See, for instance, Genevieve Azam, "What Is DeGrowth?" accessed October 10, 2018, https://systemicalternatives.org/2014/11/26/what-is-degrowth/; and Anitra Nelson and Vincent Liegey, *Exploring Degrowth: A Critical Guide*, Pluto Press, London, 2020.
33 See Gosta Esping-Andersen, *Politics against Markets: The Social Democratic Road to Power*, Princeton University Press, Princeton, NJ, 2017; Bo Rothstein, *The Social Democratic State: The Swedish Model and the Bureaucratic Problem of Social Reforms*, University of Pittsburgh Press, Pittsburgh, 1996; Rune Moller Stahl and Andreas Moller Mulvad, interview with Pelle Dragsted, "Socialism Isn't Just About State Ownership—It's About Redistributing Power," *Jacobin Magazine*, October 2021, https://jacobinmag.com/2021/10/socialism-state-ownership-redistribution-power-cooperatives-neoliberalism-social-democracy; and Goran Therborn, "The Working Class and the Welfare State: A Historical-Analytical Overview and a Little Swedish Monograph," *Papers on Labour History*, Finnish Society for Labour History, Helsinki, 2002, 1–75.
34 See Roger Goodwin, Gordon White, and Huck-ju Kwon, *The East Asian Welfare Model: Welfare Orientalism and the State*, Routledge, London, 1998; and

basic resources for survival away from the responsibility of individuals to the state unleashed unprecedented savings that could then be utilized for the development of a variety of infrastructural and productive enterprises. This also, arguably, though with a somewhat different sequence of events, might help explain China's rapid economic expansion. Simply put, the presence of a welfare system, however much under stress, meant that lower wages could be paid as opposed to those in an economy where welfare is limited and individualized.[35] The resultant freeing of scarce resources in both East Asian and Chinese instances led to unprecedented growth and infrastructural development, but on the foundation of reforms that would make those implemented under Manley's Democratic Socialism look quite moderate.

Generally, however, and on the contrary, where market reform, privatization, and austerity were pursued in an ideological manner, notably in Jamaica, and clearly in a different scale and modality in the United Kingdom, there have been decades of stagnation and limited real economic development. In brief conclusion, the more egalitarian the society and economy, with the state playing a leading role, the more cohesive the national polity, the greater the social development of health, education, and welfare, then, to revert to our analogy, the greater the possibility of the lifeboat not sinking, its denizens rowing together, and, ultimately, making some headway against the turbulent ocean.

However, even the most well-patched, well-managed, and secure lifeboats face the inexorable currents of the tempest. There is no long-term future for capital as we have known it. The carbon-carrying capacity of the world is reaching its limit. The ability to employ people and give them reasonable work is diminishing. Sheer inequality is astounding and creating a class of persons flush on financial wealth who have no connection to ordinary people's concerns and who increasingly use their resources to corrupt political systems in order to sustain the smooth accumulation of even more wealth. This situation cannot continue indefinitely. Faced with a crisis not just of production but of resources and of consumption, arising from an abundance of wealth but the inability to

Tang Kwong-leung, "Asian Crisis, Social Welfare and Policy Responses: Hong Kong and Korea Compared," *International Journal of Sociology and Social Policy* 20, nos. 5/6 (2000): 49–71.

35   See Yongxin Zhou, Nelson Chow, and Yeubin Xu, *Socialist Welfare in a Market Economy: Social Security Reforms in Guangzhou, China*, Routledge, London, 2001.

conceive the possibility of sharing that wealth and its associated resources with the people of the planet, a moment of reckoning is likely.

From a Caribbean perspective, I can only conclude that we have not been in any concerted way thinking about these matters. We have fixed our vision on the short term. Our concerns and conversations surround the next budget, the rate of the dollar, what will happen next year, how to win the next election. We have located ourselves in a world where markets are eternal, US hegemony is eternal, and the Washington Consensus is eternal. Our captivity within a certain mindset even determines the questions that can be asked and those that are outside the pale of common sense. So, for instance, a simple question that in the past might have been asked when discussing the national budget might have been, "Who do we pay first, when in crisis: the bankers, the money lenders, or the salaried employees who will face eviction without pay, or the poor who will starve without the next welfare payment?" Four decades ago, the answer might have been obvious: we pay those who cannot survive without pay first and then we pay the bankers who can afford to wait. However, after decades of neoliberal entanglement, the iron law of the Washington Consensus demands that we not even think about the obvious, intuitive[36] answer. We live in a moment of the suspension of imagination where rules are rules and all that appears solid will always be there; when in reality, to invoke Marx, who again waxed lyrical on this point, "all that is solid melts into air."[37]

Is there a way forward? I am afraid there are no simple answers, and I am not presenting a magical political path, but rather a set of considerations as part of an agenda for the future. My first suggestion is that markets, a modus of exchange, will always be with us, but we need to think about the structuring of ownership and whether the capital M Market, the market of late-afternoon capital, will always be present. If we allow our gaze to move beyond the market, then what are the kinds of social arrangements that would allow for a stable and self-sustaining growth; ample provision

---

36   For a thoughtful conversation as to how dominant hegemonic processes such as neoliberalism manufacture and utilize "common sense" in order to normalize the rules and ethics of domination, see Stuart Hall and Alan O'Shea, "Common-Sense Neoliberalism," in *After Neoliberalism? The Kilburn Manifesto*, eds. Stuart Hall, Doreen Massey, and Michael Rustin, Lawrence and Wishart, London, 2015, 52–68.

37   Karl Marx and Friedrich Engels, "Manifesto of the Communist Party," in *Marx and Engels: Basic Writings on Politics and Philosophy*, ed. Lewis S. Feuer, Collins, New York, 1974, 52.

of opportunities for people to live and prosper; a sustainable and clean environment, with respect for the other living things that share the earth with us; and for our fellow humans of whatever nationality, a meaningful involvement of all people to participate at whatever level they wish (or not) in the managing of their world and lives?[38] Here I want to underline that I am not at all suggesting that we retrace the policies of central planning. I think that János Kornai's[39] detailed study of the failures of Soviet-styled central planning severely questions the myth that there can be a single, consolidated master-plan approach to development. What I am suggesting, however, is that we need instead to think about institutionally controlled markets and popular supervision of their rules and regulations; how, importantly, capital and inherited power is transferred from generation to generation; and how capital and resources, seen globally and temporally, might be taxed to correct long-overlooked histories of exploitation. In this regard, the struggle for reparations is important on multiple levels: for the historic balancing of the scales of justice; the sheer educational importance, win or lose, of fighting the fight; and the possibility in it, if won, for the correction of global economic inequalities, if the ultimate benefits of a new reparatory balancing were managed justly and equitably.[40] Ironically and importantly, the correcting of historical injustice has psychological benefits that accrue not only to the children of the former enslaved but also to the children of those who benefited from slavery—just as radical policies that shift the scales of wealth benefit not only the inheritors of poverty but also, somewhat paradoxically, the inheritors of wealth as increasing overall wealth also increases the number of potential consumers. I suggest again that a new approach to political economy beyond capital does not mean the monopolistic ownership by the state of all the means of production, but rather an exploration of

---

38 For recent discussions on some of these themes, see Doreen Massey and Michael Rustin, "Whose Economy? Reframing the Debate," in *After Neoliberalism?*, eds. Hall, Massey, and Rustin, 116–35; and Axel Honneth, *The Idea of Socialism*, Polity, Cambridge, 2017.

39 Janos Kornai, *The Socialist System: The Political Economy of Communism*, Princeton University Press, Princeton, NJ, 1992.

40 The push for wider recognition of the need for reparatory justice has gained momentum with the University of Glasgow's recognition of the importance of slavery wealth in its development. See Kevin McKenna, "As Glasgow University Owns Up to Slavery, Others Urged to Follow," *Guardian*, September 22, 2018. See also Caribbean Community, "CARICOM Ten Point Plan for Reparatory Justice," accessed September 28, 2018, https://www.caricom.org/caricom-ten-point-plan-for-reparatory-justice/.

ways in which the popular will might be incorporated into planning and setting the ethical boundaries for human prosperity.

Moving to the specifics of the Anglophone Caribbean, and from a more overtly political perspective, we might want to think about the real limitations of Westminster-style government and how even as it has given us a degree of stability and a pathway to changing regimes constitutionally, it has at the same time entrenched too much power in the dominant parties, creating a deep and persistent tribalism that facilitates the persistence of entrenched social and political hierarchies.[41] What would a political system look like that ended tribalism, brought all the people more intimately into the governmental process, yet avoided the stifling possibilities that would arise if only one party were entrenched in power? We might want to think of these questions and their implicit answers as approaches to a new social living, even as we would want to clearly define its boundaries and the ethical concerns that we would wish to see incorporated into its framework. We might think of adding to this exercise of questioning one set of questions directed at exploring what the notion of the "end of sovereignty" (a sovereignty that we have never really had) means for the reimagining of trans-Caribbean and trans-diasporic spheres of collective self-governing and self-imagining, genuine "common-wealths" that expand beyond insular and artificial boundaries to incorporate peoples who share common histories, geographies and cultures. In my 2007 book *Envisioning Caribbean Futures*,[42] I imagined (and the title is self-explanatory) a "Constituent Assembly of the Jamaican People at Home and Abroad"[43] as a vehicle for the kinds of discussions that are required for us to begin to face the crisis that is growing around us; with the proviso, however, that the twentieth-century-notion of the sovereign, self-sustaining state was always unreal, even for the largest entities, much less the small and microcosmic ones.[44] We need to begin to imagine the alliances, formations, and collaborations that will lead to

41   See Brian Meeks and Kate Quinn (eds.) *Beyond Westminster in the Caribbean*, Ian Randle, Kingston, 2018.
42   Brian Meeks, *Envisioning Caribbean Futures: Jamaican Perspectives*, The University of the West Indies Press, Kingston, 2007.
43   Meeks, *Envisioning*, 127.
44   For wide-ranging discussions around the salience of Caribbean sovereignty and alternative approaches for the twenty-first century, see Linden Lewis (ed.) *Caribbean Sovereignty, Development and Democracy in an Age of Globalization*, Routledge, London, 2013.

new conglomerates of cooperation that will allow measures of prosperity and community self-expression to flourish alongside each other.

Critically, we need to explore and reinscribe a long-dormant set of "commonsense" language phrases, sayings, and aphorisms that, in the immediate postcolonial period, allowed us to begin emancipating ourselves from mental slavery and imagining different choices for our future; these sayings—among them, "Each one, teach one," "Touch one, touch all," "One love, one heart"—were not empty phrases, but allowed us to think, imagine, and conjure up the vague yet distinct outlines of less alienating, isolated, and individualistic futures.[45] We need to return these to our conversation, give them new life, and engage in the creative act of inventing and birthing new graphic aphorisms and codes for a future beyond neoliberalism's starkly barren and atomistic word boundaries.

Here at the end, I wish to return to what I hope is my no longer enigmatic title. There is a roadblock on Hope Road if we think of Hope Road as a metaphoric highway of possibilities running from downtown to uptown that has been impeded for more than forty years. We need to emancipate ourselves from mental slavery and think beyond the stifling and blinding boundaries that capital would wish us to stay safely within. We need to rethink notions of what, as Sylvia Wynter suggested, it means to be human,[46] as we rethink the infinite possibilities that will be unleashed if these islands in the Caribbean, these lifeboats on the hurricane currents of globalization, are allowed to patch our leaks, pull together in greater unity, mount the shore, and motor down the Hope Road of our collective imaginations.

---

45   For similar debates, see Hall and O'Shea, "Common-Sense Neoliberalism"; and Doreen Massey, "Vocabularies of the Economy," in *After Neoliberalism?*, eds. Hall, Massey, and Rustin, 24–36.
46   See Anthony Bogues (ed.) *After Man Towards the Human: Critical Essays on Sylvia Wynter*, Caribbean Reasonings series, Ian Randle, Kingston, 2006.

9

On the Question of Optimism in Troubled Times: Revolution, Tragedy, and Possibility in Caribbean History

THE LONG CARIBBEAN SEVENTIESTHE LONG CARIBBEAN SEVENTIES

This is a peculiarly Anglophone Caribbean conversation, but as with all such debates emanating from this historical crossroads of modernity, there are inevitable global resonances. The British began to withdraw from the West Indies in 1962 with independence granted to Jamaica and Trinidad and Tobago in the same month. However, the great expectations of independence were never met, and within the first decade much of the region—both independent and still colonized—was in open rebellion against the painful and sordid British colonial legacies that the new leaders inherited and failed to eliminate. The particular confluence of tributaries that contributed to an insurrectionary flood included the closure of the safety valve of migration to the United Kingdom, after the labor shortages of the immediate post–World War II years had been filled; the evident failure of the "Operation Bootstrap" style of economic policies[1] of the newly independent states to solve growing unemployment and the subsequent blossoming of extreme poverty, particularly in the cities; the continuing oppressive racial and color hierarchies of colonialism, which excluded Black people, especially the newly educated, from access to prestigious jobs and advancement in the social order; and out of this, the emergence of new movements and accompanying philosophical frameworks for radical social change—Black Power from the United

---

1 See Owen Jefferson, "Jamaica's Post-War Economic Development," in Norman Girvan and Owen Jefferson (eds.) *Readings in the Political Economy of the Caribbean*, New World, Kingston, 1971, 109–20; and Edwin Carrington, "Industrialization by Invitation in Trinidad since 1950," in Girvan and Jefferson (eds.) *Readings in the Political Economy of the Caribbean*, 143–50.

States and Rastafari in Jamaica—that seemed to provide both a theoretical and practical pathway for rebellion[2] and perhaps even revolution against the postcolonial order.

The history and arc of the Black Power movement in the Caribbean has been extensively documented and debated. In a compact sense, it began with Dr. Walter Rodney's exclusion from Jamaica in October 1968, precipitating a famous one-day urban riot,[3] after protesting students were teargassed and beaten by the police. It gathered significant steam with the 1970 Black Power demonstrations in Trinidad and Tobago,[4] with tens of thousands of people marching in the streets daily under Black Power slogans. The Trinidad "1970 Revolution," as it has come to be known, ended after Prime Minister Eric Williams declared a state of emergency, which was immediately followed by an army mutiny of disgruntled junior officers who refused to enforce it. The mutineers, however, before reaching the capital city Port of Spain, backed down and returned to their barracks;[5] loyal troops upheld the state of emergency and despite subsequent armed clashes with militants that persisted for more than two years, the Trinidad moment of popular uprising soon subsided. Further north in Jamaica, the traditional, centrist People's National Party (PNP) under the leadership of Michael Manley and in the popular upsurge precipitated by the Rodney riots, came to power in 1972 and over the course of that decade, in the face of daunting external and internal opposition, moved steadily to the Left.[6] Manley's regime implemented simple but long-delayed social reforms, advocated for a

2   See Anthony Bogues, "The Abeng Newspaper and the Radical Politics of Postcolonial Blackness," in Kate Quinn (ed.) *Black Power in the Caribbean*, University Press of Florida, Gainesville, 2014, 76–96.
3   See Rupert Lewis, *Walter Rodney's Intellectual and Political Thought*, The University of the West Indies Press, Kingston, 1998, especially 85–123.
4   See Selwyn Ryan and Taimoon Stewart (eds.) *The Black Power Revolution 1970: A Retrospective*, St. Augustine, Institute of Social and Economic Research, 1995; and Brinsley Samaroo, "The February Revolution (1970) as a Catalyst for Change in Trinidad and Tobago," in K. Quinn, *Black Power in the Caribbean*, 97–116.
5   See Brian Meeks, "The 1970 Revolution: Chronology and Documentation," in Brian Meeks, *Radical Caribbean: From Black Power to Abu Bakr*, The University of the West Indies Press, Kingston, 1996, 9–36.
6   See Evelyn Huber Stephens and John D. Stephens, *Democratic Socialism in Jamaica*, Macmillan, London, 1986; Michael Kaufman, *Jamaica under Manley: Dilemmas of Socialism and Democracy*, Zed, London, 1985; and Kari Polanyi-Levitt, *Jamaica: Lessons from the Manley Years*, Maroon Pamphlets, Kingston, 1984.

new international economic order, and, crucially, established warm relationships with the neighboring regime of revolutionary Cuba. Manley's government lost power in 1980 in a bitter and bloody election and the island resumed its post-independence policy of fealty to Washington and dependence on the international financial institutions. The final venue of this broad movement of radical insurgency occurred in the tiny southern Caribbean island of Grenada, where in 1979 the New Jewel Movement, the leading party in the parliamentary opposition coalition, overthrew the Government of Prime Minister Eric Gairy. Over the following four and a half years, the People's Revolutionary Government (PRG) under the leadership of Maurice Bishop sought to implement radical social and political policies, including, in the international sphere, establishing close relationships with Cuba and the Soviet Union.[7] The PRG, however, in an infamously tragic sequence of events, imploded in October 1983. Maurice Bishop was placed under house arrest by his own party, then shortly after was released by a huge crowd of his supporters. After marching to and occupying the island's major military base, the army sought to retake it; there was a confrontation, soldiers and civilians were killed, then Bishop and close supporters were captured and shot by members of their own People's Revolutionary Army (PRA). A week later, the United States, supported by a number of, but not all, Caribbean states, invaded Grenada. Following intense resistance from units of the PRA, the remaining leaders of the revolution were captured, arrested, and remained for more than two decades in prison under a deeply flawed trial for murder, then convicted with the threat of execution, and finally released from prison in 2009. This traumatic defeat, preceded by Bishop's killing, generated deep and lasting divisions not only in Grenada but across the Caribbean and, capped as it was by a US invasion that was welcomed by many, slammed the door shut on the Long Seventies of radical Caribbean insurgency.

---

7 See Patsy Lewis, Peter Clegg and Gary Williams (eds.) *Grenada: Revolution and Invasion*, The University of the West Indies Press, Kingston, 2015; Wendy Grenade (ed.) *The Grenada Revolution: Reflections and Lessons*, University Press of Mississippi, Jackson, 2015; Shalini Puri, *The Grenada Revolution in the Caribbean Present: Operation Urgent Memory*, Palgrave Macmillan, London, 2014; David Scott, *Omens of Adversity: Tragedy, Time Memory*, Duke University Press, Durham, NC, 2014; Laurie Lambert, *Comrade Sister: Caribbean Feminist Revisions of the Grenada Revolution*, University of Virginia Press, Charlottesville, 2020; and Brian Meeks, *Caribbean Revolutions and Revolutionary Theory: An Assessment of Cuba, Nicaragua and Grenada*, Macmillan Caribbean, London, 1993.

The invasion of Grenada also signaled the start of the era of neoliberal dominance that has lasted for more than three decades and, despite the 2008 global economic crisis, which at first seemed to signal its demise, continues to dominate policy, with no immediate end in sight. The social and political features of this period in the Caribbean are similar to other international, post-radical, and postcolonial sequences. To use Jamaica as an instance, traditional parliamentary politics, driven by IMF-inspired structural adjustment policies, has dominated and radical and revolutionary sentiments have declined. Strategies of economic development based on tourism, remittances, and market-led initiatives have, however, failed to deliver indices of credible "growth"[8]—the marker for neoliberal success. Corruption[9] has become more prominent in the absence of buoyant economic initiatives. It has proliferated both "above," through avenues of white-collar crime, and "below," where urban gangs, formed in the crucible of the internecine warfare of the 1970s, have established profitable political and economic space and autonomy for themselves in the notorious "garrison" communities[10] of the inner cities. I have elsewhere described this prolonged, fraught moment, where the old hegemonic bloc of the middle-class and anti-colonial politicians has lost control over the social direction of the country while retaining some modicum of political control, as one of "hegemonic dissolution."[11] It is both the failure of the old and newer elites to drive the country in the direction they wish, as it is the failure of the popular majorities to wrest it away from them. The result is an era of uncertainty defined by the evacuation of notions of ethical morality from political and social discourse and their replacement by atomism, dog-eat-dog sentiments, and the reversion to violence as the first move in conflict resolution. The postcolony in the Caribbean is not to be directly equated with Africa's parallel postcolonial moment,

8   See Kari Polanyi Levitt, *Reclaiming Development: Independent Thought and Caribbean Community*, Ian Randle Publishers, Kingston, 2005, 109–212.

9   Of 180 countries measured on the 2019 Corruption Perception Index, three Caribbean countries were among the most corrupt, with Jamaica at 74 and Guyana and Trinidad and Tobago tied at 85 at the bottom. (Numerous tied ratings accounted for the only 85 levels.) See *Corruption Perception Index 2019*, www.transarency.org/cpi.

10   See Mark Figueroa and Amanda Sives, "Homogenous Voting, Electoral Manipulation and the 'Garrison' Process in Post-Independence Jamaica," *Journal of Commonwealth and Comparative Politics* 40, no. 1 (2002): 81–108.

11   Brian Meeks, "The Political Moment in Jamaica: The Dimensions of Hegemonic Dissolution," in Meeks, *Radical Caribbean*, 124–43.

but anyone reading Mbembe[12] will recognize the points of commonality, even as the differences confirm that all social and political theorizing must inevitably rest on the deep understanding of a particular situation.

Much of the critical scholarship that has emerged from the Caribbean and its diaspora in this period has sought, while using different lenses and approaches, to understand the rise and fall of the long radical Caribbean seventies, the character of this articulated post-insurrectionary interregnum, and possible futures beyond it. There is, for instance, Hilbourne Watson's work[13] in political economy, which locates the Caribbean as a minor link in the worldwide cybernetic, information, robotic revolution, with deeply pessimistic implications for Caribbean sovereignty or any autonomous project of nation-building. There is Obika Gray's study[14] that explores in detail the social history of the Jamaican inner-city communities and redefines the role of the state as a predatory enterprise. Deborah Thomas also explores the Jamaican inner city to understand its denizens' complicated and contradictory culture of "modern blackness."[15] And in her more recent work *Exceptional Violence*,[16] she examines the persistence of structural violence against the urban poor, in order to consider what "repair" might look like and how the incorporation of "affect" might help in redefining the boundaries of sovereignty. There is Percy Hintzen's attempt to think through what a new democracy for

<hr/>

12 See Achille Mbembe, *On the Postcolony*, University of California Press, Berkeley, 2001. Mbembe's powerful, poetic, and subtle text doesn't present itself for easy summary. Beyond his deep cynicism surrounding the corruption, brutality, and sheer absurdity of the regimes that inhabited postcolonial Africa, particularly those of the francophone postcolony, he nonetheless leaves the door open for hope. Even as he describes the postcolonial era as "a time of unhappiness" (238) in which "force cohabits with bufoonery, caprice with brutality" (238), he imagines this as a temporary phase: "On the other hand, the time of unhappiness is like a tidal wave, and we know that a tidal wave comes and goes, flows in and out" (238). While postcolonial time is therefore one of unhappiness, it is also a time of possibilities (241). One wonders whether Scott's tragic sensibility leaves any door open for transformative possibilities in the way Mbembe so clearly does.
13 See, for instance, Hilbourne Watson (ed.) *The Caribbean in the Global Political Economy*, Lynn Rienner, Boulder, CO, 1994.
14 See Obika Gray, *Demeaned but Empowered: The Social Power of the Urban Poor in Jamaica*, The University of the West Indies Press, Kingston, 2004.
15 See Deborah Thomas, *Modern Blackness: Nationalism, Globalization and the Politics of Culture in Jamaica*, Duke University Press, Durham, NC, 2004.
16 See Deborah Thomas, *Exceptional Violence: Embodied Citizenship in Transnational Jamaica*, Duke University Press, Durham, NC, 2011.

the Caribbean based on local empowerment might look like.[17] There is Paget Henry's work on Caribbean philosophy, which seeks to open up a new, foundational archive for both historical exploration and political action, through the elaboration of what he describes as "Afro-Caribbean Philosophy." There is a buoyant and growing Caribbean feminist scholarship, led by Eudine Barriteau, Rhoda Reddock, Patricia Mohammed,[18] and many others, which, unbowed by the crisis and travails that followed the collapse of the Grenada Revolution in 1983, has sought to consolidate gender as a critical avenue through which to understand and confront the neoliberal moment.[19]

THE PROBLEM SPACE OF DAVID SCOTT'S TRAGEDY

More directly to the purposes of this chapter, there is David Scott's work, which over the past three decades has attempted to directly interrogate the meaning of the Caribbean postcolonial and elaborate alternative methodologies to understanding it. Scott's oeuvre is of the utmost importance, both for its erudition as well as the many unquestionable insights it provides into both the contemporary Caribbean condition and the theorizing around it. At its heart is the complex project of thinking through the foundations for both structural and political stasis in the contemporary Caribbean postcolony. Scott's approach travels through three phases. First, he posits the relevance of identifying time and temporality as critical theoretical variables in approaching a given social moment; second, in locating a specific temporal context, he seeks to identify and map the "generational sensibilities" that accompany it. And third, he searches for and presents for scrutiny what he considers as more appropriate and meaningful ways of reading history. Scott proposes the abandonment of what he considers the romantic, progressivist lens that

17 See Percy Hintzen, "Towards a New Democracy in the Caribbean: Local Empowerment and the New Global Order," in Brian Meeks and Kate Quinn (eds.) *Beyond Westminster in the Caribbean*, Ian Randle Publishers, Kingston, 2018, 173–98.

18 See, for instance, Eudine Barriteau (ed.) *Confronting Power, Theorizing Gender: Interdisciplinary Perspectives from the Caribbean*, The University of the West Indies Press, 2003; and Patricia Mohammed (ed.) *Gendered Realities: Essays in Caribbean Feminist Thought*, The University of the West Indies Press, Kingston, 2002.

19 For my earlier attempt to critically engage with some of these approaches, see Brian Meeks, *Envisioning Caribbean Futures: Jamaican Perspectives*, The University of the West Indies Press, Kingston, 2007.

has previously dominated Caribbean history-telling and its replacement with one imbued with what he describes as a "tragic sensibility."[20] This approach, he posits, will more accurately reflect the real world that has been far more tragic than triumphant. It will guard, he suggests, against the hubris that inevitably accompanies romantic narratives that assume that the "arc" of history bends toward justice. While these three elements are closely interrelated, it is the foregrounding of the notion of the tragic sensibility with which I have the greatest concern and which will occupy much of the rest of this chapter.

Scott's oeuvre is still very much a work in progress, though its substantial outlines are developed across three central books that one can consider a trilogy. In *Refashioning Futures*[21] he develops, through a series of neo-Foucauldian essays on postcolonial Sri Lankan and Jamaican politics, the suggested outlines and foundations for alternative Caribbean futures. In *Conscripts of Modernity*[22] he returns to C.L.R. James's classic portrayal of the San Domingo (Haitian) Revolution in order to elaborate his critical perspectives on history and history-writing and his theory of the tragic. In *Omens of Adversity*,[23] he engages in a specific meditation on the Grenadian Revolution, the third of the self-proclaimed Caribbean Revolutions (Haiti, Cuba, and Grenada, if Nicaragua is understood as a Central American phenomenon), and builds on his earlier identification of the importance of tragedy to elaborate questions of temporality and specifically to identify the importance of generational sensibilities. At the heart of this notion is the assertion that the aging Caribbean generation of the 1970s, those who were on the side of radical change, are living in a time which to them appears "out of joint."[24] They exist in a kind of time warp in which the "problem space" in which their politics of radical nationalism and revolution existed has passed. This disorientation leaves them stranded in a no man's land of political meaninglessness, "lost in space," as it were, and therefore incapable of fully grasping, much less acting upon, the new times that we are living in.

20 See especially Scott, *Conscripts of Modernity: The Tragedy of Colonial Enlightenment*, Duke University Press, Durham, NC, 2004, 170–208.
21 David Scott, *Refashioning Futures: Criticism after Postcoloniality*, Princeton University Press, Princeton, NJ, 1999.
22 Scott, *Conscripts of Modernity*, 2004.
23 David Scott, *Omens of Adversity: Tragedy, Time, Memory, Justice*, Duke University Press, Durham, NC, 2014.
24 For his use of this phrase from *Hamlet*, see Scott, *Conscripts of Modernity*, 162.

There are some substantial aspects here with which I find easy agreement. The Left of the 1970s, with its crudely Hegelian sense of imminent revolution and willingness to bypass popular opinion in favor of "historical necessity,"[25] may very well have hastened its own destruction. Had the Grenadian "comrades," for instance, been somewhat humbler, more willing to compromise, with a greater appreciation that it could all end, as it did, in tragic destruction, could they have possibly avoided the worst possible outcome? The invocation of "what-ifs" may inevitably be futile, but, nevertheless, what if Coard, Bishop, and both sides of the 1983 New Jewel Movement crisis had paused and considered tragedy as the more likely denouement? Could history have traveled along a different path? More tellingly for future seemingly irresolvable political impasses, what benefits might a tragic sensibility, driven by fear of the greater likelihood of failure and defeat, yield in the direction of eliciting caution, compromise, and possibly, survival? However, and beyond this, there is something in Scott's invocation of the tragic that takes it beyond the role of a mere warning signal and leaves one with an overarching sense of emptiness, of a political void in which radical change and revolution become dangerous chimera, leaving room only for a nihilistic and frozen politics of retreat and closure.

As such, I distinguish between Scott's "tragic sensibility," in which one's entire worldview is informed by and tilted in the direction of "the tragic," and what I would wish to advance as a necessary "sensitivity to tragedy,"[26] in which we keep the possibility of the tragic outcome as a flashing amber signal on our dashboard, for easy reference when appropriate, but not as the sole or even primary source of information and direction. In order to take this distinction beyond the immediate moment of instinctive concern and to develop an alternative approach to thinking about the contemporary Caribbean, I want to focus more attention on the second of these three books—*Conscripts of Modernity*—which is the linchpin on which the other two gain substantial support.

---

25   See this argument in chapter 5 in this volume, originally published as Brian Meeks, "Jamaican Roads Not Taken: Or a Big 'What If' in Stuart Hall's Life," *boundary 2*, December 2017, boundary2.org.

26   For further elaboration of this point, see my review of Scott's *Omens of Adversity*, in which I argue: "It is not that Scott does not identify substantial intellectual and political shifts that need urgently to be identified and addressed, but that in painting an absolute and grim picture he has also painted out the rich and varied colors of the popular movement." Brian Meeks, "Review of David Scott's *Omens of Adversity*," "After Tragedy, Searching for Liberation," *Cultural Critique* 93 (Spring 2016): 212–20.

Conscripts, as intimated previously, is set against the background of the Haitian Revolution, as famously captured in C.L.R. James's 1938 masterpiece *The Black Jacobins*.[27] In order to gain purchase on Scott's argument, but also to invoke James's deep wellspring of optimism, I am going to sketch the barest brushstrokes of James's story, as a pathway to exploring Scott's interventions and my agreements and disagreements with him. I am determined to invoke again the story of the Haitian Revolution because, as Trouillot[28] so eloquently argued, it was an impossibility in a world of white supremacy and therefore had to be silenced and erased from world history. In closing, I want to reflect on the contemporary (2020) global moment and the very notion of revolution to leave with a somewhat more optimistic approach to imagining Caribbean and, more generally, postcolonial futures.

THE HAITIAN REVOLUTION

The Black Jacobins (henceforth *BJ*) is the history of the only successful slave revolt, the only successful Black revolution against slavery, and the creation of the second independent country (following the United States) in the Americas. To the extent that this history is better known today, with the important work of scholars like Trouillot, Blackburn, Genovese, Dubois, Fick,[29] and many others, it is because of James's foundational intervention. *BJ* is simultaneously scholarly and passionate. It is reflective

---

27   C.L.R. James, *The Black Jacobins: Toussaint L'Ouverture and the San Domingo Revolution*, Vintage, New York, 1989.
28   See Michel-Rolph Trouillot, *Silencing the Past: Power and the Production of History*, Beacon Press, Boston, 1995.
29   See Trouillot, *Silencing the Past*, Robin Blackburn, *The Overthrow of Colonial Slavery*, Verso, London, 1988; Eugene D. Genovese, *From Rebellion to Revolution: Afro-American Slave Revolts in the Making of the Modern World*, Louisiana State University Press, Baton Rouge, 1979; Carolyn E. Fick, *The Making of Haiti: The St Domingue Revolution from Below*, University of Tennessee Press, Knoxville, 1990; Thomas Bender, Laurent Dubois, and Richard Rabinowitz, *Revolution! The Atlantic World Reborn*, New York Historical Society, New York, and D. Giles, London, 2011; Ada Ferrer, *Freedom's Mirror: Cuba and Haiti in the Age of Revolution*, Cambridge University Press, New York, 2014; Adom Getachew, "Universalism after the Post-colonial Turn: Interpreting the Haitian Revolution," *Political Theory*, 446, 821–45, 2016; Susan Buck-Morss, *Hegel, Haiti and Universal History*, University of Pittsburgh Press, Pittsburgh, 2009; Charles Forsdick and Christian Hogsberg (eds.) *The Black Jacobins Reader*, Duke University Press, Durham, NC, 2017; Anthony Bogues, "The Black Jacobins and the Long Haitian Revolution: Archives, History and the Writing of Revolution," in Forsdick and

of James's maturing Marxist approach to history yet reads history with a brash agnosticism rooted in his own appreciation of the particularities of the Caribbean, the profound impact of slavery and the plantation, and an acute sense of the interconnectedness between the plantation economy and the consolidating mercantilist capitalism of France and western Europe. Events in the Empire are intimately connected with her colonies and when revolution begins in France in 1789, its repercussions are almost immediately felt in the Caribbean. In the highly racialized structure of St. Domingue (San Domingo for James), on the western side of the island of Hispaniola and the richest sugar colony in the world, the whites are immediately divided between royalists and supporters of the revolution. This soon spills over to the mulatto caste, many of whom are wealthy inheritors of their white fathers' wealth but deprived by the *Code Noir*[30] of full social and political rights. Few imagine that the demonstrations, riots, and general turmoil that begins will impact the mass of Black slaves who constitute the overwhelming majority of the population.

However, as the struggle in France intensifies and becomes more radical, so, too, does the nascent unrest among the Blacks, and in 1791 there is a general rising. At first, it is inchoate and resembles other similar uprisings that have occurred across the plantation arc of the Americas—but things soon change. James underlines the entry among the rebels of an old house slave, Toussaint Breda who will soon rename himself L'Ouverture (the Opening). It is Toussaint, as general, strategist, politician, and statesman, who forges a modern, highly trained, and effective Black army. He is able to brilliantly maneuver among the various forces arrayed across the revolutionaries: the Spanish, occupying Santo Domingo to the East; the English, who have entered to capture the now-prostrate French colony for themselves; and the French, the principal enemy against whom Toussaint is initially at war. But with the shifting of French politics to the Left and the elevation of the Jacobins in Paris, the popular democratic mood in the metropole leads, finally, to the historic abolition of slavery. Toussaint, recognizing the opening provided by this epic moment, changes tack, joins forces with the contingents of revolutionary (Jacobin) France, eventually becomes the Black Council of St. Domingue, and rules effectively on behalf of France over a newly freed population of Blacks, mulattos, and the

---

Hogsberg (eds.) *Black Jacobins Reader*, 2017; and Sudhir Hazareesingh, *Black Spartacus: The Epic Life of Toussaint Louverture*, Allen Lane, London, 2020.
30 The infamous Royal Code of 1685 that defined conditions of slavery in the French colonies.

remaining whites. Notably, for the events that will soon follow, Toussaint does not at this time imagine an independent state, but contemplates a continuing relationship with France, which, in his reading, is now both the guardian of liberty and a requirement for the maintenance of "civilization," read here primarily, though in a deeply conflicted way, as access to trade, manufactures, culture, and, crucially, weapons for self-defense. Toussaint's approach, then, simply stated, believed first in freedom for the Blacks, but this required the support of France, its "civilization," and its continued economic presence.

Meanwhile in Paris, the course of and prospects for the revolution are changing. The Jacobins—guardians of the emancipation proclamation—are eclipsed and suppressed, and soon thereafter, Napoleon ascends to power. Bonaparte—racist and a state-builder—possesses none of the idealism of the previous regime, but driven by support from the powerful interests of mercantile and slave capital, as well as his own imperialist predilections, he begins preparing to reestablish slavery—and with it, profitability—in St. Domingue and the other colonies. In December 1801, the first ships, bearing an army of 12,000 men under the command of Napoleon's brother-in-law, General Leclerc, sail into the harbor of Le Cap, the main port on the colony's northern shore, with precise instructions from Paris. The generals of the Black army, most of all Toussaint, must be fooled to believe that the French army is still representative of their liberty, equality, and fraternity. Under this guise, they must land safely, entrench themselves, and then decapitate the leaders and disarm the rank and file of the Black army. This would be the necessary prelude for a reestablishment of slavery.

Leclerc is allowed to land and is at first met with uncertainty and only limited resistance. Toussaint is unwilling to commit his full might against France, but there is grave concern and foreboding as to why, if France is not hostile, such a massive army has been sent. When it becomes obvious that it is an army of enslavers, a more widespread and determined resistance begins to consolidate and Leclerc, who imagined that the powerful and triumphant French army would easily defeat these Black rebels, begins to see the extraordinary military capabilities of his foes. Then, surprisingly and unexpectedly, Toussaint yields, parlays with Leclerc for peace, demobilizes, and retreats to his own small estate. This is all and more that Napoleon could have hoped for and soon Toussaint is arrested, forced on board a French ship, and conveyed to a brutal jail in the cold Jura Mountains, where he dies of humiliation and exposure.

The capture of Toussaint, however, is not met with resignation, but alarm and more rapid mobilization among the leading Black generals as well as contingents of autonomous resistance fighters. Even more alarmingly, word reaches St. Domingue that Napoleon has restored slavery in the smaller eastern Caribbean colonies of Martinique and Guadeloupe. This leads to a new and final phase of war, in which the Black army under Dessalines, Christophe, Maurepas, and others unites with the southern, mulatto-led army under Pétion and fights the final, sanguinary but glorious War for Independence, ending with the decisive defeat of the French, the Haitian Declaration of Independence on January 1, 1804, and the inauguration of the first Black republic—the state of Haiti.

SCOTT INTERVENES

It is on this narrative presented here in miniature (and undoubtedly, in my compression, with significant damage!) that Scott builds his case. James, he proposes, wrote the history of the revolution initially as a romance. It is rooted in Enlightenment imperatives of the inevitability of progress, of right triumphing over wrong, and of redemption for the heroes at the end of the day.[31] These unilinear notions fail, he suggests, to sufficiently account for the role of contingency, of uncertainty in history-making and the fact that outcomes are seldom if ever optimal, or even good. Further, James, in writing the book, fails to consider and account for the "problem space" within which he is writing and how it differs from the problem space of St. Domingue at the time of the revolution, or with further problem spaces that have cascaded since the original volume was published in 1938. The set of problems that occupied James in 1938, Scott suggests, were related to how to encourage anti-colonial revolutions in the Caribbean, but even more notably in Africa. These were quite different from Toussaint's conundrum, of trying to find a path beyond racial emancipation to economic prosperity for a poor, isolated, singular Black state.

These, Scott suggests, are to be even further differentiated from the problem space of the early 1960s, when in the second edition of *BJ* James inserted seven new paragraphs to the final chapter—"The War of Independence." In this new intervention, Scott suggests that James

---

31   In Scott's words, James writes in a tradition of "romantic vindicationalism." See Scott, *Conscripts of Modernity*, 79.

shifts register. Instead of the story of victory against overwhelming odds, which is largely the framework for the rest of the book, James meditates on Toussaint's ultimately tragic dilemma. Torn between his burning goal to consolidate freedom for his people and his competing certainty that without France there could be no survival in a "civilized" sense, Toussaint was effectively disarmed. This moment of uncertainty, vacillation, and paralysis provided the opportunity for his laying down of arms and his capture, leading to his tragic incarceration and death. It was, in James's words, a "hamartia,"[32] a tragic flaw in Toussaint himself that cost him his freedom, his life, and very nearly the entire revolution.

Scott's assertion is that the insertion of these paragraphs, the rumination on tragedy and the tilt away from a romantic to a tragic lens, is not coincidental, but rather derives from the different problem space of the early 1960s when these were inserted, which was far divorced from the problem space of 1938. In the 1930s, the widespread labor upheaval in the West Indies in the wake of the Great Depression and the rise of anti-colonial movements in India, Asia, and the African continent all suggested the likelihood of imminent success for anti-colonial struggles. By the 1960s, these hopes had either been tempered or dashed. The specific Caribbean disappointments, with the failure of the attempt at Federation,[33] were accompanied by increasingly dismal prospects for new postcolonial advances on the African continent. James, therefore, was seeking to think through some way to temper the optimistic romanticism that permeated the earlier book, with the sobriety that the new situation demanded. Even more profoundly, Scott continues, if *BJ* is read today in a twenty-first-century post-Bandungan world, its hopeful, romantic triumphalism gives limited insight either as a model of what is to be done, or prospect of what the future might look like. To quote Scott at length:

> The Black Jacobins is an anti-colonial history written out of and in response to a particular colonial present and projected towards a particular postcolonial future ... That future which constituted James's horizon of expectations (the emergence of nation-state sovereignty, the revolutionary transition to socialism) and which the Black

---

32 *Conscripts of Modernity*, 153–54.
33 For a contemporary revisiting of the importance of federations in the failed anti-colonial attempt at "worldmaking," see Adom Getachew, *Worldmaking after Empire: The Rise and Fall of Self-Determination*, Princeton University Press, Princeton, NJ, 2019.

Jacobins anticipated, we live today as the bleak ruins of our postcolonial present. Our generation looks back, so to put it, through the remains of a present that James and his generation looked forward to (however contentiously) as the open horizon of a possible future. James's erstwhile future has elapsed in our disappearing present. But if this is so, if the longing for total anti-colonial revolution, the longing for the overcoming of the colonial past that shaped James's horizon of expectations in The Black Jacobins is not one that we can inhabit today, then it may be part of our task to set it aside and begin another work of reimagining the futures for us to long for, for us to emancipate.[34]

BEYOND TRAGEDY

Let me start with what is as yet only a partial response to this main conclusion of Scott's study by addressing his central point that "the political space for a certain kind of anti-colonial revolution no longer exists." I wish to argue with this assertion. If by this he means the likelihood of single-state Cuban or Grenadian Revolution, with intrepid guerrillas battling corrupt dictators, then I would agree that the peculiar conjuncture of the contemporary world, the power of imperial militaries, and the all-encompassing ability of finance capital to make recalcitrant regimes scream, as evident today in the instance of Venezuela, weigh heavily against the likelihood of single-state revolutions surviving. We should qualify this, however, with the recognition that the idea of a single-state revolution, of the Haitian, Cuban, Grenadian, and Nicaraguan variety, was always tentative and, in small postcolonial instances like these, predicated on close alliances with powerful patrons—Jacobin France for Toussaint, and the Soviet Union for Fidel Castro. This was Toussaint's dilemma as captured by James. Whether one wishes to read Toussaint as wedded to a false notion of the superiority of French civilization, or simply his recognizing that liberated Black people, in order to clothe, feed, build shelter, and defend themselves, would require close alliances with powerful states, it is evident that he was clear that St. Domingue on its own in a white slaveholder world would find it difficult to survive. When Napoleon took power, this one hope of support from Jacobin France—a reasonably well-intentioned power—was eliminated and the rest of Haitian history, which one cannot even begin to elaborate

---

34 Scott, *Conscripts of Modernity*, 45.

here, was largely determined by this hard fact of isolation in a white, imperialist world.

From this perspective, the world of 1804 is not so dramatically different from that of 1938, 1959, or the Long Seventies of Caribbean Black Power and popular insurrection. In all instances, locally based movements in small states, seeking to enact radical social change, faced daunting prospects in a world dominated by hostile powers. The problem space, then, as now, if such movements arise and are fortuitously able to take power, is, as most recently Venezuela illustrates, "do we have powerful allies, or not?"

What is admittedly different is that when Scott wrote *Conscripts* in 2004 and up until very recently, there has been no dominant and self-evident counter-hegemonic philosophy to guide and drive new movements. For the almost four decades since the collapse of the radical, national liberation and revolutionary movements of the 1970s, the decisive defeat of Bandung,[35] and the demise of "really existing socialism," there has been no confidence in a theory of revolution, the way in which anti-slavery thinking drove Toussaint and the masses of St. Domingue and as Fanonian perceptions, Black Power, and Marxism drove the anti-colonial radicals of the 1970s. Whether the absence of a clear, guiding philosophical frame is an indication that there can be no clear frame at all, or that there might be one in the making, there is the distinction between Scott's absolute partition of historic "problem spaces" into watertight compartments and the extent to which we might wish to take a different approach, in which historical periods overlap and leak into each other; the extent to which, in other words, there is still room to build new movements, albeit movements with new programs, and different trajectories that move beyond the boundaries of twentieth-century nationalism and the nation-state and the elevation of the "political kingdom" as the inevitable avenue to human liberation.

This segues into a second of Scott's assertions, in which he argues that we should abandon the "longing for total revolution," as this world no longer exists. One can agree that the world of the twenty-first century, certainly the Caribbean twenty-first century, a world largely beyond slavery and colonialism and deeply linked into digital networks and transnational diasporas, is not that of eighteenth-century, transatlantic mercantile capital. However, if we consider the conditions of the crisis

---

35   For Scott on Bandung, see Scott, *Conscripts of Modernity*, 30.

of the second decade of the new century, then it might be worthwhile thinking about another critical dimension of revolutions. If the economic conflicts between the interests of the aristocracy and mercantile/financial/slavery capital of the eighteenth century contributed to the collapse of feudalism and the absolute defeat of the slave system in one colony, then what are the portents for a global crisis in the second decade of the twenty-first century? I want to suggest that if we think of Lenin's[36] classic definition of a revolutionary situation and his description of the ruling classes "not being able to continue ruling in the old way" as one of the critical conditions and portents for a revolutionary situation, then it would be reasonable to propose that this aspect of his proposal is worth serious consideration in today's world.

Think of, for instance, beyond the market failures of 2008, the global environmental crisis, manifest most alarmingly in global warming, and the consolidating consensus that the earth is verging on ecological catastrophe. Think also of the vast inequalities engendered and exacerbated by financial capital and the "new economy" that on one level generate deep discontent, but at another hinder the sort of possibilities that Keynes saw in demand-led capitalist growth. Think thirdly of the potential for massive structural unemployment in an exponential increase in robotization that will only accelerate in the near future and the emerging evidence that suggests there is no answer to this new imperative.[37] I mention these three because they are burning and prominent, but they are already having a tremendous impact at the level of politics and policy, with the demise of the Washington Consensus, the rise of Trumpism[38] and the Far Right

36 Lenin's precise words were: "When it is impossible for the ruling classes to maintain their rule without any change ... " See V. I. Lenin, "The Collapse of the Second International," *Lenin Collected Works*, Vol. 21, August 1914–December 1915, Progress Publishers, Moscow, 1973, 213–14.
37 See Darrel M. West, "What Happens If Robots Take Jobs? The Impact of Emerging Technologies on Employment and Public Policy," Center for Technology Innovation at Brookings, October 2015.
38 This draft was first written in December 2020, in the moment between Joe Biden's victory at the polls and his January 2021 inauguration, with no certainty that Donald Trump would actually concede and leave office voluntarily. The unprecedented attempt to deny the electoral results, leading ultimately to the storming of the capital by the Trumpian mob on January 6, is now, of course, history. Trump eventually stepped down and Biden was inaugurated, but his denial of the election results continues, even as over five hundred would-be insurrectionists face trial in the coming months. What is certain, however, is that based on his continuing popularity in the Republican Party, the legacy of Trumpism—neo-fascist, racist nationalism—will endure. Trump's remarkable

across the globe, and the likelihood of damaging and debilitating trade wars in the near future, particularly but not exclusively between China and the United States.

So, if the dominant classes cannot rule in the old way, what of the possibilities for rebellion from below? When I first delivered these thoughts at the UCL conference "After the Event" in May 2019, my subsequent comment was that this was a frightening moment, because while structural crises were imminent, the popular response was fragmented and inchoate. At the time I wrote:

> What makes the present moment particularly frightening however, is that while we can imagine a collapse of the environment, linked into a crisis in the "forces of production" it is happening at a moment of relative weakness of popular movements, both at the national level and in the form of trans-national and global alliances. It is not that there is not deep dissatisfaction against all of these imminent signs of crisis, and nascent transnational movements like "Extinction Rebellion"[39] and the 2017 Women's March,[40] but that this fightback is too sporadic and limited. The forces of progressive resistance are a few steps behind the consolidating wave of a global right-wing insurgency. However, far from there being quiescent belief in the rightness of the present order, I suggest that popular majorities, under the weight of hard imperatives of economic survival and lacking a clear, well-defined understanding of what to fight for, remain relatively disengaged, and on the sidelines.[41]

Since then, things have moved at warp speed. "There are decades where nothing happens: and there are weeks where decades happen."[42]

---

support by some 73 million voters (Biden received more than 80 million) suggests the deep resentment felt by sections of the white working and middle classes on their perceived loss of not only the election but their social, racial, and economic status and the inherent dangers that lie ahead for the United States and the world.

39   See Matthew Taylor, "The Evolution of Extinction Rebellion," *Guardian*, August 4, 2020.

40   See Anemona Hartocollis and Yamiche Alcindor, "Women's March Highlights as Huge Crowds Protest Trump: 'We're Not Going Away,'" *New York Times*, January 21, 2017.

41   Brian Meeks, "On the Question of Optimism in Troubled Times," paper presented at the conference "After the Event: Prospects and Retrospects of Revolution," May 15–17, 2019, University College, London, 16.

42   Purportedly written by V. I. Lenin, though, with much controversy surrounding it, the saying is nonetheless aptly reflective of moments when life accelerates, as in the summer of 2020.

The dramatic 2019 anti-neoliberal and anti-authoritarian uprisings, most notably in Chile, Sudan, Lebanon, India, and Hong Kong,[43] among many others, and then in 2020 the unprecedented upwelling of anti-racist and anti-fascist sentiments, arising out of the police murder of George Floyd[44] in the United States and spreading across the globe, despite and in the face of the global COVID-19 pandemic, have upended that earlier portent. The rapidity of mobilization, the sheer scale of the popular protests, as well as the instantaneous sharing of information surrounding programs, strategies, and tactics were all present in 2019 and then immeasurably amplified in the summer of 2020. Black Lives Matter demonstrations, emanating from the Floyd murder, took place in May and June on a daily basis in cities and small towns across America and were soon described as "the broadest in US history."[45] Amazingly, the demonstrations jumped national boundaries and Black Lives Matter protests proliferated on all continents, addressing the specific question of police violence against Black people in the United States but also incorporating anti-racist and anti-authoritarian themes specific to their localities.

The epoch of quiescence and retreat, the "problem space" Scott correctly, if somewhat one-sidedly, identifies that occurred at the end of the Bandung era, at the end of the "national liberation" moment is itself drawing to a close. A new era of popular upwelling[46] has begun. The popular program is not yet written in stone, but given the centrality and salience of anti-racism to the current moment, it might be useful to peruse some of the thematic demands in the 2020 Policy Platform of the Movement for Black Lives, the driving organization behind Black Lives Matter.

End the war on Black communities
End the war on Black youth
End the War on Black Women

---

43   See, for instance, Robin Wright, "The Story of 2019: Protests in Every Corner of the Globe," *New Yorker*, December 30, 2019.
44   See Jen Kirby, "'Black Lives Matter' Has Become a Global Rallying Cry against Racism and Police Brutality," June 12, 2020, www.vox.com/2020/6/12/221285244/black-lives-matter-global-protests-george-floyd-uk-belgium.
45   See Lara Putnam, Erica Chenoweth, and Jeremy Pressman, "The Floyd Protests Are the Broadest in U.S. History—and Are Spreading to White, Small Town America," *Washington Post*, June 6, 2020.
46   I am searching for a description of the present moment that falls short of proclaiming global insurrection yet recognizes that the present upsurge of popular unrest goes far beyond the normal decades-long, sporadic resistance to neoliberalism.

End the War on Black trans, queer, gender non-conforming and
    intersex people
End the war on Black health and Black disabled people
End the war on Black migrants
End to all jails, prisons and immigrant detention
End the death penalty
End the war on drugs
End the surveillance on Black communities
End to pretrial detention and money bail[47]

Many of these are, of course, specific to the US context; but there is a central core of demands that question the permanency of national boundaries (ending the war on Black migrants), center the importance of gender and sexuality as inalienable rights, and argue for the erosion of the state as presently constituted (end to jails, prisons, and immigration detention). The emerging program of liberation is therefore distinctly anti-racist, transnational, and, if not anti-statist, certainly questioning the limits, boundaries, and powers of states as presently constituted.

How does this remarkable new turn square with Scott's proposal that the "longing for total anti-colonial revolution" should be abandoned? I am not sure where invoking this notion as originally mooted by Bernard Yack[48] really leads. If it ends in the recognition of the need to turn things upside down, then there is a lot in the present moment that requires policies and movements that will advocate for radical, upending changes—for instance, in carbon-reducing environmental policy, the taxation of financial profits to reverse gaping inequalities, the curtailment of inordinately high budgetary spending on arms, and the shift of resources to health, welfare, and, again, the environment. These, if grouped together with many of the demands as expressed in the Movement for Black Lives Platform and accompanied by new, more democratic, and inclusive modalities of governing, could be considered revolutionary and very much worth both longing and fighting for.

But undoubtedly, too, the idea of revolution is moving away from its singular location in the nation-state. The future is already evident in

---

47 Movement for Black Lives, *Vision for Black Lives—2020 Policy Platform*, www.m4bl.org.
48 See Bernard Yack, *The Longing for Total Revolution: Philosophic Sources of Social Discontent from Rousseau to Marx to Nietzsche*, Princeton University Press, Princeton, NJ, 1986.

these transnational alliances as vividly demonstrated above and that have the potential to move beyond demonstrating to build coalitions around common platforms and across differing matters of concern in areas such as saving the environment; fighting against racial, gender, and sexual structural discrimination; and fighting for fair housing, against gentrification, and for community survival and the preservation of jobs. All of these movements are already out there but lacking the common sense of purpose and program and an underlying platform as to the kind of world they are fighting for. I think of Stuart Hall's *Kilburn Manifesto*[49] written as a collaborative venture shortly before his death in 2015 as one particularly fertile source of thinking through new platforms and programs. While one of its weaknesses is that it is a proposal focusing on Great Britain, this also provides it with the strength of local specificity. Its paramount question "What and who is the economy for?" is one that resonates and could form the basis for thinking about other similar manifestos for specific places as well as transnational ones.

So, my suggestion is that while Scott is right that a particular definition of single-state-bound anti-colonial revolution may have passed its time of conceptual usefulness, the conditions for revolt are in many other respects ripe, and the mythos of "revolution," with its deeply inbuilt connotations and history of breaking decisively with the past, still has a useful purpose and shouldn't yet be abandoned.[50]

---

49   See Stuart Hall, Michael Rustin, and Doreen Massey (eds.) *After Neoliberalism? The Kilburn Manifesto*, Lawrence and Wishart, London, 2015, and the conversation in chapter 5 of this volume.

50   The question that must inevitably be posed for anyone familiar with recent Africana thought is: How is Scott's reflection on tragedy positioned in relation to the increasingly visible school of Afro-pessimism? My initial proposition is that while both emerge in an era of defeat and cynicism and share an absence of optimism for the immediate future of radical political engagement, little else is common. Afro-pessimism, certainly as expressed by Frank B. Wilderson, one of the originators of the genre, seems to altogether flatten history, equating the "social death" experienced by Black people under slavery with a permanent "paradigmatic" positioning. Thus, "For Afro-pessimists, the black is positioned *a priori*, as a slave" ("Afro-pessimism," 1). I strongly disagree with this soul-destroying conclusion, which negates almost two centuries of unrelenting post-slavery resistance, which has been interspersed by tragic defeats but also marked by many substantial advances. Closely following this assertion, there is no basis for alliance with non-Black allies, whether from the white working class or non-Black persons of color, because "subjects just can't make common cause with objects" ("The Position of the Unthought," 90), concluding that white workers, even when exploited, remain subjects, whereas Blacks are always positioned as objects. The

FREEDOM AND THE SUBLIME

In his epic composition "Concrete Jungle" on the album *Catch a Fire*, Bob Marley stakes a claim for a yet to be achieved freedom beyond the colonial moment: "No chains around my feet but I'm not free / I know I am bound here in captivity."[51] If we think of Marley's invocation, which recognizes that physical restraint is no longer the primary means of social control, then we can explore his assertion in order to recognize how notions of freedom have expanded exponentially in the postcolonial era to include freedom from male exploitation and abuse; freedom to explore, decide, and live one's chosen sexuality; freedom to move without hindrance across boundaries in search of work; freedom from pollution and the right to enjoy a clean environment; freedom from arbitrary violence and war; and freedom from want. This partial but nonetheless revealing list suggests the foundations for a further rethinking of freedoms beyond negative/positive binaries and even beyond Amartya Sen's more nuanced notions of human capability[52] to imagine new programs and policies that, while not driven by predetermined teleologies, might pioneer new horizons for human thriving.

We might define the present moment, then, using Scott's framework as a new problem space, but it is a problem space still animated by the specters of the past even as it demands new expansive definitions of freedom and requires new political forms to fight for as well as achieve its always expanding objectives. In this sense, therefore, the "longing for total revolution" is not at all a mythopoetic chimera that needs to

---

sheer impossibility of a politics of alliances and common struggle, or any politics at all from this, leads either to a solo fight of Black people always by themselves, which, in places like the United States where Black people constitute a minority, would likely be a losing one or a wholesale, nihilistic withdrawal and surrender from political engagement. Needless to say, David Scott's "problem space" is not flattening but, complicating history and far from essentializing Black people and their struggles, is underlining the importance and permanence of a politics of pluralism. I still, however, restate my disagreement with Scott's unique lean to the tragic. See Patrice Douglass, Selemawit D. Terrefe, and Frank B. Wilderson, "Afro-Pessimism," in *Oxford Bibliographies*, accessed September 30, 2021, https://www.oxfordbibliographies.com/view/document/obo-9780190280024-0056.xml; and Saidya V. Hartman and Frank B. Wilderson, "The Position of the Unthought," *Qui Parle* 13, no. 2 (Spring/Summer 2003): 183–201.

51   Bob Marley, "Concrete Jungle," *Catch a Fire*, Island Records, 1973.
52   See Amartya Sen, *Development as Freedom*, Alfred A. Knopf, New York, 1999.

be exorcised, but rather a necessary narrative that, while always under revision, can provide intellectual purchase, motivational purpose, and directional compass for ongoing projects of radical change.

At a conference in 2019 at Brown University titled "Unlearning Imperial Rights/Decolonizing Institutions," I asked the following of African American thinker Hortense Spillers: If Hegelian notions of synthesis and religious notions of redemption no longer provide illumination for our groping in the darkness, what new thinking could potentially animate us and provide direction in the storm? After a short pause, Spillers responded that we could perhaps look to the cycle of life and particularly the inspirational moment of birth as a lodestone. Birth is the ever-present new, and while bearing inevitably the options of failure and tragedy, it is also laden with possibilities of transformation and hope. The purpose of living, then, always possesses at its very core, hidden as it were, in plain sight, the foundations for optimism and hopefulness.

There is one final feature of James's reflections, which I think Scott misses altogether. It is the typically Jamesian invocation of the power and possibilities that people have when they dare to hope, see freedom within their grasp or fear that, once attained, it might slip away. I wish to refer to this as the phenomenon of the *sublime*[53] in the revolutionary moment and it is at the very heart of James's *Black Jacobins*. Under Toussaint's leadership, Black people have been living free in St. Domingue for five years. It is a difficult time; the sugar economy is in a state of collapse and there are continuing threats from the British in Jamaica and the Spanish who occupy the eastern two-thirds of the island. Further, in order to keep the economy alive, Toussaint has insisted that people return to the hated estates, though now in a new capacity as paid laborers. It is a fraught, compromised moment, but it is freedom nonetheless.

But now Napoleon's army has returned, Toussaint is captured and transported to his eventual death, and the truth is out that slavery has been restored in neighboring colonies; St. Domingue is targeted to be next. This realization signals the beginning of the Black army's final battle for liberation, which James captures in graphic, unforgettable prose, of which I mention two instances. The first is from a French soldier, Lemmonier-Delafosse, who had served during the war. James notes

---

53 I use "sublime" here in the sense in which it is understood in chemistry, as a compound that changes directly from solid to a vapor. This is to suggest the extent to which "revolution" is both ephemeral yet has been in the past and may be utilized in the future as a framework to mobilize and fight for radical change.

for emphasis that he believed in slavery, but found this to say about the character and humanity of his Black adversaries:

> But what men these blacks are! How they fight and how they die! One has to make war against them to know their reckless courage in braving danger when they can no longer have recourse to stratagem. I have seen a solid column torn by grapeshot from four pieces of cannon, advance without making a retrograde step. The more they fell the greater seemed to be the courage of the rest. They advanced singing, for the Negro sings everywhere, makes songs on everything. Their song was a song of brave men and went as follows:
>
> > "To the attack grenadier,
> > Who gets killed that's his affair.
> > Forget your ma,
> > Forget your pa,
> > To the attack, grenadier,
> > Who gets killed that's his affair."[54]

The second, is among the correspondence written by General Leclerc to Napoleon shortly before his death in late 1802. James notes that the French had arrived in St. Domingue the year before, covered with glory from the European campaigns and with the hubristic belief that they would quickly dismantle this Black army of their racial inferiors. I quote only the immediately relevant section: "I have decided to send you General Boudet … Believe what he will tell you. We have in Europe a false idea of the country in which we fight and the men whom we fight against."[55] What Lemmonier-Delafosse saw clearly and Leclerc realized too late at the end of his life, was not the bravery of Black people per se, but the heroic stance of armed and capable Black women and men in the throes[56] of social revolution, who were unwilling under any circum-

---

54   James, *Black Jacobins*, 368.

55   *Black Jacobins*, 353.

56   Scott Henkel convincingly develops this notion of the extraordinary power generated through revolutionary enthusiasm, and the ability of oppressed people under peculiar circumstances to rise to unprecedented levels of collaboration and accompanying self-sacrifice. He starts, interestingly, with C.L.R. James's quote from General Leclerc, that removing Toussaint from Haiti was insufficient, and, indicating the depth of revolutionary fervor, that some two thousand leaders would have to be taken out of the equation in order to defeat the revolution. See

stances to yield and return to a life of slavery and degradation.[57] This romantic, mythopoetic, but also ultimately true and compelling portrait of a moment in Haiti's revolution provides a powerful coda and reminder that whether the struggle is to secure a free foothold on the western side of Hispaniola, to secure the civil rights of Black people in the United States, or to oust a ruthless kleptocratic dictator in the Sudan, the majesty of mobilized people transcends historical eras. James sought to invoke that intangible spirit of revolution as a motivation and source of optimism for twentieth-century anti-colonial struggles. Twenty-first-century revolutionary transnational movements in an entirely different problem space might wish nonetheless to learn from, while not being transfixed by, the tragedies of history and instead draw inspiration from the archive of revolution, even as they fight for significantly new objectives, though in necessarily modified forms, against both old and new opponents.

Scott Henkel, *Direct Democracy, Collective Power, The Swarm and the Literatures of the Americas*, University Press of Mississippi, Jackson, 2017.

57   From a different time and place, the moment after the taking of power in Grenada in 1979, think about this sentiment expressed by Theresa Simeon, suggesting a time of untethered possibilities, when anything, against any odds, might be achieved: "Then when the revolution happened, I was in the States. So I came back here, I really wanted to make up for not being here. I started going to the rallies ... I was so impressed I'd never seen people so together and united like that before in Grenada. I was thinking, how can I help? I knew we needed a lot of money and I wondered, how can I raise some? Then in November 1979 we heard about the international airport idea. So I called my friends together, and twenty-two of us decided to form the St. George's development committee ... All this involvement has changed my life so much ... We are much more involved in the revolution and always being called upon to help." Interview with Theresa Simeon in Chris Searle and Merle Hodge, *Is Freedom We Making: The New Democracy in Grenada*, Fedon Publishers, St. George's, Grenada, 1982, 73.

Index

ill refers to an illustration; *n* to a note; NWM to Norman Washington Manley

Abu Bakr Muslimeen movement 98
Achong, Corina Aurelia *see* Meeks, Corina
Adams, Grantley 37, 39
Africa 166–7
    post-colonial era 185–6, 186*n*
African Caribbeans 147–8
African diaspora 25, 167
African women 167
African Party for the Liberation of Guinea-Bissau and Cape Verde (PAIGC) 57
Afro-pessimism 201–2*n*
After the Event Conference (2019) 198
Albert, Michael *Parecon: Life After Capitalism* 142
Allende, Salvador 55, 57, 61, 65, 174
Almagro, Luis 15
Amazon Corporation 152
Andy, Bob 'I've Got to Go Back Home' 48
Anglophone Caribbean *see* Caribbean Community
Angola 55, 58–9, 63, 65, 173
Anthropocene era 169
anti-colonial movements 194, 195–6
Antigua Caribbean Liberation Movement (ACLM) 112
Antillean Caribbean 133
Arendt, Hannah *The Origins of Totalitarianism* 161
Argentina 10
Aristide, Jean-Bertrand 6, 17
Asia, economic growth in 176
Augier, Roy 90
Augusto, Geri 163

Bahamas 15
Bandung Conference (1955) 196, 199

Barbados 12*n*, 16, 101, 113, 135, 172–3, 174*n*
Barbuda 144
Barriteau, Eudine 21, 187
Belize 26
Bennett, Louise 44
Berlin Conference (1884–5) 71
Best, Lloyd 106
Biden, Joe 8, 31, 197–8*n*
Biko, Steve 164
Bishop, Maurice 99, 101–2, 113, 122, 184, 189
    arrest and execution of 46, 60, 99, 105, 184
Black Lives Matter 1, 3–4, 32, 158, 172, 199
Black Marxists 110
Black Panthers 2, 148
Black people, representation in art of 86
Black Power movement (US) 61, 164, 182–3
Black radicals 166–7
Black Writers Conference (1968) 111
Blake, William 73–4, 81
    The Body of Abel Found by Adam and Eve (painting) 73
Bobo Dreads 48
Bogle, Paul 66
Bogues, Anthony 21, 108–9, 111
Bonilla, Yarimer 17–18, 20
Boudet, General Jean 204
Boxer, David 70*n*
    Edna Manley ; sculptor 69
Bramwell, Neville 41–2
Brathwaite, Kamau (Eddy) 42–4
    'Arrivants' trilogy 43
    'Rites of Passage' 43–4

Brexit referendum (2016) 1, 129, 130, 172
British colonialism 105, 134–5, 147–8, 182
British Guiana (later Guyana) 17
British Virgin Islands 134–5
Brooks, Cedric 51
Brother Valentino (singer) 45
Brown, Dennis 51
Brown, Wayne 69, 72, 76, 80, 88
Brown University. Department of African Studies 45
Burnham, Forbes 99, 100
Burning Spear (singer) 142
Bustamante, Alexander 30, 36, 37–8, 39–40, 82, 91, 98
Byron, George Gordon, Lord Byron 'The Prisoner of Chillon' 41

Cabral, Amílcar 66
capitalism 27–8, 32, 116, 121–2, 141, 153, 167–73
Cardenal, Ernesto 101
Carey, Henry 2
Caribbean 4, 134, 172–5, 178–89
  corruption in 13–14, 185
  and indigeneity 26–7
  meeting of leaders with Trump (2019) 15–16
  migration from 13, 148, 182
  murder rate in 14
  sexual assaults in 13
  and sovereignty 14, 17, 18–20, 180
  Westminster-style government in 21, 27, 59, 137–8, 139, 180
Caribbean Artists Movement 44
Caribbean Community (CARICOM) 10–11, 12–17, 29, 59, 64, 180
Caribbean Federation project 36–9, 82, 194
Caribbean feminists 187
Caribbean Feminist Action Network (CAFRA) 10
Caribbean Festival of the Arts (Carifesta) 35n
Caribbean Left 112–5, 114n, 189
Caribbean Marxism-Leninism 19, 106, 113, 114–5, 119, 121–2

Caribbean poetry 42–6, 67
Carlos, John 164
Castro, Fidel 8, 57, 101, 136
Cayman Islands 134
Centre for Caribbean Thought Conference (2004) 111
Ceremony of Souls 101, 105
Cesairé, Aimé 20, 167
Chamberlain, Mary 95
Charlottesville rally (2017) 157
Chauvin, Derek 3
Chen, Kuan-Hsing 110
'Chicago Boys' 61
Chile 2, 10, 55, 57, 61, 65, 174
China 176, 177
Christophe, Henri 193
Chronixx (singer) 11
Citizens United (US) 171–2
Clarke, Bobby 114
Clarke, John 129
Claude, Bed-Ford 7
climate change 23, 169
Clinton, Bill and Hillary 158
Coard, Bernard 114, 189
Code Red feminist movement 10
Coke, 'Don' Christopher 18
Coleridge, Samuel Taylor 'Christabel' 41
Communist Party of Cuba (PCC) 8, 136–7
'common sense' 47, 117, 128–9
Conference on the Jamaican Seventies (2017) 32, 41, 61
Constituent Assembly of the Jamaican People at Home and Abroad 23, 138, 180
Coral Gardens massacre (1963) 91
Corruption Perception Index (2019) 13–14
Count Machuki (deejay) 42
Count Ossie and the Mystic Revelation of Rastafari 51
  'Grounation' 51
  'Oh Carolina' 51
Covid-19 pandemic 3, 24, 199
Cox, Oliver 167
Creole nationalism 147, 148

Cuba 8–10, 57, 64, 65, 99, 101, 121,
    136–7, 173, 184
  health service in 9, 24
  Special Period 8, 136
cultural studies 123, 127–8

Dakota Access Pipeline 159
Daley, Leonard (Bra Daley) 50, 65–6
Davis, Angela 66, 167
decolonization 14–15
Dessalines, General Jean-Jacques 193
Dominguez, Jorge 11
Dominica Liberation Movement
    (DLM) 113
Dominican Republic 15, 22
Drummond, Don and the Skatalites 51
Du Bois, W.E.B. and 'double con-
    sciousness' 153n
dub poetry 44n
Duval-Carrié, Edouard Le Royaume de
    ce Monde (artwork) i

education 24
English poetry 41–2
environment 23–4, 28n, 143–4, 169,
    197
Extinction Rebellion (XR) 198
extractivism 23–4

Fabian Society 74–5
Fairclough, O.T. 88
Fanmi Lavales Party (Haiti) 6
Fanon, Frantz 2
feminist movement 10–11, 167, 187
financial sector 130, 137–40, 152–3,
    168–9
Floyd, George 3–4, 199
Fordism and post-Fordism 118
Foucault, Michel 108
France 2
  uprisings (1968) 164
Francis, Donette 41
French colonialism 17–18, 20, 135,
    191–2
  Code Noir 191
French Guiana 135
French Revolution 191, 192
Frente Sandinista (FSLN) 99–100

Front for the Liberation of
    Mozambique (FRELIMO) 57

Gairy, Eric 59, 113, 184
Garvey, Amy Jacques 66
Garvey, Marcus 66
Gaye, Marvin
  'Let's Get It On' 52–3
  'What's Going On?' 52–3
gender and capitalism 167
Gerbaudo, Paolo 3
Getachew, Adom 14
Girvan, Norman 14
Gleaner, The 15, 55
Glissant, Edouard 18
Global Financial Crisis (2008) 1, 4, 23,
    127, 130, 140, 151–2, 158, 185
globalization 130, 143, 152, 172
Goldsmith, Oliver 'The Deserted
    Village' 41
Gonsalves, Camillo 16
Goodison, Lorna 43
Gordon, Lewis 21
Gramsci, Antonio 47, 117–8, 128–9n,
    145n, 160–1
Gray, Obika 186
Greater Antilles 27
Green Economy 143
Green New Deal 130
Grenada 13
  US invasion of (1983) 17, 46, 60, 67,
    81, 123, 184–5
Grenada Revolution (1979) 12, 59–61,
    65, 99, 101–2, 105, 113–4, 133,
    163, 187, 189
Guadeloupe 17, 135, 193
Guevara, Che 2, 66
Guiado, Juan 17n
Guinea-Bissau 65
Guyana 12, 13–14, 26, 99, 103

Haile Selassie 1, Emperor of Ethiopia
    45, 48
Haiti 6–7, 15, 17, 18n, 22, 27
  Ceremony of Souls 105
Haitian Revolution 27, 101, 190–3,
    203–5

Hall, Stuart 26, 31, 47, 71, 110–1, 114–23, 127–8, 140–1, 146, 150–1, 168, 201
  'Domination and Hegemony' 132*n*
  'Through the Prism of an Intellectual Life' 132*n*
  'The Toad in the Garden' 115
  'What is this 'Black' in Black Popular Culture?' 117
  for topics discussed by Hall, *see* the topic, e.g. hegemony
Hanna, Miss 73
Harewood, Guy 46, 57, 65
Hariri, Saad 2
Harris, Wilson 108
Harvard Opinion Poll (2016) 155–6
Hayek, Friedrich 61
Hearne, John 38
Hector, Tim 112
hegemony 47, 116–7, 128*n*, 132*n*, 145–51, 160–1
Henry, Ariel 7
Henry, Claudius 90
Henry, Paget 21, 108–9, 187
Henry Rebellion (1963) 90–1
Hintzen, Percy 186–7
  'Towards a New Democracy in the Caribbean' 21–2
Hispaniola 6, 22, 191, 205
Holness, Andrew 16
homophobia 11, 25
Hungarian Revolution (1956) 118, 119
Hurricane Irma (2017) 135, 144
Hurricane Maria (2017) 4–5, 134, 135

Iceland 142*n*
Iké, Lila 11
Indo-Caribbean 26
Intergovernmental Panel on Climate Change (IPCC) 28*n*, 169
International Labour Organization (ILO) 87
International Monetary Fund (IMF) 6, 9, 13, 133, 170, 174
Iran 65
Iran/Contra funding 61
Iraq 2

Jacobins 191–3
Jacques, Martin 118
Jagan, Cheddi 102, 113
Jah9 (singer) 11
Jamaica 13–14, 22–3, 173–4, 174*n*
  1970s ('Long Seventies') 12, 41, 46–7, 47*n*, 57, 61, 149, 163
  attitudes to colonialism 15, 15*n*
  attitudes to women in 78
  electoral system 12
  independence of (1962) 29, 30, 39–40, 97–8, 182
  Institution of Crown Colony government 71
  migration from 37
  racial hierarchies in 78
  referendum on independence (1961) 36, 39
Jamaica Independence Day 35–6, 39–40
Jamaica Labour Party (JLP) 36, 37–8, 82, 98, 133, 147*n*
Jamaica Observer 'Turn out for What?' 13
Jamaican flag 30, 35*n*, 35–6
Jamaican music 11, 42, 51
  reggae 11, 51, 66
Jamaican poetry 42–6
James, C.L.R. 19, 97, 101, 102–3, 111, 112*n*, 123, 166, 167, 188, 203
  The Black Jacobins 32, 166, 190–5, 203
James, Marlon 55*n*
Jones, Beverley 65–6
Jones, Claudia 66, 167
Jones Town, Jamaica 55, 56

Kamugisha, Aaron 20
  Beyond Coloniality 13, 19
Kennedy, Mark 105–6
Keynes, John Maynard 61, 157, 170, 197
Khrushchev, Nikita 118, 119, 120
Kilburn Manifesto, The (2015) 31, 127–32, 137, 139–44, 201
King, Martin Luther 164
King Stitt (deejay) 42
Koch Brothers 171

Koffee (singer) 11
Kornai, János 179
Kwayana, Eusi 112

Labour Party (UK) 75
Lamming, George 19, 20, 30–1,
    95–109
    on culture 104–5, 107
    on place 105–6
    on the role of the artist 107
    on the self 105
    political views of 102–4
    WRITINGS
    In the Castle of My Skin 95, 104
    Of Age and Innocence 95–7, 104
    On the Enterprise of the Indies
        106–7
    'The Plantation Mongrel' 100–1
    Season of Adventure 95–7, 107
Lebanon 2
Leclerc, General Charles 192, 204–5
Lemmonier-Delafosse, Jean-Baptiste
    203–4
Lenin, V.I, 197
Lewis, G.K. 114
Lewis, Hopeton 'Take t Easy' 41–2,
    42*n*, 43
Lewis, Linden 17, 20
Lewis, Patsy (wife of Brian Meeks) 45
LGBT people 11, 25
*Life in Leggings: Caribbean Alliance
    Against Gender-Based Violence*
    11
Livingstone, Bunny 52
Lyannaj 18, 20
Lorde, Audre 19
love, ethic of 19, 21
Lumumba, Patrice 66

Macron, Emmanuel 2
Maduro, Nicolás 15, 174
Malcolm, Carlos 51
Manley, Carmen (wife of Douglas) 38
Manley, Douglas (son of NWM) 38–9,
    77, 93
Manley, Edna (wife of NWM) 30, 39,
    69–94
    character of 73

meets and marries NMW 73, 75–6,
    77–80, 79*ill*, 93
    place in Jamaican society 78–80
    political views of 70, 74–5, 81*n*,
        81–2
    ARTWORKS 81
    'Adam and Eve' 84*ill*, 86
    'Beadseller' 77
    'Boy with Reed' 82, 83*ill*, 86
    'Brother Man' 90*ill*, 91–2
    'Dawn' 77
    'Diggers' 85*ill*, 86
    'Eve' 77, 82
    'Ghetto Mother' 92*ill*, 92–3
    'Market Women' 86–7, 87*ill*
    'Negro Aroused' 84*ill*, 86
    'Strike' 89*ill*
    'Voice, The' 91*ill*, 92
    'Youth' 88*ill*
Manley, Joseph (son of Michael) 69
Manley, Michael (son of NWM) 14,
    30, 69–70, 98–9, 100
    defeat in 1980 election 31, 61, 80,
        93, 147*n*, 148–9, 184
    and Democratic Socialism 93, 99,
        139, 148–9, 177
    wins 1972 election 45–6, 98–9, 183
    The Politics of Change 93
    The Struggle in the Periphery 93
Manley, Norman (grandson of NWM)
    38–40
Manley, Norman Washington 14, 30,
    39–40, 82, 90–1
    meets and marries Edna Swithin-
        bank 73, 75–6, 77–80, 79*ill*, 93
Manley, Rachel (granddaughter of
    NWM) 72, 73, 92
    Horses In Her Hair 69
Manley, Thomas 78
Manley, Vera (sister of NWM) 76
Margaret, Princess 39
Marley Bob 44, 51, 52, 64, 65, 66
    attempted assassination of 55
Marley, Bob and the Wailers 52–3, 92
    'Burnin'' 52
    'Catch a Fire' 52
    'Concrete Jungle' 202
    'Revolution' 64

maroons and marronage 19, 20
Mars, Perry 114*n*
Martelly, Michel 6
Marti, José 101
Martinique 17, 135, 193
Marx, Karl and Marxism 61, 64,
    102–3, 116–8, 141, 145*n*, 165–7
  Capital 167
  see also Caribbean Marxism-Lenin-
    ism
masculinism 65–6
Massey, Doreen 127, 128, 129
Massey, Doreen and Martin Rustin
    'Whose Economy?' 129
Maurepas, Jacques 193
Mbembe, Achille 186
McCabe, Colin 116
McKay, Claude 167
Meeks, Brian 45–6
  'Envisioning Caribbean Futures' 22,
    137–40, 180
  Paint the Town Red 55*n*
  POEMS 47, 63, 66–8
  'Angola Poem' 58–9, 63
  'Brother Man' 90*ill*, 91
  'Count Mystic' 51, 65
  The Coup Clock Clicks 30, 41, 56, 67
  'Greetings Two' 48–50
  'Grenada' 60–1, 67
  'Langwidge and Culcha' 53–4
  'March 9, 1976' 55–6, 67
  'October 80 Night' 62
  'One Love for Bra Daley' 48–50
  'Shattered Glass' 62–3, 67
  'To a Guy I Knew but Didn't Meet'
    57–8, 65–6
  'Trench Town Assault Case' 53, 63,
    65
  'Tundahstaam' 52
Meeks, Corina (mother of Brian) 38*n*,
    45
#MeToo movement 172
Mighty Sparrow (singer) 44
Mills, Charles 21, 115, 115*n*, 122*n*
Mohammed, Patricia 187
Moïse, Jovenal 6–7
Monbiot, George 132

Montreal, student uprising in (1970)
    97–8
Morales, Ed 6
Morant Bay Rebellion (1865) 71
Morley, David 127
Morris, Mervyn 44, 44*n*
Mottley, Mia 12*n*, 16
Movement for Black Lives 200
Movement for National Liberation
    (MONALI) 113
Movement for the Assemblies of the
    People (MAP) 112
Mozambique 57, 65
Munroe, Trevor 102, 114
  *Social Classes and National
    Liberation* 119, 119–20*n*
Mutabaruka (Allan Hope) 44

Napoleon 1, Emperor of the French
    166, 192, 195, 203, 204
nation language 54
nation state, the 14–15, 27
national liberation movements 120
National Stadium, Kingston 30, 35,
    39
National United Freedom Fighters
    (Trinidad and Tobago) 46, 57,
    65–6
nationalism 106
neoliberalism 61, 128–31, 132–3, 139,
    153, 170–1, 185
  resistance to 130–1, 131*n*, 199
Nettleford, Rex 35*n*, 90
New Beginning Movement (NBM)
    112
New Jewel Movement (Grenada) 59,
    99, 102, 112, 113, 122, 184, 189
New Left (UK) 110, 118
New York Times 3
New Yorker 1–2
Newman, Janet 129
Newman, Janet and John Clarke
    'States of Imagination' 129
Nicaragua 65, 99–100, 101
Nixon, Richard 164, 174
Nkruman, Kwame 14
Nove, Alec *Feasible Socialism* 141–2
Nyere, Julius 14

O'Shea, Allan 128
Obama, Barack 3, 9, 136, 158
oil crises 98, 174
Olympic Games (1968), Black Power
    salute in 164
Onuora, Oku (Orlando Wong) 43
Operation Bootstrap 134, 182
Orange Lane fire 55
Organization of American States
    (OAS) 15, 17n

Pacific Islands 144
Padmore, George 167
Pan-Africanism 25
Pan-America 26
Pan-Asia 26
Paquet, Sandra Pouchet 104, 107
Parboosingh, Karl 38
Patterson, Orlando 174n
Penguin Book of Caribbean Verse in
    English 44
People's National Congress (Guyana)
    99
People's National Movement (Trinidad
    and Tobago) 97
People's National Party (PNP) 13, 17,
    37, 39, 67, 70, 82, 93, 113, 133,
    148,183
    election defeat (1980) 67, 148
    election win (1972) 98–9
    and the Four Hs 120n
    referendum on Federation 36
People's Progressive Party (Guyana)
    102, 113
People's Revolutionary Army
    (Grenada) 60, 184
People's Revolutionary Government
    (Grenada) 99, 113, 184
Pétion, Alexandre 193
Petrocaribe Agreement (2005) 15
Philip Sherlock Centre for Creative
    Arts 43
Piketty, Thomas 141
Pinochet, Augusto 2, 10, 57, 61, 65
Polanyi, Karl 141
    The Great Transformation 171
Policy Platform of the Movement for
    Black Lives (2020) 199–200

Popular Movement for the Liberation
    of Angola (MPLA) 57
Portuguese Africa 57, 61
Prague Spring (1968) 119, 164
Prince Buster (deejay) 42
Productive Organisation for Women
    in Action (Belize) 11
Protoje (musician) 11
protest movements 2–4, 11–12,
    199–201
Puerto Rico 4–6, 7, 134, 135
    Financial and Oversight
        Management Board 4, 134
    plebiscite on statehood 5–6n
pwofitasyon 18, 28

race and racism 25, 71–2, 76–8, 77n,
    117, 151, 182–3
racial capitalism 141, 167–8
Rastafari 19, 21, 43, 48, 66, 89–92, 110,
    148, 165, 183
Rastafari language 46, 48
Rastafari mysticism 45, 48, 49
Rastafari philosophy 48
Red Thread feminist movement 10
Reddock, Rhoda 187
religious right 154
Republican Party (US) 146, 154
Revolutionary Marxist Collective
    (Jamaica) 112
Rhys, Jean 44
Right, the 1, 172
Roberts, Neil 20
Robinson, Cedric 141
robotization 152, 169–70, 197
Rodney, Walter 26, 61, 100, 103, 163,
    165–7
    assassination of 61, 100
    expulsion from university post 43,
        45, 46, 98, 111, 163, 183
    History of the Guyanese Working
        People 103, 108
    How Europe Underdeveloped Africa
        167
Rojek, Chris 115, 115n, 119, 127
Romeo, Max 92
Roopnarine, Rupert 112
Roselló, Ricardo 5

Ruglass, Joe 51
Rustin, Martin 127, 129

St Domingue (later Haiti) 166, 191–3, 195, 203
St Lucia 15
St Vincent and the Grenadines 12, 16
Sanders, Bernie 131, 158
Santamaría, Haydée 66
Savacou (journal) 44, 44*n*
Scandinavia 176
Schumpeter, Joseph *Capitalism, Socialism and Democracy* 171
Scott, David 21, 32, 61*n*, 108, 187–90, 196, 199–203
   on *The Black Jacobins* (James) 193–6
   Conscripts of Modernity 32, 188, 190, 196
   Omens of Adversity 188
   Refashioning Futures 188
Scott, Dennis 44
Scott, James *Domination and the Arts of Resistance* 149*n*
Seaga, Edward 147*n*
Sen, Amartya 202
Sewell, Anna *Black Beauty* 121
Shaw, George Bernard 74
Shearer, Hugh 98
Sheller, Mimi *Island Futures* 22
Shervington, Pluto 'I Man Born Ya' 35, 35*n*
shiprider agreements (1997) 17
Silá, Ernestina Titina 66
Singapore 176
Singh, Rickey 100–1
Sir Arthur Lewis Institute of Social and Economic Studies (SALISES) 29
Sis D (wife of Leonard Daley) 65–6
Sistren Theatre Collective 10
slavery 7, 166–7
   impact on children of 179
   reparations for 179
Small, Jerry 43
Small Axe Collective 32, 61*n*
   Conference on the Jamaican 70s (2017) 41, 61

Smith, M.G. 90
Smith, Mikey 44
Smith, Tommy 164
socialism 131, 131*n*, 133, 142, 159–60
Solow, Robert 169*n*
Soundings Group 127
South Africa 55, 63, 164
South Korea 176
sovereignty 14, 17, 18–19 18*n*
Soviet Union 8, 64, 102, 118, 119–20, 142
Spillers, Hortense 203
Stalin, Joseph 118, 119
state, the 20, 129
Streeck, Wolfgang 151, 152
Sugar Duties Act (1846) 71
Suriname 26
Swithenbank, Edna *see* Marley, Edna
Swithenbank, Ellie (wife of Harvey) 71–2, 76
Swithenbank, Harvey (father of Edna) 70–2
Swithenbank, Lena (sister of Edna) 74

Taino people 27
Taiwan 176
Tambourine Army (Jamaica) 10
Tamùkke Feminist Rising (Guyana) 10
Tea Party movement 3
Tennyson, Alfred Lord 'The Lotos-Eaters' 41
Thame, Maziki 77*n*
Thatcher, Margaret and Thatcherism 150–1, 157, 159, 170
Thomas, Deborah 18–19, 20
   Exceptional Violence 186
Tivoli Gardens, invasion of (2010) 18
Toledo Maya Women's Council (Belize) 11
Tosh, Peter 51, 52
totalitarianism 161–2
Toussaint L'Ouverture, François Dominique 191–3, 194, 203–4
Trinidad and Tobago 13–14, 17*n*, 26, 46, 97–8, 99, 134
   Black Power Revolution (1970) 43, 46, 97–8, 111, 163, 183
   independence of 29, 97–8, 182

Trouillot, Michel-Rolph 190
Trump, Donald and Trumpism 5, 8,
    31–2, 131–2, 136, 152, 155–7,
    160, 197–8
  meeting with Caribbean leaders
    (2019) 15–16
  wins 2016 election 1, 130, 146, 155
Turks and Caicos Islands 134
Twelve Tribes of Israel 48
twin barrel bucky 66

Uber 152
unemployment 152, 170, 197
Unidad Popular (Chile) 57
United States 31, 151–62, 171–2
  attitudes in 154–6
  civil rights movement 164
  election (2016) 131, 150, 156
  invasion of Grenada by 46, 60, 67,
    81, 184–5
  policy on Cuba 8–9
  political attitudes in 131
University College of the West Indies
    (UCWI) 37, 38, 113, 163, 165
  Creative Arts Centre (CAC) 43
University of Guyana 165
Unlearning Imperial Rights/Decolo-
    nizing Institutions Conference
    (2019) 203

Venezuela 8, 9, 15, 174, 195, 196
Vergerio, Claire 25–6n
Vietnam 57
Vietnam War 65, 155, 163–4
violence 65, 186
VOX (news website) 4

Wailers, The see Marley, Bob
Walcott, Derek 38, 44
Walters, Ewart 39n
Washington Consensus 158, 172, 178,
    197
Washington Post poll (2017) 155
Watson, Hilbourne 106n, 108, 186
Webb, Beatrice and Sidney 74
Wells, H.G. 74
Wesleyan Church 72
Westphalian Order 25–6n
Wilderson, Frank B. 201–2
William, Duke of Cornwall (later
    Prince of Wales) 11
Williams, Eric 14, 37, 39, 46, 97–8,
    166, 183
  Capitalism and Slavery 97, 166
Windward Islands 27
Womantra (Trinidad and Tobago) 11
Women's March (2017) 3, 198
Workers Party of Jamaica (WPJ) 102,
    108, 113, 121
Workers Revolutionary Movement (St
    Lucia) 113
Working Class Party, The (WPJ) 121–2
Working People's Alliance (Guyana)
    112
World Bank 133
World Health Organization 3
Wright, Robin 1–2
Wynter, Sylvia 19, 181

Yack, Bernard 200
Youlou Liberation Movement (St
    Lucia) 113
young people 66